Housing Improvement and Social Inequality

Case Study of an Inner City

PAUL N. BALCHIN
Thames Polytechnic

SAXON HOUSE

Published by Saxon House
Teakfield Limited,
Westmead, Farnborough, Hants., England

ISBN 0 566 00274 4

Printed in Great Britain by David Green (Printers) Ltd, Kettering Northamptonshire

Contents

Tables

Figures

Preface

This book is about housing improvement, and particularly about its effects upon the residential population of the inner areas of west London. The economic and social rationale of improvement is explained, and the role of landlords, developers and local authorities is analysed. Although there was a temptation to dwell on individual cases of speculative gain and illegal or dubious methods of displacing tenants, this has been largely avoided, and the book concentrates both on the defects of the improvement process as a whole, and on the application of housing legislation within a specific geographical area. An attempt is made to relate housing improvement to the general debate about the inequality of wealth by implicitly posing the question: who benefits and who loses from improvement policy?

The subject matter of the book progresses from the general to the particular. Chapter 1 provides an introductory background account of residential location theory insofar as it is relevant to the inner areas of cities. Chapter 2 deals with the renewal of urban housing and examines policies, and the economic and social justification for improvement in contrast to redevelopment. Chapter 3 considers some of the problems of housing in inner London, and Chapter 4 reviews the progress of improvement legislation as applied to the metropolis. Chapters 5 and 6 set out to explore the relationship between the distribution of improvement grants and social and economic variables in west London in general, and in General Improvement Areas and Housing Action Areas in particular. Chapter 7 seeks to identify the connection between grant distribution and socio-economic change within these declared areas within the period 1969-75. Chapter 8 concludes by questioning whether prevailing legislation is likely to achieve its main objective - the improvement of housing for the benefit of existing residents.

In producing this book it soon became very evident that it was difficult to keep up to date. Some of the research dates back to the mid 1970s, but the gathering of data and information is a necessary prerequisite to analysis. However, every effort has been made to ensure that legislative and statistical detail is accurate at the time of writing.

Acknowledgements

I would like to acknowledge the invaluable help given to me by
Professor Eila Campbell of Birkbeck College, University of London,
in the preparation of my doctoral thesis on which this book is
based.   I am also indebted to Professor Peter Hall, University of
Reading, for providing constructive criticism of the original work.
I would like to thank the many local government officers, residents
and others connected with improvement grant policy for the
considerable amount of assistance given me in collecting data and
information, and the students in the School of Surveying, Thames
Polytechnic, who assisted in social and economic surveys of areas
of west London.   Considerable help, for which I am very grateful,
was also given by my wife, Maria.

Abbreviations

CBD	Central Business District
ED	Enumeration District
GIA	General Improvement Area
GLC	Greater London Council
HAA	Housing Action Area
LBA	London Boroughs Association
RNI	Rehabilitation-Need Index
RPI	Rehabilitation-Potential Index
RRI	Rehabilitation-Realisation Index
SEG	Socio-Economic Group

1 Introduction

RESIDENTIAL LOCATION THEORY AND THE PROBLEMS OF PRIVATE HOUSING IN THE
INNER CITIES

In an attempt to explain why there are extensive areas of deteriorated
residential properties in our cities and to comprehend the consequences
of housing improvement policy in a specific area, it is necessary
initially to analyse the working of the urban housing market and to
consider some of the interdependencies which define the urban system.
The housing market is unlike the market for other goods and services in
that the product is spatially unique, very durable and heterogeneous.
In considering the housing market, the spatial distribution of the product
is one of the principal factors of the analysis. But the market is not
perfect; government intervention in the form of zoning restrictions, rent
control or regulation, subsidies and public housing development have
greatly influenced the forces of supply and demand. The institutional
arrangements for mortgage· finance and income tax allowances on mortgage
interest payments have also had a major effect. In this analysis these
factors will be mainly ignored and simplifying assumptions will be made.
These are: an urban area with a single centre, perfect knowledge on the
part of sellers and buyers, rational behaviour and the assumption that the
seller or producer of the dwellings aims to maximise revenue, and the
buyer aims to maximise his satisfaction or utility. It is recognised
that although:

> the internal structure of any city is unique in its particular
> combination of detail...in general there is a degree of order
> underlying the land use patterns of individual cities. (Garner,
> 1970, pp.338-339).

THE CONCENTRIC ZONE AND SECTOR MODELS

The rapid growth of cities in the United States during the late nineteenth
and early twentieth centuries was characterised by an outward 'invasion'
of low income households into formerly high income areas. The concentric
zone model illustrates this process, and has often been used to explain
the pattern of urban land uses throughout the industrialised world. The
model is particularly relevant to the problems of the inner city.

It is assumed that accessibility and values diminish with equal
regularity in all directions from a central point in an urban area.
Distortions caused by variations in topography and differential accessibility are ignored and it is argued that patterns of land use will be
arranged in regular concentric zones. Based on his studies of Chicago,
Burgess (1925) stated that at any moment of time, land uses within the
city differentiate themselves into zones according to their age and
character (Fig.1 A).

The transitional zone is the main area of dilapitated housing, and it
also includes light manufacturing, wholesaling and other (mainly small)

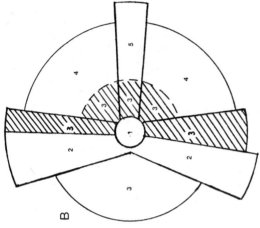

A

1 CBD

2 WHOLESALE LIGHT MANUFACTURING AND
LOW–CLASS RESIDENTIAL

3 MEDİUM–CLASS RESIDENTIAL

4 HIGH–CLASS RESIDENTIAL

5 COMMUTERS' ZONE

B

1 CBD

2 WHOLESALE LIGHT MANUFACTURE

3 LOW–CLASS RESIDENTIAL

4 MEDIUM–CLASS RESIDENTIAL

5 HIGH–CLASS RESIDENTIAL

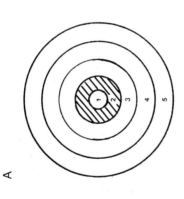 MAIN AREAS OF DILAPIDATED HOUSING

Figure 1.1   The concentric zone model (A) and
sector model of urban structure (B)

2

businesses.   Blighted conditions and slums result in much of this zone
being referred to as 'the twilight area'.   It is the zone in which there
is the greatest need for renewal.   It surrounds the central business
district (CBD) which forms the heart of the city's commercial, cultural
and social life as well as being the focus of urban transport.   The
transition zone is surrounded by the low class residential zone which,
according to Burgess, is:

> inhabited by the workers in industries who have escaped from the
> area of deterioration but who desire to live within easy access
> of their work (p.55).

This in turn is surrounded by a zone of middle and high income housing
characterised by single family dwellings.   Around this there is an outer
zone beyond the city limits, a commuter belt of suburban and satellite
communities.   Burgess acknowledged that neither Chicago nor any other
urban area fit exactly into this ideal scheme.

With population and economic growth, urban land use is influenced first
by centripetal forces of attraction, second by centrifugal forces of
dispersion and third, by forces of spatial differentiation.   There is,
according to Burgess, the:

> tendency of each inner zone to extend its area by the invasion of
> the next outer zone.   This aspect of expansion may be called
> succession, a process which has been studied in detail in plant
> ecology ....   In the expansion of the city a process of
> distribution takes place which sifts and sorts and relocates
> individuals and groups by residence and occupation (p.56).

A result of this process is that the oldest residential property will be
centrally located (in parts of the CBD but mainly within the zone of
transition) and the newest housing will tend to be in the commuter zone.
Whereas the higher income groups are able to afford the newest property
and so locate mainly in the outer urban area, the lowest income groups
are only able to afford the oldest property which will be mainly within
the 'twilight' areas of the transition zone.

Unlike the concentric zone model, sector models assume that urban land
use is conditioned by the pattern of radial routeways.   Variations in
accessibility cause sectoral difference in property values and the
arrangement of land uses.   Hoyt (1939) hypothesised that similar land
uses concentrate along particular radial routeways to form sectors
(Fig.1 B).

A low income residential sector would extend outwards by the addition
of new growth on its outer arc.   The same process would occur on the
outer edge of the high income sector, although Hoyt (like Burgess)
explained that as residential structures deteriorate and become obsolete
with the passage of time they are 'invaded' by lower and intermediate
rental groups who replace higher income households who have mainly moved
to the outer edge of their sector.   But Hoyt noted that the inner areas
still attract a few high income households:

> de luxe high-rent apartment areas tend to be established near the
> business centre in old residential areas ....   When the high-rent
> single family home areas have moved far out on the periphery of
> the city, some wealthy families desire to live in a colony of
> luxurious apartments close to the business centre (p.118).

Evans (1973) suggested that as the size of the urban area expands so the proportion of the high income group who wish to live near the centre increases:

> as the size of the city increases .... so the distance from the centre to the edge of the city increases, and so the cost of giving up proximity to the centre increases relative to the benefit of living in the high income neighbourhood at the periphery. For both these reasons, the large city is likely to have a high-income neighbourhood, at, or near, the centre, while in a small town all members of the high-income group will locate in the outer part of a sector of the city (p.132).

It can be assumed that both on the periphery of cities and within the central areas high socio-economic groups (and, to a diminishing extent, other groups) will pay a higher price or rent for a location amongst others in the same group. *True of London esp in parts*

Stone (1964) noted that the value of land in London generally falls regularly with distance but in the case of areas with special attractions as residential locations – such as Hampstead – the rent gradient is disrupted. This suggests that in order to locate in a high income neighbourhood a 'neighbourhood premium' has to be paid over and above the 'normal' rent or price. The premium is zero at the edge and usually highest in the centre, the whole neighbourhood perhaps being topographi-cally attractive, for example being on high ground or on a river front, or being very accessible to central area employment and services. In most cities there will be some high income households who find their optimal location in the intermediate areas of cities and who group themselves into neighbourhoods at various distances from the centre. Maximum benefit will be realised if these neighbourhoods coalesce into a single sector of the city – an underlying factor causing the creation of high income sectors even when the city is very large, examples are the Knightsbridge/Kensington and Hampstead/Highgate sectors in London.

With the increased cost, time and inconvenience of commuter travel since the 1950s, the process of outward 'invasion' described by Burgess and Hoyt has been supplemented by an in migration of higher income households willing to pay a neighbourhood premium to acquire accommodation in the inner city. A consideration of the relationship between commuter costs and housing costs by means of trade-off models provides the rationale underlying this recent trend.

TRADE-OFF MODELS

Instead of regarding the location of a household as being determined by the availability of housing, economists in the 1950s began to assume that a household would find its optimal location relative to the centre of the city by trading-off commuter costs (which mainly increase with distance from the centre) against housing costs (which generally decrease with distance from the centre). It was recognised that a continual trade-off outwards was impossible, Schnore (1954) assuming that:

> the maximum distance from significant centres of activity at which a household unit tends to locate is fixed at that point beyond which further savings in rent are insufficient to cover the added costs of transportation to these centres (p.342).

4

Further versions of the theory were developed by Hoover and Vernon (1959), Alonso (1960, 1964) and Wingo (1961a, 1961b). Alonso (1960) argued that households choose their location to maximise their utility and in so doing balance:

the costs and bother of commuting against the advantages of cheaper land with increasing distance from the centre of the city and the satisfaction of more space for living (p.154).

Adapting the classical theory of economics, Alonso (1964) devised an individual's bid-rent curve, and argued that an individual's income was a function of his expenditure on land, the commuting costs of travelling from his home to the centre of the city and his expenditure on all other commodities.

$$Y = P(t)\ q + K(t) + P_Z z$$

where

Y	=	income
Pq	=	price x quantity of land
t	=	distance from the centre of the city
K	=	commuting costs per unit of distance
$P_Z z'$	=	all other expenditure

The price of land declines with distance from the centre of the city while commuting costs rise. As a household moves away from the centre of the city it can purchase more land for the same amount of money, but this gain will be offset by the increase in commuting costs. Thus an expansion in demand for space will be partly expressed through higher expenditure on transport. Conversely, the price of land increases towards the city centre and commuting costs fall. If households move towards the centre they purchase less land for the same amount of money, but this may be compensated by lower commuting costs.

In order for a household to maximise its utility two conditions must obtain: the marginal utility of the household's expenditure on housing and all other forms of consumption must be equal, and no move can increase the household's real income. For equilibrium to be reached under these conditions either the saving derived from moving from the inner city must decline with distance otherwise the household could always increase its income by moving even further from the inner city, or the saving derived from moving towards the centre must decline otherwise households could maximise their incomes by acquiring accommodation in the city centre rather than in the inner surrounding areas.

Low income households have a narrow choice of expenditure on housing, commuting and on all other goods and services. With less money available for commuting they would live close to their employment but could only afford to pay for small amounts of high value housing near the city centre. Higher income households can afford to live in either the outer urban areas acquiring larger amounts of lower value properties and incurring high commuting costs, or in the inner urban areas where low commuting costs offset the acquisition of small but expensive properties. There is thus the anomaly of poor people living close to the city centre on high value land, and the higher income households living mainly at the periphery where land is less expensive but also in the inner areas in

5

competition with low income households. As with many other forms of consumption it is only the higher income groups who have a freedom of choice.

The trade-off hypothesis was extended by Evans (1973) who suggested that if the demand for household space increased, the household would have to move further out from the centre to find its optimal location; but if the rate of pay of the head of the household increased, but his demand for space remained constant, the household would move nearer the centre to find its optimal location. The increase in the rate of pay and the resultant increase in the valuation of travel time further means that the total savings in travel costs would offset higher house prices.

When the wage or salary increases there are two opposing forces influencing his locational choice. First, the increase in the household's demand for space pushing the household away from the centre; secondly the increase in the rate of pay pulling the household's location towards the centre because of the increase in the value of travel time. The direction of the change in location, if any, will depend upon the relative strength of these two opposing forces. Evans explained that if:

> the household's demand for space increases very little when the rate of pay is increased, the household will move towards the centre; if the demand for space increases very greatly when the rate of pay is increased, the household will move out from the centre. The direction of the move can be said to depend upon the household's elasticity of demand for space with respect to income. Now it is obvious that there is some elasticity at which the two opposing forces are exactly equal, so that any increase in the householder's rate of pay would not result in a move either away from or towards the centre (p.118).

If this elasticity is denoted $\bar{E}$ and the household's income elasticity of demand for space is more than $\bar{E}$, Evans argued that:

> the household would move outward since the outward push generated by the increase in demand for space will outweigh the inward pull generated by the increase in the value of travelling time. On the other hand, if the household's income elasticity is less than $\bar{E}$, the household will move inward since the inward pull generated by the increased travel costs will outweigh the outward push of the increased demand for space (p.120).

Evans argued that the highest income groups would have elasticities of demand for space both greater and less than $\bar{E}$ and would be able to out-bid other income groups for housing both within the outer and inner areas of cities. With lower levels of demand and less extreme elasticities of demand for space the lower and middle income households would locate in intermediate positions within the urban area - lower income households having the lower elasticity of demand for space and consequently locating within the inner areas.

Evans showed that this pattern of distribution exists in the major British cities. Referring to the 1961 Census, he showed that within the Greater London, West Midlands, South-east Lancashire, Merseyside, Tyneside and Clydeside conurbations the very high income groups were over-represented in the conurbation centre, and underrepresented in the rest of the conurbation. The next highest income groups were overrepresented in both the conurbation centre and outer area but underrepresented elsewhere

in the conurbation, and the lowest income group was overrepresented in
the conurbation centre, and the proportion in any area declined with a
greater distance from the centre.

Evans referred to the importance of the 'neighbourhood premium', an
amount a high income household is willing to pay to reside in a high
income neighbourhood. This desire for a location in an 'exclusive' area
partly explains why the same is not true of house prices and travel
costs, although there is an inverse correlation between site values and
travel costs around many cities, for example London. High income
commuters do not have to trade-off travel costs and housing costs as they
can afford both. In general it is assumed that house buyers will
attempt to acquire a house as expensive as they can afford with the
maximum mortgage that they can raise, in an area of their choice.
Increasingly, high income households are choosing the inner areas of
cities as their residential location. This book shows how housing
improvement policy is facilitating this choice and it examines some of
the repercussions.

2 Urban housing renewal

Despite the attraction of the inner urban areas for an increasing number
of high income households, the urgent need for urban renewal implies that
the price mechanism has not functioned properly in these areas over the
past half a century.   It is argued that intervention is essential because
private activity has not resulted in renewal, and desirable if the total
benefits from renewal exceed the total costs.   A comprehensive urban
renewal programme would have many aims.   Rothenberg (1967) identified
the following:

a) The elimination of slums.
d) The provision of decent, safe and sanitary housing in a
    suitable environment.
c) The attraction and maintenance of an adequate middle class
    component in the inner areas.

While these aims relate directly to residential renewal other aims
indirectly affect the quality of the housing stock.   These are:

d) The enhancement of the financial strength of city government
    through the broadening of the rate base - thus enabling the
    provision of better community services.
e) The attraction of additional, clean and light industry to
    the central area diversifying employment opportunities.
f) The mitigation of poverty.

Urban renewal usually takes three forms - 'redevelopment' - usually
undertaken on a large scale and integrated with a programme of demolition
and clearance; 'rehabilitation' - involving the improvement of properties
over a wide area or in more specific locations, and 'conservation' -
involving both limited clearance and rehabilitation in order to upgrade
an area.

The legislative framework of urban housing renewal in Great Britain
dates back to the nineteenth century, but has had more extensive and
implicit effects since the Town and Country Planning Act of 1947 and
Housing Act of 1949.   The policy base has been the compulsory purchase
powers of the local authorities supported by annual grants and long term
loans from central government.   But the pace of housing renewal has been
slow, due mainly to the many competing demands on resources at national
and local level, the rapidly rising cost of sites and the scale of the
housing shortage within the inner urban areas.

SLUM CLEARANCE AND REDEVELOPMENT

With approximately one third of Britain's housing stock built before 1919
there is a very great need to replace slum dwellings and other obsolete
housing.   Both residential development and redevelopment usually take
place at ever decreasing densities even within the inner urban areas.
In 1881 the average density of development was at about 67 dwellings per

Table 2.1

Houses closed or demolished, Great Britain, 1963-77

Year	England and Wales	Scotland	Great Britain
1963	61,445	12,058	73,503
1964	61,215	14,392	75,607
1965	60,666	15,534	76,200
1966	66,782	16,650	83,432
1967	71,152	19,087	90,239
1968	71,586	18,768	90,354
1969	69,233	17,847	87,080
1970	67,804	17,345	85,149
1971	70,057	20,554	90,511
1972	66,098	18,518	84,616
1973	63,553	16,479	80,032
1974	41,698	11,615	53,313
1975	49,083	10,646	59,729
1976	46,146	6,881	53,027
1977	37,108	6,004	43,112

Source: Department of the Environment,
          Housing and Construction Statistics

hectare (28 per acre), between 1881 and 1921 it was at 49 dwellings per hectare (20 per acre) and between 1921 and 1941 it had fallen to 31 per hectare (13 per acre). Demolition, clearance and redevelopment there-fore tends to produce a deficiency of adequate housing within the confined inner areas thus creating more pressure for local authorities who, since the Housing Act of 1930, have been obliged to adequately rehouse displaced households. About 0.5 per cent of the housing stock is demolished each year due to slum clearance and for such reasons as road building and the provision of open space. From 1861 to 1961 about two million demolitions occurred, of which over half took place after 1931.

It is doubtful whether slums will ever be completely eliminated. Slum clearance - the result of local government action and assisted by central government subsidies - is a continuing process. The level of slum clearance varies greatly over the country. The real value of subsidies vary between authorities and over time, and local authorities have very different attitudes towards slum clearance depending upon their political philosophy, the quality of local housing and general economic activity. Nationally the rate of slum clearance fluctuates (Table 2.1) reflecting both the size of the central government subsidy and the general economic situation. By the late 1960s there were 1.8 million slum dwellings in Great Britain and another 2.5 million lacked at least one basic amenity (Housing Condition Survey, 1967). Referring to the state of repair, stability, freedom from damp, lighting, ventilation, water supply and drainage the Housing Repairs and Rent Act of 1965 laid down the criteria to define whether a house was unfit for human habitation. Because of the substandard nature of stock, demolitions are likely to continue but probably at a reduced rate. Circular 13/75 of the Department of the Environment confirmed the need to demolish 'areas of irredeemably unfit housing where clearance is the only reasonable solution', but it also emphasised the need to retain as much as possible of the existing fabric. It advocates gradual renewal seeing it as:

> a continuous process of minor rebuilding and renovation which sustains and reinforces the vitality of a neighbourhood in ways responsive to social and physical needs as they develop and change - (and accepting that).. some houses of low quality meet a real need of cheap accommodation which might otherwise not be satisfied (paragraph 12).

Since 1969 there has been a clear shift of emphasis towards rehabilitation and away from clearance, though in varying degrees housing improvement has always been regarded as a complementary rather than an alternative method of renewal.

HISTORY OF HOUSING REHABILITATION POLICY TO 1969

The substantial increase in population in the first half of the nineteenth century, the growth in the proportion of the population living in urban areas and the almost complete absence of controls over building and public health brought forth unprecedented congestion and squalor. Within the cotton and wool towns of the north and the coalfield areas, and in much of London the rationale of housing development was to get as many dwellings as possible on to a site at the least cost and as close as possible to places of work. From the 1840s there was a partial movement away from laissez-faire attitudes and policies concerning the urban environment. By the 1860s much of the first generation of housing developed in the industrial revolution was in a state of obsolescence physically (if indeed it was ever 'satisfactory' socially) and later housing was showing obvious signs of decay and dilapidation. The Artisans Dwellings Act of 1868 was the first Act empowering local authorities to repair or improve houses in default of such action by their owners. But the powers were rarely used.

Throughout the late nineteenth and early twentieth centuries suburbanisation was seen as the main answer to the housing problem of the inner cities. Population growth, the extension of public transport, the development of the motor car, the transmission of electricity, the availability of relatively cheap land and the activity of speculative builders led to urban sprawl and lower densities. Some order was brought to this trend by the Public Health Acts of 1872 and 1875, the Housing of the Working Classes Act of 1890, the Housing and Town Planning Acts of 1909 and 1919 and the Town and Country Planning Act of 1932. The Garden City Movement likewise focussed attention on 'building' rather than 'rebuilding' - Ebenezer Howard propogating the desirability of garden cities, founding Letchworth and Welwyn Garden City and influencing the built-form of much of the emerging suburban environment. Except for some public sector infilling and development by charitable bodies, housing within the inner areas remained largely neglected up until the second world war. By the Public Health Act of 1936, local authorities were however empowered to compulsorily purchase 'working class' houses which were unfit and to rehabilitate them so that they would have a further life of 20 years, but as no subsidies were given for this task the Act produced few results. Additional powers given to local authorities to enforce the repair or improvement of unfit houses (with default powers to undertake the work and recover the expense) similarly had little impact.

Improvement policy 1949-69

Throughout the 1950s and most of the 1960s there was very little rehabilitation. In the immediate post war period there was official opposition to improvement or 'patching up' as the process was then termed. The White Paper, Capital Investment (1948) stated that:

> it is implicit in the object of the investment review that the volume of maintenance and small works in 1948 must continue to be strictly controlled, since any significant expansion of this class of work would clearly impede the transfer of resources to more essential purposes (paragraph 14).

In the same year the Ministry of Health Circular 40/48 stressed that:

> work on existing houses calling for the use of sanitary ware, baths and pipes must be limited due to scarcity and the effect use of such materials would have on new building construction (paragraph 7).

Resources were clearly to be steered towards local authority housing development and the redevelopment of blitzed city centres. Yet within a year, the Housing Act of 1949 introduced improvement grants to private owners and subsidies to local authorities in an attempt to make rehabilitation attractive or at least feasible. In part this was seen to be necessary as sub-market rents reduced the ability of both private and public landlords to maintain or improve their tenancies. Grants were available to private persons up to half of the cost of improvement or conversion where the estimated cost of the work was between £100 and

£600.   Three-quarters of the cost of the grant was paid by the central government.   Local authorities received commensurate assistance for the refurbishing of their own properties.   But very little improvement (whether by local authorities, owner occupiers or private landlords) resulted, the Ministry of Housing and Local Government (1955) reporting that between 1949 and 1954 only 5,463 dwellings had been improved and only 624 new dwellings were produced by grant aided conversions.

Local authorities were perhaps still influenced by former restrictions on patching up and more specifically by current policy which firmly placed improvement in a secondary role behind new development, the Ministry of Health (1949) Circular 90/49 recommending that:

> it will be much better to secure a smaller number of good homes than to fritter away the building resources and expenditure on the patching of houses which would remain unsatisfactory in many respects (p.3).

Many local authorities, moreover, were prejudiced against allocating grants for private improvements and used their discretionary powers to the full.   To prevent any use of public money for private profit improvement grants were offered subject to a complex web of conditions:

(i)   that the new dwelling would comply with the required standard;

(ii)   that the new dwelling would have a future life of not less than 30 years;

(iii)   that the applicant had an interest in the property for that period;   and

(iv)   that the local authority would fix the maximum rent which could be charged for the dwelling which in general would equal 6 per cent of the cost of improvement to the landlord.

These onerous (though possibly fair) conditions and the bureaucratic delays to which they gave rise, resulted in private property owners being reluctant to take advantage of the grant facility.

The change from a Labour to a Conservative government in 1951 brought about a shift of emphasis from public to private housing.   Not only did the completion of new houses rise by 63 per cent from about 200,000 in 1951 to 326,000 in 1953 (of which 56,000 were for private owners - the number of private completions achieving parity with public completions by the late 1950s), but the improvement grant scheme was made more flexible in an attempt to attract private landlords and owner occupiers. The government appreciated that if resources were to be available for private house building, rehabilitation would be a way of partly offsetting the necessary rundown in local authority house building.   The proposals of the White Paper, Housing - The Next Step (1953) were largely implemented by the Housing Repairs and Rents Act of 1954 and were intended to increase the pace of housing improvement.   The top limits on the cost of work eligible for an improvement grant (£100-£600) were removed (though the local authority limit remained at £400);   the maximum grant was fixed at £400;   the minimum life of an improved dwelling (in approved cases) was lowered from 30 to 15 years;   and permitted rent increases were raised to allow a landlord to charge an additional rent of 8 per cent of the cost to him of the improvement.

Although in 1954 the number of grant aided improvements and conversions showed a 100 per cent increase over previous years there was a small take-up of grants as conditions were still unfavourable. A high element of repair work was required prior to grant aided improvements, and as there were still limitations imposed on additional rents chargeable, landlords had little incentive to improve their properties. It was not surprising that 90 per cent of improvement grants were awarded to owner occupiers in the mid 1950s. It was probable that the extent of the housing problem of the inner area, was not fully appreciated by the Ministry of Housing and Local Government. The White Paper, Slum Clearance (1955) showed that there were 847,112 unfit houses in England and Wales and forecast that 375,484 would be demolished between 1955 and 1960. But these figures greatly underestimated the true situation. The government might have believed that by extending the role of housing associations the pace of rehabilitation would be speeded up towards the assumed required level. The Housing Act of 1957 enabled housing associations to obtain loans for house purchase and conversion from building societies, local authorities and other public lending bodies. Like private owners they could now apply for improvement grants for property to be converted into rented dwellings after consultation with the appropriate local authority. The 1950s was not however a period of improvement - from 1949 to 1958 only 159,869 dwellings in England and Wales were rehabilitated with improvement grants.

By the late 1950s the slow pace of improvement was officially recognised. The Housing Purchase and Housing Act of 1959 enabled rents to be increased by 12.5 per cent of the landlord's cost of improvement or up to the rent of similar dwellings in the area where property did not contain controlled tenants. Standard grants were introduced which could be claimed as a right. These were available in specific amounts for the installation of the standard amenities - bath/shower, wash handbasin, hot water supply, W.C. and a food store - the total grant available was £155. The Housing Act of 1961 brought houses containing controlled tenants under the Rent Act of 1957 into line with all others by permitting rent increases of 12.5 per cent of the landlord's cost of improvement. It was further recognised that there was a disincentive to improve a house if other houses within the same street or area remained in an unfit condition or at least severely dilapidated. The Housing Act of 1964 was designed to improve areas of poor housing. Local authorities were empowered to declare 'improvement areas' if dwellings lacked the standard amenities and where at least half of the dwellings could be brought up to the approved standard and be expected to last 15 years or more. Local authorities could require landlords to improve their tenancies in these areas with the consent of their tenants. Local authorities could also apply these powers of compulsion outside of the improvement areas. The use of improvement grants was encouraged by a relaxation of conditions of allocation. Standard grants could be used to offset part of the cost of installing some of the standard amenities (but only where it was not practicable to provide all five at reasonable expense); the period over which the grant conditions applied was reduced from 10 to three years; the maximum grant for converting houses of three or more stories was raised from £400 to £500 per unit, and the rent limit was increased for improved dwellings not subject to controlled tenancies. The 1964 Act also strengthened the powers of local authorities for dealing with undesirable conditions in multi-occupied houses.

Although between 1958 and 1968, 1,147,875 dwellings were improved with discretionary and standard grants (a six fold increase over the previous ten year period), the pace of rehabilitation in relation to the number of poor houses remained very slow. From 130,832 grants being awarded in 1960 (the highest number up to that date) the number fell to 108,938 in 1969 (Table 2.2). The economic incentive for landlords to use improvement grants was insufficient. Despite a gradual relaxation in the conditions of grant provision and the slight increase in the permitted rate of return, landlords remained reluctant to undertake improvement. Local authorities were also unwilling to undertake modernisation programmes especially where this would have required the acquisition of properties. The lack of a government subsidy coupled with low rent levels proved to be major constraints.

Coming into office in 1964 the Labour Government had (according to the Party's election manifesto of the same year) a housebuilding target of half a million dwellings per annum. In 1965 the White Paper, The Housing Programme, 1965-1969, confirmed this target and proclaimed that the post war emphasis on new house building (rather than on improvement) was to continue. But devaluation in 1967 and the accompanying disinflationary measures made the government revise its housebuilding programme - in January 1968 the public sector's target being reduced by 16,500 per annum. The number of houses built in the public sector consequently declined by 9.2 per cent from 203,918 in 1967 to 185,090 in 1969 and the total number of houses built - after reaching a peak of 404,356 in 1967 - fell by 9.3 per cent to 366,793 in 1969. Although it might have been argued that as a result of the high level of housebuilding in the mid 1960s it was now possible to plan for a shift of emphasis in the housing effort, it was more likely that the decline in housebuilding in the late 1960s made the shift inevitable.

Since the scale of housebuilding would not have raised the standard of the whole stock and because there was insufficient maintenance of the existing stock to prevent a decline in standards, Stone (1970) stated that:

> even in the short run, stabilising output of new dwellings at 375,000 a year, reducing standards temporarily below full Parker Morris levels and stabilising the proportion of dwellings with garage provision would not provide sufficient resources to raise the current stock faster than they are actually declining (p.273).

The rate of slum clearance and replacement had been slow - about 90,000 houses per annum by the late 1960s. At this rate it would have taken nearly forty years to clear the existing slums apart from new ones formed in the meantime. It would not have been feasible to increase the rate of clearance and replacement up to 270,000 houses per annum as was proposed by Donnison (1967, p.248) on the basis of information drawn from the 1965 National Plan. The capacity of the building industry and its resources were almost certainly inadequate for this task. Even if slum clearance had been undertaken on a scale only marginally greater than that of the late 1960s, there would have been the danger that a growing number of households including former owner occupiers would add to the length of local authority housing lists or buy elsewhere with relatively little compensation. It was almost certain that many low quality pre 1919 houses would be occupied for a further 30 years as at the prevailing rate replacement and growth of stock the normal life of a house is about 140 years.

Recognising therefore that the balance of need between new housebuilding and improvement was changing and that there had to be a corresponding change in local programmes, the White Paper, Old Houses into New Homes (1968) proposed that:

within a total of public investment in housing at about the level it (had) now reached a greater share should go to the improvement of older houses (p.1).

Focussing attention on the need for extensive rehabilitation, the Housing Condition Survey (1967) had revised the number of unfit houses in England and Wales up by 125 per cent from 0.8 million to 1.8 million and it showed that 2.3 million lacked one or more of the basic amenities (780,000 dwellings without a bath/shower and 1.5 million without an inside W.C. or wash basin) and that 3.7 million dwellings – although not unfit – required over £125 million to be spent on essential repairs. Out of a total housing stock of 15.7 million the proportion of poor dwellings was not inconsiderable.

THE HOUSING ACT OF 1969

Stemming from the 1968 White Paper, the Housing Act of 1969 was intended to substantially hasten the pace of rehabilitation. The Minister of Housing and Local Government, Mr Anthony Greenwood (1969a) clearly stated that a major goal of the provisions of the Act was to raise the standard of living of those residing in areas of bad housing which had the potential for improvement:

The idea of continuing to live year after year without basic amenities .... is totally unacceptable at this period in our history. Older people may have got used to a settled way of life, and in many cases it would be wrong to disturb them, but we should do everything we can to see that children are brought up in better than substandard conditions (col.964-5).

Improvement was to be encouraged by increased grants and a relaxation of the conditions attached to them. For private housing, standard grants were to be raised from £155 to £200 to assist in the provision of the standard amenities. Discretionary grants were also increased – from £400 to £1,000 – to enable such work as essential repairs, damp-proofing and rewiring to be done in addition to the installation of the standard amenities. Discretionary grants could also be used for conversions – up to £1,000 per dwelling being available for a conversion into two flats or up to £1,200 per dwelling for conversion into three or more flats. In all cases the grants would have to be matched pound for pound by the applicant's authorised expenditure and the discretionary grant would be conditional on improvement up to a 12 point standard (see Appendix A).

The government contribution towards the improvement of local authority and housing association properties was £1,000 per dwelling if improvements alone were to be done and £1,250 per dwelling if acquisition was necessary in addition. The grants were calculated at 50 per cent of the cost of improvement and acquisition. The intention was to provide local authorities with the equivalent assistance for the purchase of houses for improvement as they received from the subsidy for building new houses under the Housing Subsidies Act of 1967. The Housing Act of 1971 adjusted the amount of the improvement subsidy available to private owners, local authorities and housing associations. Discretionary grants paid by local authorities to private owner occupiers and landlords in development and

intermediate areas were increased to 75 per cent of the approved expense
of improvement works, but the government's share of the cost of improving
local authority housing fell to 3/8 of the cost, the local authority
having to meet the remaining 5/8 (75 per cent and 25 per cent in development and intermediate areas).   Where local authorities acquired properties
for conversion or improvement their acquisition costs were included in the
approved expense for improvement contributions, together with the costs of
works, and were subject to higher cost limits.   Housing associations
could receive either cash grants in the same way as private owners or
contributions in the same way as local authorities, but, outside of
development or intermediate areas, the proportion of government contribution was higher than that to local authorities, one half instead of
3/8 of the total approved cost.

    It is important to note that as a result of inflation, the discretionary
grant of £1,000 in 1969 was in real terms worth only £500 as compared with
1949 when improvement grants (up to a maximum of £300) were first
introduced.   The real increase in the grant over these years was thus
about 67 per cent rather than approximately 233 per cent - the absolute
increase.   But the principal incentive for improvement may not have been
the size of the grant but that the grant did not have to be repaid.

    Further encouragement was given to improvement by the rent provisions of
the Housing Act of 1969.   If grant aided improvements were carried out
in the case of regulated tenancies then the rent could rise to a new fair
rent level as certified by the Rent Officer (under the provisions of the
Rent Act of 1968), with the increase phased over three equal annual
stages.   Where improvements to controlled tenancies reached the quali-
fying standard, the local authority would issue a qualification
certificate.   Upon receipt of the certificate a landlord could apply to
the Rent Officer who would determine a fair rent.   Increases in rent
would have to be phased over five years.   If the property was rated at
over £90 in London or over £60 elsewhere the increases could start in
January 1971;   and lower rated properties - once improved - were eligible
for rent increases from July 1971.   In the case of furnished tenancies,
the Rent Officer could supply and give guidance on the completion of
application forms which could be submitted to the Rent Tribunal, which
might then fix a rent limit and grant security of tenure to a tenant for
a maximum of six months.   If a property was empty when improvement or
conversion took place and was then let unfurnished, the Rent Officer was
required to establish a fair rent.

General Improvement Areas

The 1969 Act re-enforced the idea of area improvement introduced by the
1964 Act, and placed great emphasis on the declaration of General
Improvement areas (GIAs) - areas which in scale could vary widely from
small and compact areas of say 300 houses up to larger areas of between
500 and 800 houses.

    Local authorities were invited to consider which mainly residential
areas could be upgraded;   to subsequently declare GIAs and to concentrate
their activities on the improvement of those areas.   Prior to the
declaration of a GIA, it would be desirable if a large element of
corporate planning could be established, combining those activities
of the local housing, planning and environmental health departments which
had to be integrated into a total policy of urban renewal.   The local

16

authority needed to refer to a report concerning the physical potential of the area, its planning future and the general attitude of residents towards improvements. At the outset both the Labour and Conservative parties in Parliament had agreed that the benefits of area improvement should be enjoyed by the residents of the chosen areas. This fundamental condition was incorporated into Circular 64/69 accompanying the Act stating:

> it is much to be hoped that from the beginning of their enquiries local authorities will make it absolutely clear that what is under consideration is a programme of action designed to raise the standards of comfort and amenity for the residents (p.5).

An important aim of area improvement was to realise the potential of housing so far as was feasible and with this aim a local authority might have insisted on issuing full improvement grants rather than standard grants. This would have been justified according to Mr Anthony Greenwood (1969b) who stated that:

> if the standard grant was available as of right the local authority would be in a very weak position in its discussions with the owners. What we are trying to do here is to put the local authority in a stronger position, so that the owners of property in the area will not simply be able to fall back on the very minimum requirements. The local authority will be able to set out to persuade them to achieve a higher standard of improvement than would otherwise be the case (col.310).

But the 1969 Act already contained the condition - even for the allocation of standard grants - that after an improvement a dwelling would be required to be in good repair, having regard to its age, character and locality. The public interest in a GIA might have been adequately protected by this requirement without any 'persuasive' powers being granted to local authorities, powers which may have deterred many owners (especially owner occupiers) from improving their properties at all.

The Act envisaged that housing associations would make a very useful contribution to rehabilitation by buying houses which came on to the market within the GIAs and improving or converting them under arrangement with the local authority.

Under the 1969 Act local authorities received reserve powers enabling them to acquire property compulsorily especially if owners threatened the success of a whole scheme by failing to take up improvement grants. Yet it was emphasised that encouragement and voluntary action should be the underlying principle. Local authorities would provide improvement and conversion plans and would seek co-operation from builders. Acquisition by agreement or compulsory purchase would only be used at the last resort - the latter requiring the approval of the Department of the Environment.

But the improvement of housing was not sufficient. The improvement of the residential environment was also important. Government grants of one half the cost of environmental improvement were to be available up to a limit of £50 per house in the area. The Act enabled local authorities to improve amenities and to acquire land for this purpose. Improvement works specified in the circulars included tree planting, the grassing or paving over of open space, the provision of play spaces, parking facilities and garages and the repairing and renewing of fences. In addition an

Table 2.2

Improvement/standard grant* approvals,
England and Wales, 1960-77

	Improvement grants (discretionary)	Standard grants (and special grants)	All grants
1960	48,013	82,819	130,832
1961	47,945	79,831	127,776
1962	41,768	68,738	110,506
1963	42,701	77,278	119,979
1964	45,050	76,635	121,685
1965	40,100	82,893	122,993
1966	39,960	67,760	107,720
1967	46,606	66,536	113,142
1968	46,178	68,038	114,216
1969	49,376	59,562	108,938
1970	87,398	69,159	156,557
1971	137,608	59,873	197,481
1972	260,007	59,162	319,169
1973	316,438	44,516	360,954
1974	207,561	24,357	231,918
1975	115,718	11,170	126,888
1976	114,232	11,399	125,631
1977	115,128	10,695	125,825

*Intermediate grants since 1974

Ministry of Housing and Local Government, Housing Returns, and
Department of the Environment, Housing and Construction Statistics.

area might be improved by the exclusion of through traffic, pedestriani-
sation of highways, the repair of road surfaces and the renewal or re-
siting of street lighting.   The importance of area improvement was
clearly recognised by the Dennington Committee which had been set up to
examine the standards for slum clearance and the improvement and repair
of the housing stock.   Its report, Our Older Houses: A Call for Action
(1966) argued that a dwelling is not satisfactory unless it stands in a
satisfactory environment and when improving a dwelling, the local
authority should also attempt to improve the environment.

   It was consequently acknowledged by the 1969 Act that the resources and
effort devoted to rehabilitation would produce a better return if they
were directed to whole areas rather than to individual and dispersed
dwellings.   It was also important that continuity was seen to be an
essential element on which improvement policy was based, therefore a
GIA should not be an area which was subject to major structural change
or redevelopment in the foreseeable future.

Some effects of the Housing Act of 1969

The 1969 Act was a major factor in restoring many properties which
otherwise would have remained in poor condition or have been demolished.
Between 1969 and 1973 the number of improvement grants approved increased
by about 230 per cent from approximately 108,938 to 360,954 (Table 2.2).
In England and Wales discretionary grant expenditure over the same period
increased from almost £40 million per annum to over £300 million.   By
1973 total housebuilding had fallen to 295,000 completions from 319,000
the year before - rehabilitation now being on a greater scale.   Even as
early as 1971 the Housing Condition Survey showed the extent of
improvement (Table 2.3).   The number of unfit dwellings had been reduced
by 31.0 per cent from 1.80 million in 1967 to 1.24 million while 2.87
million still lacked one or more basic amenities; the highest proportion
of unfit housing, 51.8 per cent being rented from private owners.   By
the end of 1973 less than 2.5 million dwellings lacked basic amenities.
At the 1973 rate of rehabilitation it would have taken probably only a
decade to rectify this deficiency.   Some regions witnessed a faster rate
of improvement than others.   In the North East virtually every pre war
local authority house was modernised, in the period 1970-72, and by 1972
the Assisted Areas were allocating about half of the national total of
grants received by owner occupiers and local authorities.   Progress was
also being made with the declaration of GIAs.   By September 1973, 733
GIAs had been set up in England and Wales comprising 223,000 dwellings -
of which approximately 50,000 had been approved for improvement grants.
But there are many side effects of improvement.   Mr Anthony Crosland (1972),
then Shadow Minister for the Environment, argued that:

> Improvement grants (although) highly successful in improving
> the housing stock, (also) operate regressively.   They are
> overwhelmingly taken up by better off owner-occupiers and
> speculative property developers, who receive not only the
> amount of grant, but also the appreciation in the capital value
> of the house.

   Within GIAs these trends and comparisons were especially pronounced,
Babbage (1973) argued that:

> by declaring a general improvement area in an area of housing
> stress .... the local authority may just as well have been putting

a flag on the developer's office wall map to show where he
might operate with the best return on investment (p.279).

Improvement grants also enabled private landlords to raise rents and
thus increase the capital value of their investments. At first they
were reluctant to take up improvement grants because many tenants could
neither afford nor wished to pay higher rents. This was particularly
evident in the case of controlled tenancies - only 4,000 dwellings being
improved to the standard of repair and maintenance from 1969 to October
1971. The White Paper, Fair Deal for Housing (1971) explained that this
was because:

> the landlord of a controlled dwelling who wishes to improve it
> has to undergo a daunting procedure before obtaining the right
> to charge a fair rent; and must wait four years after the
> improvements have been made before the rent can be obtained in
> full.

The subsequent Housing Finance Act of 1972 enabled improvement work to
proceed as soon as the landlord obtained approval for a grant. As soon
as the improvement works were carried out, the landlord would then be
able to charge a rent increase - its annual rate being 12.5 per cent of
the amount (net of grant) spent on improvement. A further rent increase
up to the fair rent level (if not yet reached) would then be permitted -
after the dwelling had been certified as being up to the qualification
standard of repair and amenity - the increase being spread over a two
year period. The 1972 Act probably had some effect on the rapidly
increasing number of improvement grants taken up in 1972 and 1973, but
this should not be over emphasised.

Although it was the intention of the Labour government in 1969 that
tenants would benefit from housing improvement with landlords being
rewarded by getting fair rents, few small landlords could afford improvement despite the relaxation in conditions. Landlords had to match grants
pound for pound, and taking into account allowances, it was forecast that
average rents would increase by only 35p per week in 1972 and by 25p in
1973. Landlords would therefore either look forward to vacant possession
or would sell to larger landlords who would increase the capital value of
their newly acquired property if it became vacant. Comparatively low
rent tenancies would be converted into high rent furnished luxury flats
or maisonettes. New higher income tenants could afford the furnished
rents at the market level without recourse to the Rent Tribunal and the
authorised eviction which such action frequently provoked. Both for the
purpose of development for sale and for the creation of 'up market'
tenancies, owners usually felt it necessary to displace their tenants.
Results of social research by the Department of the Environment (1975)
have shown that over 60 per cent of households were displaced from
properties owned by landlords in receipt of grants for improvement or
conversion. Although many of the affected tenancies were furnished,
housing young transient occupiers, many contained families who had made
their homes over many years in the less expensive furnished accommodation
typical of a high proportion of lettings in stress areas. Babbage (1973)
described how 'winkling' was a common method used to encourage tenants to
quit:

> Offers of as much as £5,000 were made to tenants to give up
> their statutory tenancy. The greatest worry was the larger
> proportion of cases where, particularly with older people,
> an offer of a few hundred pounds was made. To the poorer

Table 2.3

House condition survey, England and Wales 1971,
stock of dwellings lacking basic amenities
by region

Condition	Thousand dwellings	%
Unfit dwellings	1,244	7.3
All dwellings not unfit	15,856	92.7
Total dwellings	17,100	100.0
Lack of basic amenities Dwellings lacking		
W.C. inside dwelling	2,032	11.9
fixed bath in a bathroom	1,630	9.5
wash basin	2,043	11.9
sink	84	0.5
hot and cold water at 3 points	2,374	13.9
one or more of these amenities	2,866	16.8
Dwellings with all these amenities	14,234	83.2

Source: National House Condition Survey, 1971

family it seemed a large sum and they were tempted to move out only to find it insufficient to assist them in finding another home. In some cases winkling was combined with an agreement that the landlord would 'evict' the tenant on the presumption he would then have to be rehoused by the local authority as 'homeless' (p.280).

Harassment was a further process used to displace tenants. It was probable that the degree of alleged harassment - when compared to that affecting non grant properties - was much greater in the case of properties which were either already or later to be the subject of discretionary grant application. Although prosecution was often inhibited by inadequate evidence there was usually enough of it to link allegations of malpractice to the owner's desire for vacant possession.

Inevitably the displaced low income tenants would seek homes in an ever shrinking pool of privately rented accommodation. Many of these households shifted to the already overcrowded furnished areas. Here they joined those destined to become eventually homeless. But some became immediately homeless. It fell to the local authority social services:

> to find temporary accommodation (usually at high cost in hotels
> and boarding houses) and then to the housing department
> permanently to rehouse them ... How absurd that the same hand
> which dangles the carrot should then pay the bill for bed and
> board and lose a dwelling at the expense of the waiting list,
> at the expense of conversion schemes which showed no housing
> gain and very often, a housing loss (Babbage, p.279).

The then Secretary of State for the Environment, Mr Peter Walker (1972) became aware of this dual and conflicting responsibility of local authorities - the statutory duty (or so it was believed) to provide improvement grants on the one hand and the duty to house the homeless on the other. But he did not accept that tenants should be displaced immediately an owner acquired a grant:

> I recognise that certain tenants in rented properties have been
> told they have to go because of improvement grants .... In their
> ignorance they have gone. So I am writing to all local
> authorities to ask them in future where they approve an
> improvement grant for tenanted property that they should inform
> the tenants of their basic legal rights (col.349).

It can be questioned however whether tenants faced with eviction, and perhaps subjected to the pressures of 'winkling' or harassment would be prepared to claim their legal rights to the full, especially when the end result might not just be security of tenure but a large increase in rent - not withstanding the availability of rent allowances for unfurnished accommodation provided by the Housing Finance Act of 1972.

The large increase in property values between 1971 and 1973 - which in the inner areas of large cities resulted largely from the demand of the speculative developer - jeopardised the plans of local authorities and housing associations. Rents and repayments on improved properties would have been greatly in excess of the ability to pay of those in need. Higher grants were clearly required to reduce the amount of expenditure which had to be recouped from tenants.

Whereas the need to eliminate rapidly rising commuter travel costs provided the motive, improvement grants partly provided the means for middle and higher income households to acquire and renovate poor housing within the transitional zone. Developers attempted to satisfy this demand, but not without far reaching repercussions. Mr Anthony Crosland (1972) as Shadow Minister for the Environment – argued that:

> The manic rise in prices fosters a speculative investment demand for houses .... creates a hideous two-nation pattern of housing .... through the middle class takeover of previously working class areas.

Improvement grants intended to benefit the residents of areas of substandard housing were manifestly not benefitting those residents. They were adding to the profit of developers, increasing the capital value of the properties of often non-resident landlords and helping to provide new homes for former commuters. Simultaneously communities were being destroyed as quickly as if major clearance schemes had been undertaken – many former residents doubling-up in increasingly multi-occupied dwellings, becoming homeless or moving elsewhere, often without trace. Within the GIAs – particularly in areas of high stress – these trends were magnified, improvement grants causing:

> massive socio-economic change (and) leaving a juxtaposition of affluence and squalor with the extremes of the social index in neighbouring properties, only some of which are improved (it is evident that) the professional and managerial classes are keen to move into an area being socially and environmentally upgraded and are happy to live next door to a working class family in the expectation that 'they will eventually move away'. (Babbage, p.280).

A body of opinion evolved in the 1970s which either ignored the social effects of the 1969 Act or actually welcomed them.

The 'bricks and mortar' approach, applied before official research had indicated the social implications of rehabilitation, doubtless prompted the Minister of Housing and Construction, Mr Julian Amery to state that 'the name of the game is improvement'. He referred (1972a) to the distribution of improvement grants nationally – 75 per cent to owner occupiers and 25 per cent to private landlords/developers thus underestimating the real effects of improvement especially within the inner areas of cities where the distribution of grants was the reverse of the national pattern.

The Estates Gazette (1972) similarly saw improvement mainly in physical terms:

> One of the great assets bequeathed by Victorian enterprise is a large stock of solid buildings. Many of these have another century of worthwhile life in them, and by adaption, conversion and modernisation – or in other words by improvement – they can make an extremely valuable contribution to the total number of homes available .... Certainly a proportion of the grants may be considered by some to be misdirected, but this may be a cheap price to pay for an overall increase in the available housing stock (p.1647).

The journal implied that even if improvement benefitted initially the middle classes:

the cumulative process of filtration would benefit all sectors
of the community.   Every addition to the housing stock provides
an extra home for someone, somewhere.

Yet, as was discussed above, this process is very imperfect and it is
questionable whether it works at all within the transitional zone where
both rehabilitation and redevelopment usually result in lower density
and more expensive housing.

   In theoretical terms an argument can be presented for the assimilation
of socio-economic groups within the same areas of housing, indeed this
was a basis of public housing policy in Britain in the years just after
the second world war.   The Housing Act of 1949 deliberately omitted
virtually all reference to the working classes because it was believed
that housing should be an indivisible subject;   it is unlikely that there
would be any great demand to restructure housing policy on the class
basis which existed before this Act.   More positively, middle class in-
migration could reinvigorate both the economic and social structure of
the transitional areas.   Referring to the East End of London, Bermant
(1973) suggested that:

   it would bring more money, a greater variety of life styles,
   better shops and restaurants, a broader social cross section
   in the schools, a wider choice of candidates for the councils,
   a higher yield on the rates.   It might even give the East End
   something it has never had, a decent English bookshop, and
   restore something it used to have - children playing in the
   street.

This prediction might also be applicable to the large number of other
inner city areas where over the years mass deprivation and the formation
of low income ghettoes have occurred.   But the cause of concern is not
that improvement grants may be associated with the creation of more
balanced communities, but that certain areas may be taken over by middle
and higher income groups - the poorer classes being displaced.

Proposals for reform 1972-74

The consequences of the 1969 Act were becoming increasingly identified -
but at first not openly acknowledged by the government.   Mr Julian Amery
(1972b) thought that:

   the landlords of the country are doing a very good job (and) it
   is very difficult to judge which developers should qualify for
   improvement grants and which should not.

Yet within the Conservative Party there was growing recognition of the
social consequences of grant approval.   Mr David Hunt (1972) Young
Conservative national chairman thought it necessary to:

   impose strict conditions on the availability of improvement
   grants to ensure that they are repaid if the property is resold
   after five years.

   Shelter (1972) advised greater protection for households especially
tenants of unfurnished lettings in improving areas.   It was necessary,
argued Shelter, that those living in improvement areas benefitted from
improvement (the intention of the Act).   Where compulsory purchase was
required for this purpose (and for the acquisition of empty property)
100 per cent grants should be made available.   Shelter proposed that,

to deter eviction, private property left empty pending improvement should be rated at 200 per cent. But the Association of Public Health Inspectors (1972) was concerned with the pace of rehabilitation. In a memorandum to the Department of the Environment it drew attention to the shortage of available builders to undertake improvement work. It proposed that rehabilitation would only be effective in helping to eliminate substandard housing if improvement grants were increased up to 75 per cent throughout the United Kingdom, and that the £200 - £300 standard grant were raised and its 50 - 75 per cent (of cost) limit relaxed. It was also argued that there were too few general improvement areas - comprising only about 2.75 per cent of poor housing in England and Wales, and that the size of a typical GIA (about 300 houses) was too small.

The Housing Condition Survey (1971) published in 1973 indicated that it would take until 1982 to eliminate all the unfit housing - a prediction based on the rate of improvement over the previous $4\frac{1}{2}$ years. Although the numbers of unfit dwellings and those lacking basic amenities had fallen from 1.8 to 1.2 million, and 3.9 to 2.9 million respectively from 1967 to 1971, one in six households still lacked at least one basic amenity. The government consequently accepted that the improvement grant system should be subject to thorough scrutiny.

In 1972, a House of Commons Select Committee on Expenditure was appointed for this task and it was to consider specifically:

a) Who was receiving grants, how and for what.

b) The effects of improvement grants on the housing stock, its condition, its ownership and its price.

c) Whether the legislation was achieving its purpose.

A major supplier of evidence to the Committee, the Royal Town Planning Institute (1973), emphasised that:

the problem of 'gentrification', the movement out of existing tenants and their replacement by groups with higher incomes .... poses important questions about what and who the present legislation is for? Is it intended to upgrade existing areas of sub-standard housing or is it to improve the conditions of the existing residents of these areas? This becomes an urgent problem when those tenants displaced as a result of improvement, by the need for vacant possession by landlords or higher rents, suffer a decline in their housing standards (paragraph 2.3.4).

The Association of Municipal Corporations (1973) making recommendations, regarded it reasonable and helpful if local authorities were empowered to:

impose conditions when making improvement grants as to repayment on sale within a defined term of years .... to nominate a tenant to occupy a dwelling improved with a grant (and) to prescribe the type of applicant for a tenancy, or the nature of the letting (paragraphs 13-14).

Being disappointed with the low take up of grants within the general improvement areas, the Association suggested that local authorities should also be given powers requiring the improvement of houses beyond the limited power they had under section 19 of the Housing Act of 1964; and being concerned that rent increases under the Housing Finance Act of 1972 could take place without obligations being imposed on the landlord, proposed that 'certificates of provisional approval' (introduced by the 1969 Act) be reintroduced enabling local authorities to secure that at least a minimum standard of repair and improvement was carried out before a landlord obtained a rent increase.

The White Paper, Better Homes - The Next Priorities (1973) included some of the recommendations of the witnesses to the Select Committee. The White Paper proposed that where improvement grants were awarded to landlords, local authorities should have the right to insist that the dwelling was let for at least seven years, and if a property was sold after improvement (assuming the owner had vacant possession) the grant should be repaid with compound interest to the local authority. It was also proposed that local authorities should have discretion to compel owners to improve their properties (and if they refused the authorities should undertake the work themselves and impose a charge). Local authorities should also be given powers to buy up empty properties using compulsory purchase orders. Perhaps the most important aspect of the White Paper was the proposal to declare Housing Action Areas (HAAs). These would be inner stress areas of about 400 - 500 houses where developers and large landlords have displaced lower income tenants; where house prices are rapidly rising, and where communities are being broken up and homelessness is increasing. There would be a high proportion of furnished tenants, occupancy rates would be over 1.5 persons per room and multi-occupation would be substantial. There would also be large families, a high proportion of elderly occupants and housing would generally lack basic amenities. Within the HAAs the new powers of the local authorities (specified above) would be exercised to the full but in addition landlords would be prevented from selling their properties to speculators or any private individual without first offering them to the local authority or a housing association. Local authorities would have the responsibility of rehousing tenants evicted as a result of an improvement, and local authorities should also be able to nominate tenants when landlords left rooms empty. GIAs would continue to be declared but specifically within areas free of stress - unlike many which had been declared in the past, often with unsuccessful results. The proposals provoked criticism. From the left it was thought that HAAs would involve another degree of area fragmentation - total community action and neighbourhood renewal being preferred, and from the right it was thought that improvement would slow down as the proposals would deter the activities of developers and speculators.

Prior to subsequent legislation, the government considered it necessary to ensure that improvement grants in certain circumstances would not merely be added to developers' profits. Clearly the government was not convinced that if the proposals of the White Paper were implemented developers would cease to convert or improve. Circular 99/73 stated that the refusal of an improvement grant would be justified where its only effect would be to add to the profits flowing from a development scheme which would have proceeded as a commercial venture even without the grant. Since at least 1969, local authorities had discretionary powers but most had been reluctant to use them, and in 1973 the Minister for Housing and Construction, Mr Paul Channon became more willing to give permission for compulsory purchase orders realising that this was perhaps the only way to prevent the wholesale eviction of traditional working class communities. The Secretary of State for the Environment Mr Geoffrey Rippon (1973) reiterated official support for rehabilitation declaring that:

> we should now turn away from a policy of massive and widespread
> redevelopment and give the first priority to providing people
> with fit, modernised, comfortable houses where they now live
> .... (their) .... familiar surroundings contain a community
> structure that has taken generations to build up.   It cannot
> be recreated quickly on remote new estates.

The Housing and Planning Bill of January 1974 seemed a half hearted
attempt to apply the proposals of the White Paper.   It accepted that
improvement rather than redevelopment was to receive top priority, and
HAAs were to be declared specifically for this purpose.   The Bill
proposed that grants would have to be returned at a compound rate of
interest if an improved house within a HAA is sold within seven years
(and if located elsewhere within three years);   that generally
compulsory purchase could be used solely to protect tenants, and that in
many cases compulsorily acquired tenancies would be handed over to
housing associations and then assisted by funds from the Housing
Corporation – the corporation being able to borrow up to £300 million
from the government for this purpose.   The Bill also proposed that
improvement grants should no longer be available for second homes.   But
many of the recommendations of the White Paper were omitted especially
those applicable to HAAs.

Mrs Gladys Dimson, Chairman of the GLC's Housing Development Committee
(1974a) thought that:

> overall the measures will tickle rather than tackle the enormous
> problem....   Furnished tenants will still be vulnerable to
> eviction by landlords seeking to get vacant possession in
> advance of an action area being declared.

The Bill did not propose that landlords wishing to sell their properties
should first inform the local authority or a housing association giving
them first option to purchase;   it did not give local authorities power
to compel a landlord of an empty tenancy to accept appointed tenants;
nor did the Bill give local authorities the responsibility of rehousing
tenants evicted as a result of improvement.   The general election of
February 1974 and the return to office of a Labour government prevented
the Bill from being enacted.   New legislation had to be drafted.

REHABILITATION POLICY SINCE 1974

Introducing an alternative Bill, the Secretary of State for the
Environment, Mr Anthony Crosland, (1974) stated:

> I have for long been a passionate opponent of indiscriminate
> clearance, which I believe has gone too far .... in many areas.
> I believe that indiscriminate clearance can be appallingly
> destructive of existing communities and frequently a very
> expensive solution (col.53).

To emphasise the continuing shift of emphasis of public policy the
Housing Act of 1974 therefore extended the Housing and Planning Bill of
the former government.   The Act prevented recipients of improvement
grants from selling their properties (or leaving them empty) within five
years unless the grant was repaid to the local authority at a compound
rate of interest (this contrasted with the three year limit prescribed

27

by the previous Bill). A seven year restriction within the HAAs was also imposed (as the previous Bill had required). Local authorities were empowered to demand the improvement of individual rented properties - a nine month period being imposed on landlords for this purpose. If landlords failed to improve their tenancies, the local authority is able to purchase the properties with a compulsory purchase order if necessary and then to hand the municipalised accommodation back to the original tenants. To alleviate the 'disincentive' effect on owners of the new conditions attached to grant approval, grants and limits of eligible expenses were increased. Improvement grants were raised from £1,000 to £1,600, or, where a building of three or more storeys was being converted, from £1,200 to £1,850. These amounts represented 50 per cent of the increased level of eligible expenses - £3,200 and £3,700 in respect of the above cases. Within the GIAs improvement grants were increased up to £1,920 and £2,220, and in the HAAs they were raised up to £2,400 and £2,775. Intermediate grants were introduced replacing standard grants. These were at a higher rate and equal to 60 per cent of eligible expenses up to £700. Repairs or replacement grants were to be made available at 60 per cent of eligible expenses up to a maximum of £800. There were many other provisions of the grant system which were amended by the 1974 Act (Appendix B), but the principle that improvement grants should give a house a life of at least 30 years was retained. After improvement a dwelling should, if practicable, have all standard amenities and meet a 10 point standard (see Appendix C).

Policy towards the GIAs was modified in the light of the problems which had emerged since 1969. Except in some of the larger urban authorities there had been an absence of any systematic attempt to integrate GIA policy with planning in general. Planning staff were very rarely involved with GIAs and little research was undertaken into the relationship between GIAs and for example slum clearance, new housing, local rent levels and employment opportunities. Both the 1973 White Paper, Better Homes, the Next Priorities, and the House of Commons Committee on Expenditure expressed dissatisfaction with the rate of progress in declaring GIAs and the rate of improvement within these areas. Circular 13/75 issued under the 1974 Act therefore stressed that confirmation for housing renewal schemes within the GIAs would not be forthcoming unless they are part of a well formulated overall strategy. The same circular advised local authorities to formulate fresh renewal strategies and where appropriate to declare housing action areas as integral parts. In areas of acute stress HAAs would become the principal part of renewal policy. HAAs were seen by Pickup (1974) as:

> holding operations, designed to produce a swift amelioration in basic living conditions .... In most cases it is hoped that major rehabilitation of the area may turn out to be feasible, perhaps reinforced by its subsequent conversion into a general improvement area (p.55).

But other HAAs will have lesser prospects, the object being to make conditions reasonably tolerable towards the end of an area's useful life during which redevelopment will gradually take place.

The 1974 Act soon provoked criticism. Shelter (1974) predicted that landlords without the aid of improvement grants and using their own funds would continue evicting tenants of furnished flats and converting the accommodation into expensive luxury flats. This fear was proved in part groundless as the Rent Act of 1974 introduced tenure security in respect

28

of most furnished lettings, though of course it provided an incentive for some landlords to obtain vacant possession by winkling and harassment. There were also fears that compulsory purchase orders would be used only in the last resort because of the severity of the prevailing economic conditions. It was proposed by the North Islington Housing Rights Project in association with Shelter (1974) that the government should stress the importance of compulsory purchase orders in the new HAAs especially where properties were in a poor condition; where landlords were known to be negligent; where councils are informed of intended evictions; where housing was offered for sale on the expiry of a tenancy; where overcrowding was acute, and where properties were left empty or under-occupied.

The White Paper, Public Expenditure to 1978-79 (1975) announced that although expenditure on improvement works was to be reduced from £423 million (in 1974-75) to £297 million (in 1975-76) the emphasis would be on improving the worst housing. The acquisition of property for improvement would therefore increase at the expense of refurbishing existing local authority stock - especially inter war flats. There was also to be a continuing shift of emphasis away from building new council housing to the rehabilitation of substandard houses. In part this was due to the very high cost of managing and maintaining local authority estates. In 1974 this amounted to about £500 million - much of it being spent on repairs and damage caused by vandalism - a comparatively rare phenomenon in areas of rehabilitation. Yet Shelter (1974) accurately foresaw that local authorities acquiring rundown tenancies would not have enough resources to modernise the properties - the houses remaining empty in consequence. Despite increased local authority waiting lists and increased homelessness, the number of local authority dwellings acquired for improvement but standing empty has rapidly increased - reaching 500,000 in England and Wales in 1975 out of a total of 675,000 empty dwellings.

There was also a sharp decline in the number of improvement grants taken up, a decrease of 65.2 per cent from the record number of 360,954 in 1973 to 125,825 in 1977 (see Table 2.2). Although the recession in the property market, high rates of interest and the financial difficulties of the construction industry were all contributory, it is probable that the more stringent conditions of grant approval introduced by the 1974 Act also had an adverse and possibly major effect upon applications for grants.

A further and far reaching shift of emphasis in housing (and planning) policy was announced by the Secretary of State for the Environment, Mr Peter Shore (1976). He stated that there would be a reversal of the decentralisation policy of the last 30 years to one of concentrating resources on the improvement of the inner areas of the major cities - not least London.

While decentralisation has meant better living standards and improved employment opportunities for thousands of families - within the inner areas poor housing, overcrowding, one parent families, social polarisation and high unemployment remain very great causes of concern. It is questionable whether the 1974 Act is meeting its objectives notwithstanding the constraints imposed upon it by economic conditions. The comprehensive reinvigoration of the twilight areas, involving a more co-ordinated national urban renewal policy, would in large measure require an even greater commitment to rehabilitation by future legislation.(1)

It has often been economically more feasible for a house owner to improve rather than demolish and rebuild. Rebuilding might have cost for example £10,000 and the house would last 80 years whilst rehabilitation might have cost about £4,000 and the building would have had an additional life of at least 20 years. The difference of £6,000 invested say at 5 per cent after tax would have yielded £16,000 after 20 years. The finance and resources saved by rehabilitation would then be available for other projects. Higher costs and rates of interest in the last few years would not have greatly altered the comparative advantage of improvement.

Private landlords are interested initially in increasing capital values and then the flow of rents (unless they are going to sell their property). They would probably undertake improvement if the post renewal value of the property was greater than the pre renewal value plus the net capital expenditure incurred in improvement. This belies many of the complexities of replacement theory such as alternative forms of investment related to different rates of return.

Davis and Whinston (1961) argued that the value of property not only reflects its own value but also the condition of the immediate area in which it is located. Using an example from game theory, known as the 'prisoner's dilemma', they assumed that there was a neighbourhood which included two property owners each of whom had half their capital invested in shares. They were at position D in the table below in which the left hand figure in the bracket refers throughout to the average return of Owner 1.

		Decision of Owner 2	
		Invest in improvement	Not invest in improvement
Decision of Owner 1	Invest in improvement	(0.07,0.07)A	(0.03,0.10)C
	Not invest in improvement	(0.10,0.03)B	(0.04,0.04)D

Each owner had to decide whether or not to transfer some capital from the sale of his shares to his property in order to renovate the property. Each owner's decision was determined by the action of the other owner. If only one of the owners renovated his property his return decreased because his house was in a decayed neighbourhood, and he had foregone an income from his shares. Meanwhile the owner of the non-renovated house benefitted as he still received an income from his shares and also derived a higher return on his investment in property due to the improvement of the neighbourhood. This is illustrated in position C and B. In position C, Owner 2 no longer benefitted from investing in his property as this would have lowered his return from 10 per cent to 7 per cent as shown in position A. Unless the two owners agreed that they should both renovate their properties simultaneously and move to the optimum position (position A), they would probably remain at position D, because if either took the initiative and renovated his property his return would be reduced. Davis and Whinston defined this uneconomic use of resources at position D as 'blight', and suggested that it exists:

> whenever (i) strictly individual action does not result in redevelopment, (ii) the co-ordination of decision making via some means would result in redevelopment, and (iii) the sum of the benefits from renewal could exceed the sum of the costs (p.59).

If this situation existed in the inner areas of cities, there would either be an incentive for owners to co-ordinate their property investment decisions or for a developer (private or public) to purchase the properties and improve them. The developer would thereby internalise the externalities and derive a profit surplus.

Local authorities take a broader view of the comparative costs of re-development and rehabilitation and are more concerned with maximising net social benefits. The Department of the Environment in its Supplementary Memorandum to the House of Commons Expenditure Committee (1973) accepted that:

> all costs and benefits .... should ideally be taken into account. The method requires that rationally one should select that scheme which provides the greatest excess of benefit over cost and, in so doing, one should – through discounting – take account of the different lengths of time of investment schemes and the unequal instance of cost and benefits over time (paragraph 4).

But the Department acknowledged that there are major difficulties in measuring the benefits of a scheme:

> Even if free market conditions existed it would involve measuring benefits that accrue to people not directly affected. But most housing investment decisions are taken in circumstances very far removed from free market. A method outlined in Appendix B to Circular 65/69 .... attempts to overcome this difficulty by reducing the benefit assessment to a judgement of the quality of an investment relative to some standard where practice or opinion suggests that all cost and benefits are equal. New local authority dwellings are taken as this standard (paragraph 5).

The implication of this is that if rehabilitation is less expensive than public sector housebuilding there will be a surplus of benefits over costs assuring that benefits will be broadly comparable.

Some of the more important cost factors which are taken into account when an authority has to decide whether to improve or rebuild an existing block of houses comprise:

(i) Foregone housing cost. If the houses are replaced or improved then the existing housing services are lost. Allowances have to be made for this by including the value of the existing structures (i.e. the acquisition price of the building less the value of the cleared site) as a cost in both options. Where the acquisition costs have increased this will reflect the increased value of the structure and the site.

(ii) Transaction costs. All transaction costs incurred in acquiring the property should be included.

(iii) <u>Site value</u>. Redevelopment is usually more costly than improvement because the site lies unoccupied for much longer than if rehabilitation occurs. This is taken into account by charging the site an annual cost some years prior to occupation and compounding it at the rate of interest. Thus if the site is expected to be unoccupied for four years the site value, say £60,000 will then be £60,000 $(1.1)^4$ = £87,846, i.e. £60,000 compounded at 10 per cent per annum. If the rehabilitation scheme did not necessitate the site being unoccupied, the site value for improvement cost would be £60,000 - a relative cost saving of £27,846.

(iv) <u>Improvement costs</u>. These include the cost of planning, design and environmental improvements.

(v) <u>Building costs</u>. These include the costs of new building plus the cost of demolition and the cost of new roads, services and other community facilities on the site.

(vi) <u>Repair cost</u>. Despite improved houses being brought up to a high standard their subsequent repair costs will probably be higher. Separate estimates of the discounted value of these costs should be made of each type of investment.

Taking into account these costs and government financial support for redevelopment and improvement the Department of the Environment considered that it was:

difficult to see how one could arrive at the conclusion that improvement puts a greater financial strain on the rate payers than redevelopment, given that a higher proportion of the total cost of improvement is met by the government and that improving an older house is generally cheaper than building a new one (paragraph 23).

Relative cost advantage was of course fully appreciated before the 1969 Act was passed. Hillman (1969) referred to the £600 million per annum expenditure necessary to construct 200,000 local authority houses compared with the £115 million (only half being paid through rates and taxation) needed for the improvement of 230,000 homes (a realistic target in 1969 for 1972).

Had there continued to be a concentration on the building of new homes, this would have done little to provide housing for about 20 per cent of the population who could not afford new houses. These houses would have been built mainly for the higher income groups. Needleman (1965) and Stone (1970) concluded from this that the best way to improve the minimum standard of housing with the available resources was to concentrate upon rehabilitation up until at least the 1980s.

Paradoxically, as the national income per capita increases, less households are able to afford the housing which they believe they need. Required standards have tended to have risen at a faster rate than the productivity of the building industry with resulting increases in real costs.

It is frequently argued that when higher income households acquire new homes this creates mobility, whereby each income group is able to filter through to the former housing of the next higher income category. The 'filtering hypothesis' would imply that as the poor move into better standard dwellings there would be an overall surplus of housing -- albeit the lowest quality stock. But there is little evidence to suggest that this has been the case. The building industry has not had the capacity to supply an adequate surplus for filtering to work. For this process to occur there would have to be a fall in the price of old (former high income) houses so that they could be purchased by lower income groups. Yet a fall in the old house prices would adversely affect the price of new houses and developers would suspend building until the resulting scarcity produced price increases.

The 1969 Act, it was agreed in Parliament, would increase the supply of minimum standard private accommodation. While preferring the municipalisation of all private rented property, Mr Anthony Greenwood argued (1969a) that in his view the management and financial problems involved were prohibitive and that landlords would only maintain their property if they derived a profit on the capital they invested. The government regarded the maintenance of the private rented sector as necessary rather than desirable, as an expediency rather than a goal. Provisions were thus made in the Act to permit an improved property to be changed from a controlled to a regulated tenancy.

The Conservatives saw the Act as a stimulant to the private market. Placing greater reliance on the market system than on public intervention, the Conservatives have continually argued that the private rented sector declined as a consequence of rent control. They predicted that the Act by diminishing the number of controlled tenancies would reduce the pace of this decline. This prediction was supported by the argument that within a relatively free market the private tenant would be the most mobile of all households.

Because of their belief in a 'capital owning democracy', the Conservatives viewed the Act with its grant concession as a means of achieving one of their principal housing goals - an increase in the proportion of owner occupiers. The Conservatives considered that about 50 per cent of the housing stock being owner occupied was too low a proportion. A Conservative spokesman, Mr Peter Walker (1969), further believed that:

> it is the owner-occupier who takes the greatest pride and care
> in the maintenance of his home. It is the owner-occupier who
> makes the major improvements so as to provide the modern amenities
> of a bathroom and a kitchen. It is the owner-occupier who takes
> the most positive interest in the decisions affecting the entire
> community.

The Conservatives therefore regarded the Act as a means of both preserving privately rented housing by reducing rent control and encouraging an increase in owner occupation through improvement grants.

The economic rationale for development with the aid of discretionary grants can be illustrated by the following developer's 'balance sheet' (quoted by Kilroy 1972a, pp.79-80) in respect of a private conversion of two houses into 22 flats in North Kensington:

		£
Cost of houses		43,000
Conversion costs		100,000
Fees and interest charges		17,500
	Total outlay	160,500
22 grants of £1,200		26,400
Sale price of	£8,000 per unit	176,000
	Total receipts	202,400
	Profit	41,900

Not only would there have been a return of over 25 per cent to the
developer but nearly two thirds of that return would have been provided
by investment grants. Although this particular scheme did not go ahead
as the developers failed to get vacant possession, a large number of other
similar developments were undertaken where the improvement grants
accounted for a substantial proportion of profits. In many cases because
of the inelasticity of supply, grants were added completely to the capital
value of the house or the profit of the speculator. Resultant house
prices would for the most part be beyond the reach of former tenants.
Yet housing associations could provide dwellings of comparable quality to
privately rehabilitated properties and generally each unit would not be
sold much in excess of £5,000. Similar improved private flats would
fetch £8,000 to £10,000 reflecting the extent of the profit to be realised.

Merrett (1976) proposed that gentrification divided into two political-
economic types, the 'mediated process' and the 'unmediated process'. He
identified the social groups which entered into the mediated model as:
low income residents; high income residents; landlords; estate agents;
and developers. The process is in five stages (Fig.2.1 A). In the
first stage (the base period) the low income residents rent their dwellings
from a group of landlords. In the second stage the landlords sell their
properties to developers, with estate agents acting as middlemen. The
landlords sell for a number of reasons; the institutional landlord may
decide to switch to an asset with a higher rate of return net of management costs and taxes; the small landlord may prefer to forego the future
stream of net rents (along with management problems) for a cash sum to
place at interest without administrative responsibilities; government
policy may slow down rent increases and consequently encourage asset
switching; the landlord may wish to retire or the landlord may die and
the sale of the property is effected by the heir. Developers are willing
to buy as they regard gentrification as an opportunity for profitable
activity. In the third stage –

> the existing low-income residents must be displaced to give the
> developer vacant possession of his property. This leads to
> 'winkling' (the payment of possibly large cash sums to tenants to
> encourage them to leave), harassment and eviction (either) legal
> with a court order (or) illegal eviction by force and threat
> (Merrett, pp.44-45).

The fourth stage involves the renovation (and possibly conversion) of the
vacant property, possibly with part of the cost being offset by an improvement grant (see pp. 15, 28, 40), and if house prices are rising the
developers will increase the pace of renovation. The final stage is the
rental or sale of the dwellings generally to high income residents. The

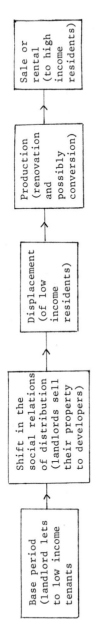

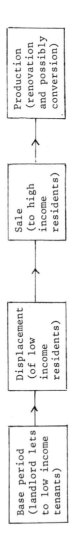

A. The mediated process

B. The unmediated process

Figure 2.1   The mediated and unmediated processes of gentrification

Source: Based on Merrett S., 'Gentrification' in Edwards M., Gray F.,
           Merrett S. and Swann J. (eds.), Housing and Class in Britain,
           1976.

The boxes in A. (the mediated process) read:

Base period (landlord lets to low income tenants) → Shift in the social relations of distribution (landlords sell their property to developers) → Displacement (of low income residents) → Production (renovation and possibly conversion) → Sale or rental (to high income residents)

The boxes in B. (the unmediated process) read:

Base period (landlord lets to low income tenants) → Displacement (of low income residents) → Sale (to high income residents) → Production (renovation and possibly conversion)

relationship between outlay and return from the second to the final stage is shown in Fig.2.2.   In an inner urban area at any one time different dwellings will be at different stages of gentrification and many buildings may never leave base.

In the unmediated model (see Fig.2.1 B) the landlord (having secured vacant possession, either by methods described above, or at the end of a lease) sells his property for the reasons already suggested.   Rising house prices will be an added incentive to sell.   The buyer will almost certainly have a higher income than the former tenant. With an improvement grant, the new resident quickly renovates his property.   Merrett defined this process as unmediated as there is no intervention by the developer, although the estate agent still acts as an intermediary between the landlord and new owner occupier.   In both processes, there may be other intermediaries such as solicitors and surveyors.

Former low income residents would either have been unable to afford higher rents after renovation, or (being without savings or mortgage finance) have been unable to buy the freehold or leasehold of their dwellings.   New high income residents would have been attracted to the inner areas of cities either because the production structure was changing (for example from manufacturing to service activity), or as was suggested by Merrett (expanding upon Evans' hypothesis):

> residence in the inner city has become relatively more attractive
> for example because of the cultural interests of teachers,
> architects and so forth are changing to favour the cosmopolitan
> centre more and suburban life less or because the relative price
> and time of travel to the centre to work and the unreliability of
> that passage are increasing .... raising the attraction of an
> inner city dwelling (pp.47,48).

THE SOCIAL ASPECTS OF IMPROVEMENT

It has become increasingly acknowledged that a major weakness in planning – not least in the context of housing – is that it fails to take social considerations sufficiently into account.   Cherry (1970) pointed out that the planner has been continually preoccupied with the physical condition of housing and the environment.   Only recently has it been realised that residents are the most important aspect of this environment.   The 1969 Act was seen by the government not only as a means of implementing its housing programme but as an important element in its social policy.   Mr Richard Crossman (1969), as Secretary of State for Social Services, stated that 'improvement was safer than building new houses because it created fewer social problems', a passive but nevertheless valid recognition of the social value of rehabilitation.

The sociological importance of good housing cannot be overstated.   The relationship between poor housing and man's opportunities in society have been demonstrated frequently.   The home environment in which a child spends its early life can have a profound effect upon his educational attainment and social adjustment.   Circular 64/69 acknowledged the social as well as the economic aspects of improvement, and recognised that although:

> in some instances there may be little economic justification
> for the improvement, (there would be) an overwhelming social
> case where the installation of one or more standard amenities

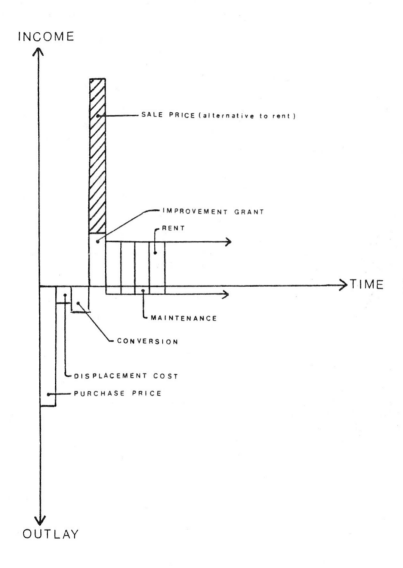

INCOME

SALE PRICE (alternative to rent)

IMPROVEMENT GRANT

RENT

TIME

MAINTENANCE

CONVERSION

DISPLACEMENT COST

PURCHASE PRICE

OUTLAY

Figure 2.2 Gentrification – outlay and income

would help to make life tolerable for a family living in a
house with a comparatively short estimated life (paragraph 2).

Yet in general the Act was mainly concerned with encouraging the use of
discretionary grants as a means of realising a property's full potential -
an extended life of at least thirty years. Comprehensive improvement up
to the 12 point standard (see Appendix A) rather than patching up was
seen as a preferable way of attempting to meet the accommodation needs of
households who would otherwise be living in substandard dwellings.

The social benefits of rehabilitation are not just confined to the sum
of household satisfaction resulting from the improvement of individual
homes. There is in addition the benefits - often intangible - of the
preservation of the local community. Following research undertaken in
east London, Young and Willmott (1957) argued that the community feeling
which existed in areas of bad housing should be retained by accommodating
the existing residents in the same redevelopment scheme. The research
showed that:

> the sense of loyalty to each other amongst the inhabitants of a
> place like Bethnal Green is not due to buildings. It is due
> far more to ties of kinship and friendship which connect the
> people of one household to the people of another. In such a
> district, community spirit does not have to be fostered, it is
> already there. If the authorities regard that spirit as a
> social asset worth preserving, they will not uproot more people
> but build the new houses around the social groups to which they
> already belong (p.198).

It was becoming accepted that people generally wish to live in the same
neighbourhood as others of the same socio-economic group. There are many
explanations for social agglomeration. First, as Anderson (1962) noted,
people in a specific socio-economic group may prefer to interact with
others in the same group rather than among people in other groups. It
is probable, that ceteris paribus, the greater the proportion of a group
living in the same area, the greater the advantages to that group.
Secondly, social agglomeration can be explained using the concept of
social space. If the household has a preference to interact with others
in the same socio-economic group its neighbourhood space will be smallest
in area if it locates in the same neighbourhood as others in the same
group. Buttimer (1969) noted that research has shown that there are:

> thresholds in space beyond which certain groups cannot travel
> without experiencing frustration, tensions and feelings of
> anomie (p.421).

Each household would wish not to cross this threshold within its daily or
local movement (i.e. its neighbourhood space). Only by locating in the
same area as others in the same socio-economic group can it achieve this.
Thirdly, people in different socio-economic groups have different
consumption characteristics. Households will be able to minimise their
cost of shopping journeys by living in the same neighbourhood as others
in the same group. Similarly, if people locate in the same local
authority area as others in the same group they may get the public
services they prefer. These explanations justify the preservation of
existing neighbourhoods, not least the areas of low income housing.

Redevelopment in the 1950s and 1960s usually involved the provision of
lower denisty housing than that which it replaced. It may also have

involved the insensitive relocation of low income communities and severe planning blight between the announcement and completion of a plan.   The distress suffered by the residents of slum clearance areas has provoked opposition to redevelopment schemes.   Improvement policy was seen as a means of avoiding these problems, Mr Anthony Greenwood (1969a) launching the Housing Bill stated that:

> it is remarkable how much attraction many older areas have for
> their inhabitants.   They are familiar, and their friends live
> there.   Slum clearance means disruption, scattering or
> beginning again.   This is not a plea to slow down slum
> clearance, far from it, it is a plea that whenever possible we
> should step in well before slum clearance is necessary - 10 or
> 20 years before - and give suitable areas a longer span of life
> (col.965).

Both political parties saw economic advantages in the Act, and both believed that the social goals were as desirable as the economic implications.   Following the Conservative victory at the general election, the Secretary of State at the Department of the Environment, Mr Peter Walker (1970) reiterated the emphasis which the previous government had placed on improvement:

> New houses are not enough.   We need many more new houses, but
> it should be remembered that whilst new homes take a matter of
> months to build, it takes much longer to build a community....
> We have established communities, with their local churches,
> their local schools, their local pubs and their local football
> teams, where the inhabitants are friends and neighbours of
> each other.   It is important that, where possible, instead of
> using the bulldozer we retain the community and improve the
> whole quality of the housing and its environment.

To help realise these objectives the Circulars to the Act had referred previously to the great stress laid by the Minister in Parliament on the obligation of local authorities both to advise the residents of the planning proposals for their area and to be receptive to the ideas and attitudes of the inhabitants themselves.   Public participation would necessitate that the improvement proposals for the area were sufficiently detailed to be intelligible, but adequately flexible to permit modification in response to popular feeling.   By means of public meetings and personal visits to households, local authorities were to make every effort to secure the confidence of residents and gain their co-operation. Local authorities should also encourage the formation of residents associations which would focus attention on the problems of rehabilitation and provide a further channel of communication.   In areas of housing stress local authorities were faced with further obligations.   Circular 65/69 to the Act ended by acknowledging that:

> there are a limited number of areas, mainly in large cities,
> where the problems of physical decay are combined with problems
> of overcrowding and multiple occupation and other severe and
> intractable problems.   They have been called twilight areas
> and coincide in some areas with what have been called in another
> context areas of multiple deprivation.   The social reasons for
> taking action in such areas may be imperative even if the
> economic prospects are doubtful (col.5).

The Circular suggested that in order that improvement should take place

in such areas it might be necessary to make more use of compulsory purchase than would be usual in, for example, most general improvement
areas.   The references in the above Circulars both to the need for
public participation and the social reasons for taking action in twilight
areas further stresses the intention of the legislation that it was the
needs of the residents which had to be considered.

NOTES

(1)   In July 1977, the government announced that the maximum cost limits
       for house improvement grants were to be raised from £3,200 of
       which an owner could receive at best £1,600 assistance in the
       modernisation of his property, to £5,000 and £2,500 respectively.
       In GIAs, where applicants qualified for 60 per cent approved
       expenditure, grants were increased to £3,000.   In HAAs, where the
       level was 75 per cent (or 90 per cent in special cases), owners
       could receive up to £3,750 or £4,500.

3 Housing stress in inner London

Although the population of inner London – the Group A boroughs (1) – decreased from a peak of 5,003,000 in 1911 to 2,743,000 in 1976, the housing market has not been able to satisfy demand. As the _Economist_ (1977, p.27) stated:

> London's population is falling and new housing is continually being built (but) that does not mean London's housing problem is on the way to being solved. Redevelopment generally results in fewer dwellings (one big old house that contained 20 ill-equipped bed-sitters may well be replaced by a block of eight self-contained flats with all mod-cons).

In addition, as Merrett (1976) pointed out, the conversion of large dwellings into bed-sit accommodation or into very small flats suitable only for couples without children reduces the number of residents, for example:

> in 1-9 Colville Gardens North Kensington the 'before' population was 210 in 72 units; the 'after' population was 120 people in 93 units (p.47).

High densities nevertheless remain. The GLC (1966) found that the residential density in Inner London (2) was 27 dwellings per acre (11 per hectare), with for example 43 dwellings per acre (17 per hectare) in Kensington and Chelsea and 33 per acre (13 per hectare) in Hammersmith. This compared with 12 per acre (5 per hectare) in Outer London (3).

The concentration of the lower social classes in the inner areas and the 'invasion' of these areas by upper classes underlie many of the housing problems of inner London. Using data from the 1966 Census, Willmott and Young (1973) suggested that the spatial distribution of the lower social classes (Fig.3.1) did not conform with Burgess' concentric zone model. Their analysis indicated that inside Greater London:

> the class pattern formed the shape of a cross. The three elements distinguished are the Central Residential District, the Cross itself and the suburban Quarters bound by it. The Cross, into which the working people were concentrated, is from the east to west along the Thames Valley, to the north along the Lea Valley and to the south, coinciding to some extent with the valley of the River Wandle. This pattern of distribution is explained mainly by the location of docks, industry and communication routes, which have mostly been located on low land. The more favoured residential areas, conversely, are commonly on higher ground. Thus the physical geography of London has helped to shape its class geography (p.190).

Willmott and Young acknowledged that their hypothesis was broadly similar to Hoyt's sector theory, but they put greater emphasis on the formative power of physical geography over the shape of the city. In common with Hoyt's model, Willmott and Young's hypothesis takes account of low social class areas being 'invaded' by a higher class population (4). Comparing

the proportions of occupied and retired males in Social Classes I, II,
IV and V in 1951 and 1966, they found that within the Central Residential
District and, for example, within the Cross West boroughs there had been
an increase in the proportion of Social Classes I and II and decreases in
Social Classes IV and V (Table 3.1 A).   It is notable that the greatest
percentage increase occurred in the Central Residential District and the
lowest increase was in the Outer Cross west sector (Fig.3.2 and Table 3.1 B).
Reference to the Census of 1966 and 1971 enables this process of socio-
spatial change to be further examined.   In the period 1966-71, the number
of economically active males in socio-economic groups (SEGs) 1-4 increased
by eight and five per cent in the boroughs of Kensington and Chelsea, and
Westminster respectively, by 29 per cent in Hammersmith, and by one per
cent in Willesden (5).   There were decreases in the numbers in SEGs 7-12,
14, 15 in each of these areas, but especially within the Central
Residential District (Table 3.1 C).

   Lower income households remain the principal group of households in inner
London.   The GLCs Annual Abstract of Statistics (1974) show that in 1974,
although the mean wage of males in London was £48 per week, 78 per cent
received less than this.   This high percentage of low paid workers is
attributable to the high proportion of personal service and public authority
employment (especially in transport), and the relative immobility of
employees in these categories.   Eversley (1973) stated that:

> as London becomes .... increasingly devoted to the provision of
> services .... so the number of people in manual, unskilled and
> semi-skilled jobs is bound to rise proportionately...   These
> lower echelons usually live in Inner London .... because their
> hours of work make it impossible for them to live far from their
> work, and because their wages are insufficient to allow for
> commuting over long distances.   London is rapidly losing its
> former mainstay of steady incomes for manual workers:
> manufacturing industry is declining rapidly and looks like
> continuing to do so...   Distributive trades employment,
> another former mainstay of the un- and semi-skilled .... is also
> declining very rapidly...   For these people the service trades
> are probably the main alternative, but offer much lower earnings
> levels (pp.27-28).

There is thus the possibility of London becoming a city of the very rich
and very poor, with the middle classes moving away and the low income
workers becoming isolated within the inner areas.   Harris (1973) referred
to a cluster analysis by Kelly (1971) based on 1961 and 1966 Census data,
and concluded that whereas:

> in 1961, there were few if any wards in Greater London which
> contained, simultaneously, high concentrations of social classes
> at the two extremes of the social class distribution (bi-polarity)
> .... between 1961 and 1966 several wards of Inner London boroughs
> characterised by flat and bedsitter accommodation .... experienced
> a moderate increase in uni-polarity towards the top end of the
> social scale.   This finding lends some support to the hypothesis
> that there are some areas .... which are experiencing an increase
> in the concentration of the 'rich' or 'prosperous' (pp.179-182).

Harris reviewed the many economic, political and social arguments in
favour of social balance, but considered that they should be treated with
caution because the ideal social composition pattern in any area, and the
size of the area in which the mix should take place, are largely unknown.

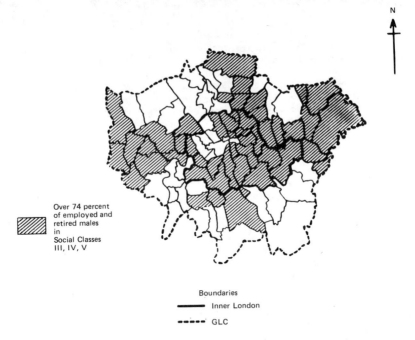

Over 74 percent
of employed and
retired males
in
Social Classes
III, IV, V

Boundaries
——— Inner London
------ GLC

Figure 3.1 Working class areas in Greater London, 1966

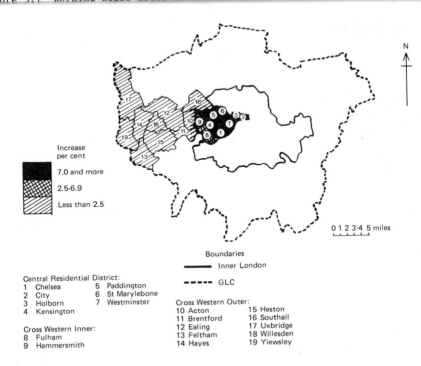

Increase
per cent

7.0 and more

2.5-6.9

Less than 2.5

0 1 2 3 4 5 miles

Boundaries
——— Inner London
------ GLC

Central Residential District:
1 Chelsea   5 Paddington
2 City   6 St Marylebone
3 Holborn   7 Westminster
4 Kensington

Cross Western Inner:
8 Fulham
9 Hammersmith

Cross Western Outer:
10 Acton   15 Heston
11 Brentford   16 Southall
12 Ealing   17 Uxbridge
13 Feltham   18 Willesden
14 Hayes   19 Yiewsley

Figure 3.2   Rates of increase in occupied and retired males in
Social Classes I and II in the west London boroughs,
1951-66

The Report of the Committee on Housing in Greater London (the Milner Holland Report, 1965) emphasised the strong correlation between the concentrated areas of the lower social classes and income groups, and overcrowding and poor housing. The report provided much information about the conditions of rented housing in London and about landlord and tenant relations. But a more comprehensive study of the capital's housing and household characteristics was provided by the GLC's Housing Survey 1967. The results of the first part of the survey were contained in The Condition of London's Housing (GLC, 1970,a). In this report, the GLC differentiated between the Inner Boroughs and Outer Boroughs. Table 3.2 shows that the principal difference between the housing stock of the Inner Boroughs and Outer Boroughs was their age. The Inner Boroughs and the inner west London boroughs in general had poorer housing than the Outer Boroughs or the average for Greater London.

The GLC survey (p.40) found that:

> most of the dwellings with a useful life of less than eight years are terraced houses or tenaments... A high proportion are rented privately, some 72 per cent are poor or unfit and .... nearly all of them were built before 1920. Only a quarter of those dwellings are found in the outer boroughs... The dwelling units with a life of eight to fifteen years do not vary very greatly from those of a life of less than eight years .... the predominant dwelling type is the terraced house (60 per cent); 11 per cent are flats which are not self contained.

It is largely from these dwellings that the GLC calculated that with the addition of a bath or inside W.C., 39,200 units could be improved in the Inner Boroughs and 40,200 units could be improved in the Outer Boroughs. Terraced houses would be the principal dwellings affected (Table 3.3). Particularly in the Inner Boroughs, privately rented dwellings showed the greatest potential for improvement by the addition of both a bath and an inside W.C. Both in Hammersmith and Westminster, nine per cent of dwellings could have been improved by the addition of a bath, a W.C. or both. In Kensington and Chelsea, and Brent the proportions were four and three per cent respectively (Table 3.4). The GLC survey also calculated the number of dwellings which could have been converted into new units (Tables 3.3 and 3.4). The Inner Boroughs contained the highest proportions of dwellings suitable for conversion and also the highest proportion of potentially new units after conversion amounting to 68 and 70 per cent respectively, of the total for Greater London. In Hammersmith 19 per cent of the dwellings were suitable for conversion, in Kensington and Chelsea, and Westminster five per cent and in Brent two per cent. The Inner Boroughs would have gained the greatest number of dwelling units resulting from conversion, 100,600 compared with 42,700 in the Outer Boroughs, proportional gains of 115 and 109 per cent respectively. Hammersmith, Kensington and Chelsea, Westminster and Brent would have increases of 109, 139, 169 and 106 respectively. Within the Inner Boroughs, the principal type of dwelling unit suitable for conversion was the terraced house, and in the Outer Boroughs the semi-detached house. The survey showed that conversions would result in a reduction in the number of rooms per dwelling. Whereas before conversion, the average size of a dwelling (suitable for conversion) was 8.7 rooms, after conversion the average size would be only 3.8 rooms. In addition it was calculated that there would be a loss of nine per cent of the total number of rooms in the converted buildings.

Table 3.1

Changes in Social Class, 1951-66;
and in Social Economic Groups, 1966-71 in West London

A

| | Social Class of Occupied and Retired Men (Percentage) | | | |
| | 1951 | | 1966 | |
	I & II	IV & V	I & II	IV & V
Central Residential District:				
Chelsea, City, Holborn, Kensington, Paddington, St.Marylebone, Westminster	29	31	36	25
Cross, Western:				
Inner:				
Fulham, Hammersmith	12	36	15	22
Outer:				
Acton, Brentford, Ealing, Feltham, Hayes, Heston, Southall, Uxbridge, Willesden, Yiewsley	16	26	18	24

B

| | Percentage change in the number of Occupied and Retired Men, 1951-66 Social Classes | |
	I & II	IV & V
Central Residential District:	+7	−6
Cross, Western: Inner	+3	−4
Cross, Western: Outer	+2	−2

C

| | Percentage change in the number of economically active males 1966-71 SEGs | |
	1-4	7-12,14,15
Kensington and Chelsea	+ 8	−21
Westminster	+ 5	−22
Hammersmith	+29	− 7
Willesden	+ 1	−13

Sources: Willmott P. and Young M., Social Class and Geography,
           Tables 6.4 and 6.5, in Donnison D. and Eversley D.
           (eds), London: Urban Patterns, Problems and Policies,
           Heinemann (London), 1973;   and 1966 and 1971 Census.

Table 3.2

The condition of housing in selected boroughs and Greater London 1961

Percentage of dwellings:	Hammersmith	Kensington & Chelsea	Westminster	Brent	Inner Boroughs	Outer Boroughs	Greater London
with 3 rooms or less	18	34	36	12	19	6	11
with 8 rooms or more	20	10	10	13	14	6	10
as flats	40	69	76	25	47	19	30
as flats converted	8	29	20	5	9	3	5
as flats - not self-contained	8	11	10	4	6	3	4
built before 1919	73	79	66	38	63	30	43
unfit or in poor condition	4	2	3	3	9	2	5
in fair condition	23	17	28	21	29	19	23
without a bath & W.C.	7	1	3	2	9	5	7
without an inside W.C.	5	4	5	2	6	4	5
privately rented	54	60	59	31	44	21	30

Source: The Condition of London's Housing - a Survey
         GLC Department of Planning and Transportation
         Intelligence Unit, Research Report No.4, August 1970

46

Table 3.3

The condition of housing in the Inner and Outer Boroughs 1961

	Inner Boroughs	Outer Boroughs
Type of dwelling unit which could be improved by the addition of a bath or an inside W.C.	%	%
Detached & semi-detached houses	2	14
Terraced houses	44	66
Maisonettes & purpose built flats	33	9
Flats converted	8	4
Flats not self-contained	11	7
Tenements	2	-
Number	39,200	40,200
Tenure of dwelling units which could be improved by the addition of both a bath and inside W.C.	%	%
Owner-occupied	14	29
Rented privately	74	69
Rented from the local authority	12	2
Number	27,600	48,900
Dwelling units which could be converted		
Dwelling units suitable for conversion	87,000	39,100
New dwelling units after conversion	187,600	81,800
Number of dwelling units gained by conversion	100,600	42,700
Type of dwellings units suitable for conversion	%	%
Detached houses	3	20
Semi-detached houses	17	42
Terraced houses	78	37
Flats and maisonettes	2	1

Source: The Condition of London's Housing - a Survey

47

Table 3.4

Dwellings suitable for improvement and conversion in West London, 1967

	Number of dwellings which could be improved by the addition of a bath, a W.C. or both		Dwellings suitable for conversion		Total number of new dwelling units after conversion	Number of dwelling units gained by conversion	
	Number	% dwellings	Number	% dwellings	Number	Number	% dwellings
Hammersmith	5,300	9	10,800	19	22,600	11,800	21
Kensington & Chelsea	2,400	4	3,400	5	8,100	4,700	7
Westminster	6,800	9	3,600	5	9,700	6,100	8
Brent	2,200	3	1,600	2	3,300	1,700	2

Source: The Condition of London's Housing – A Survey

The results of the second part of the GLC Housing Survey were contained in The Characteristics of London Households (GLC,1970,b). Summarising the chief distinguishing characteristics of the Inner and Outer Boroughs, this report showed that in the Inner Boroughs there were high proportions of pre 1920 flats (often having been converted) with three or four rooms, overcrowding and one-person households. Heads of households were younger than those in the Outer Boroughs, and they would probably be in manual occupations. In the Outer Boroughs, there were high proportions of large (six roomed) houses, low occupancy rates, and three or four person adult households. Heads of households, with higher than average incomes, would probably be in non-manual occupations. Table 3.5a shows the broad differences in overcrowding, occupation and incomes in the Inner and Outer Boroughs.

Although the Milner Holland Committee identified separate indices of housing stress which were intended to show clearly the condition of housing in the worst housing areas, the various symptoms of stress were not evenly distributed. Thus some areas suffered particularly from overcrowding, some showed a predominance of multi-occupation, while others were deficient in amenities. The GLC devised the Housing Stress Index to bring together these separate indicators in order to produce a means of identifying areas with the worst overall housing conditions. The Housing Stress Index combined the following separate indices calculated from 1961 census data:

a)   Number of households with more than 1.5 persons per room;

b)   Number of sharing households;

c)   Number of sharing households with 3 or more persons per room;

d)   Number of households with no bath;

e)   Number of households without exclusive use of hot and cold water, bath and W.C;

f)   Number of households of 3 or more persons, with more than 1.5 persons per room;

g)   Number of sharing households without exclusive use of a stove and sink.

Source: Greater London Development Plan: Report of Studies, 1969, Table 2.22.

The GLC designated the highest stress areas as those enumeration districts with stress indices falling in the top ten per cent. In 1967 approximately 293,000 households lived in these areas equal to about 11 per cent of all households in London.

To find the relationship between the cost of housing, income and the pressure for separate accommodation within certain types of housing, a sample survey was conducted in 30 groups of enumeration districts, each of about 300 households. The numerical values of the stress index in these districts ranged from a group average of 24,851 in Islington to 469 in Redbridge. Table 3.6 shows that the stress indices for the sample west London enumeration districts ranged from 23,244 in Kensington to 1748 in Brent. Information obtained in the survey (by interviewing households) was 'grossed up' in order to reflect the characteristics of households in London as a whole. Table 3.5b summarises the findings of this process. It is evident that there are very major differences between the high stress

49

Table 3.5

a. Housing characteristics in the Inner and Outer Boroughs

Percentage of households:	Inner Boroughs	Outer Boroughs	Greater London
Living at more than 1.5 persons per room	6	2	4
In manual occupations	65	51	57
In non-manual occupations	35	49	43
With incomes less than £10 per week	25	23	24
With incomes £10-19 per week	45	34	38
With incomes more than £40 per week	5	10	8

b. Housing characteristics in High and Low Stress Areas

Percentage of households:	High Stress Areas	Low Stress Areas
Living at more than 1.5 persons per room	16	1
Of three or more persons living at more than 1.5 persons per room	29	1
Living in pre 1919 dwellings	96	8
Living in flats	42	14
Living in privately rented accommodation	77	9
Lacking a bath/W.C.	33	2
Without exclusive use of a bath	71	4
Without exclusive use of a W.C.	33	4
With incomes less than £10 per week	22	18
With incomes £10-19 per week	55	29
With incomes more than £40 per week	2	14
Paying rents (as private tenants) of:		
Less than £100 per annum	34	12
£100-149	25	25
£150-199	14	18
£200-299	17	17
£300 and above	10	28

Percentage of population aged:		
15-24	6	1
25-34	21	14
35-44	22	20
45-54	18	23
55-64	15	24
Over 64	18	18

Source: The Characteristics of London's Households
           Greater London Council Department of Planning and Transportation
           Intelligence Unit, Research Report No.5, August, 1970.

Table 3.6

Six sample areas of west London used in the survey of
London's households, 1967

New borough	Old administrative area (1961 Census)	Wards	No. of 1961 Enumeration Districts	Average stress index
Kensington & Chelsea	Kensington	Pembridge Golborne	10	23,244
Hammersmith	Hammersmith	Grove	9	21,638
Brent	Willesden	Kilburn	10	20,175
Westminster	Paddington	Maida Vale South Church Hyde Park	11	8,805
Hammersmith	Fulham	Munster Town	11	5,958
Brent	Wembley	The Hyde	11	1,748

Source: Characteristics of London's Households
          Greater London Council, Department of
          Planning and Transportation Intelligence Unit,
          Research Report, No.5, August, 1970, Appendix A.1

N

0 1 2 3 miles

——— Group A boroughs

Brent

Residential areas suffering from
excessive overcrowding and
sharing of accommodation

Residential areas with houses
in poor physical condition

Residential areas suffering from
both the aforementioned categories

Figure 3.3   Housing Problem Areas, Group A boroughs and Brent, 1966

and low stress areas in overcrowding, the availability of basic amenities, the type of dwelling, income and rent levels and age distribution.   In general it is the households with the lowest incomes and paying the lowest rents which live in the poorest housing.   The high stress areas also contained a higher proportion of population aged 15-44.   The GLC intended to analyse the relationship between housing stress and household characteristics using data from the 1966 Census, but as the results would probably have been very similar to the previous findings, the analysis was not completed.

Areas of housing stress were, however, identified on the basis of 1966 census data.   There were 68 wards within the top decile of the Housing Stress Index.   With the exception of 13 wards in the boroughs of Brent, Ealing and Haringey, these wards were entirely within the Inner Boroughs. But these areas of housing stress were defined mainly on the criteria of overcrowding and sharing.   By establishing Housing Problem Areas the GLC went further in analysing the condition of London's housing.   The Greater London Development Plan: Report of Studies (1969) divided the Housing Problem Areas into north, west, south and east zones;   and further divided the Housing Problem Areas into three categories (Fig.3.3):

   a)   Residential areas suffering from excessive overcrowding
          and sharing of accommodation;

   b)   Residential areas with houses in poor physical condition;

   c)   Residential areas suffering from both the aforementioned
          categories.

The population of the Housing Problem Areas was 1,356,000 (1966) and these areas contained high proportions of young transient adults, privately rented accommodation, manual and unskilled workers and households sharing dwellings - especially in the north and west.   The GLC considered that in the north and west, where there was a high degree of overcrowding and sharing, rehabilitation should be the solution to the problems of poor housing.   In the east, where many dwellings were in an advanced state of obsolescence, redevelopment should be the solution;   and in the south where there were characteristics of the other three areas, various forms of renewal were desirable.   The Ministry of Housing and Local Government (1970) reported that it was estimated that in Greater London in 1969 there was a housing shortage of 233,000 dwellings.   It was probably impracticable to attempt to reduce this deficit (most of which was in the Inner Boroughs) by a policy solely of either rehabilitation or redevelopment.

The 1971 Census further confirmed the disparities between inner and outer London.   Table 3.7 shows that the Group A boroughs contained higher proportions of households living in privately rented dwellings, and at a high occupancy rate, sharing and without exclusive use of basic amenities. In general, Hammersmith, Kensington and Chelsea, and Westminster had even greater proportions of their households with these characteristics, and Brent had higher proportions than Group B boroughs in respect of house-holds living in private furnished tenancies, at a high occupancy rate and sharing.

THE SUPPLY AND DEMAND OF PRIVATE HOUSING IN INNER LONDON

In inner London, the coincidence of low quality housing, multi-occupation, private rented property and residents with low income and unskilled employment suggest that poor and unfit dwellings are a result of low income demand. This situation in London is paradoxical, the Milner Holland Report (1965) stating that:

> Greater London is one of the wealthiest cities in Europe ....
> incomes are rising; population within the built up area is
> falling and the number of dwellings is growing; the quality
> of housing and the general standard of housing conditions are
> both improving. Yet conditions in some neighbourhoods and
> for some people remain bad, and are probably becoming worse
> (p.200).

This situation (which still obtains) is aggravated by demand and supply factors. To a great extent, the demand for housing will depend on the labour force employed in inner areas. The Milner Holland Report examined the structure of employment in London:

> Although the work for which these people are needed ranges
> through all wage and salary levels, a high proportion appears
> to be at the extremes of the income scale: at one end, the
> new executive and professional jobs in for example private
> businesses and central government, and the expanding fields
> of modern communications - television, journalism and
> advertising; at the other, low-wage jobs in the service
> industries which must support and keep pace with metropolitan
> growth - building, transport, clerical work, catering and
> retail distribution (p.60).

Social polarisation is thus mainly a consequence of the employment structure, but to a large extent it is also due to two migratory trends, one outward, the other inward.

The GLC (1970c) indicated that the continual migration out of London consisted disporportionately of young, skilled workers or the upper working and lower middle classes. This process is partly attributable to the relocation of manufacturing firms and employment away from inner London, and is also a result of these groups purchasing a house in a commuter village beyond the Green Belt. Pahl (1970) , in analysing the new residents of a commuter village, concluded that they were highly status-conscious, having risen to the housing class of owner occupier, a process assisted by tax subsidies to mortgage payers. Out migration would accelerate if real transport costs into London were reduced and travelling convenience improved. Since they could not afford to purchase the equivalent space, standard of dwelling or privacy within inner London, these households generally will not be attracted back to even an improved inner area neighbourhood.

There is, nevertheless, in inner London a large demand for low cost housing together with a demand from the high income groups for more accommodation. The total demand for inexpensive units is likely to increase. The GLC (1970c) predicted that:

> If London is to have more hotels and restaurants, more places
> of entertainment and a greater range of personal services of
> all kinds, with more shops, we shall have an increasing demand
> for the workers who now receive the lowest 25 per cent of
> personal incomes in the metropolitan area (p.24).

This low income demand is likely to be concentrated in the private tenancy

Table 3.7

Household characteristics, 1971

Percentage of households:	Hammersmith	Kensington & Chelsea	Westminster	Brent	Group A boroughs	Group B boroughs
Living in owner-occupied dwellings	17.9	15.9	10.0	48.2	19.4	55.7
Living in private unfurnished tenancies	39.7	36.9	42.7	21.9	33.2	16.6
Living in private furnished tenancies	21.7	38.0	25.7	16.5	16.0	6.5
Living at more than 1.5 persons per room	8.2	9.7	1.3	7.7	4.4	1.4
Sharing	30.2	13.9	11.7	23.5	21.2	7.7
Without exclusive use of:						
Hot water	26.1	16.8	17.2	17.0	20.1	8.1
Fixed bath	39.2	30.8	26.9	23.3	30.3	11.4
Inside W.C.	21.0	26.9	18.7	15.3	16.2	5.7
All three basic amenities	44.6	37.2	32.3	26.6	36.5	15.9

Source: 1971 Census

market.   The GLC's Annual Abstract of Statistics (1975) showed that
whereas there were 229,554 families on London council housing lists, the
number of families housed by the local authorities from their waiting
lists decreased from 25,000 in 1970 to 10,000 in 1975.   Owner occupation
was probably even less of a solution to the housing needs of low income
families.   Although the 1975 Family Expenditure Survey showed that the
average household income was £83.21 a week gross £4,327 per annum), The
Economist (1977) stated that by 1976:

> the average deposit on a first house in London was £2,617, and
> the average price was £12,897.   London's new buyers had to have
> an annual household income of £5,300 (p.28).

These facts lead to the conclusion that the low income households will
probably remain the less priviledged tenure class.

Research undertaken recently in Chicago by Muth (1969) suggests that
with rising incomes, the higher and middle income groups move to the outer
areas of the city where they can acquire more housing space.   There was
little evidence that out migration occurred because of the undesirable
physical or social conditions of the inner city.   He did not accept the
'traditional theory of slums' which state that there is a decrease in
demand for high quality housing in certain inner areas as a result of the
obsolescence of the buildings or the decay of the area, or the reduction
in real transport costs diverting demand away from the inner city, or as
Jacobs (1961) argued because of the lack of diversity in the neighbourhood.
If Muth's hypothesis was relevant to London where would have to be a
diminishing proportion of SEGs 1-4 resident within the inner area, but
census data shows that there have been increasing percentages of these
groups, resulting from recent in migration.   Whereas Muth believed that
since the average income elasticity of demand for space is high, all
households would respond to an increase in income by moving further out,
Evans (1973) argued that:

> even though the average (income elasticity) is high, some
> households may have low income elasticities and will therefore
> respond to an increase in income by moving further in.

When the city is of sufficient size:

> the number of high-income households wishing to locate at the
> centre will be enough to make a high-income neighbourhood viable
> at the centre.   These households will not ring the CBD but will
> form the neighbourhood on one side of the CBD, so that the house-
> holds will have the advantage of proximity to each other.   Thus,
> in large cities we would expect to find – and do find –high
> income areas bounded on one side by the CBD, and on the other by
> very low income areas (p.139).

If the size of the high income group wishing to locate at the centre
increases, its neighbourhood is more likely to expand radially and
circumferentially into low income areas than into the CBD (which might
itself be expanding in area) or into the existing highest income
neighbourhoods.

Although in the United Kingdom there may be several factors (for example
the effects of improvement grants) which favour renovation which are
absent in the cities of other countries, renovation of poorer inner area
housing in the private sector elsewhere takes place probably in a spatially
similar manner, for example in the United States.   Abu-Lughod (1960) used

data which incicated that if a high income neighbourhood formed, the very high income group would locate in the core of the neighbourhood adjacent to the CBD, while the next highest income group would occupy its outer area (Fig.3.4). Of the higher occupation classes those with the lower incomes would generally reside in renovated houses in the outer periphery and those with higher incomes would live in flats in the inner core. An increase in population or in the number of households would tend to push the outer periphery further out with resultant renovation of former low income housing. It might be suggested that this process occurs in parts of inner London.

Attention has been drawn to Davis and Whinston's theory. It states that since the owner would not fully recover his capital, a badly maintained property is unlikely to be renovated when surrounded by property which is similarly decayed. While the plausibility of this argument must be acknowledged, it does not explain why property in low income areas does get renovated and why high socio-economic groups do move into the transitional areas. It has been suggested by Evans that:

> the high income households who are willing to move into low income areas and renovate property are (initially) architects, journalists, TV producers, etc. (who) will be able to obtain proximity to the centre at reasonable cost... As more and more houses in the area change hands and are renovated, the status of the area rises and it becomes permissable for business executives to move in (pp.140, 141).

The process of gentrification is akin to the process of 'upward trans-possession' (shifts in the residential balance of an area or dwelling from low income to high income households). It also involves the increase in property values, and it is because of their inability to compete for a fairly fixed supply of accommodation that low income households are forced out. The Davis-Whinston argument is thus only partly correct.

Gentrification is consistent with Muth's analysis if it is assumed that above a certain income some people place a higher value on their time than on dwelling space in order to be near the CBD. These groups will compete with the low income demand for accommodation in the inner city.

Donnison (1967) dealt with a major factor very relevant to the London situation. He suggested that a household will often move in order to adjust housing consumption to changing requirements over its life cycle. The value a household places on travel time and space will vary over the life cycle. A young single person or couple will probably be fairly dependent on the leisure facilities of the city centre, and may also spend less time at home. They will probably have a greater preference for living near the city centre than for acquiring a spacious dwelling. A family with children is relatively tied to their home and will thus consider space particularly important. The old will be less mobile, and will generally wish to reside in familiar surroundings near relatives and well known neighbours, and with easy access to shops and services. Thus inner London is likely to be attractive to its elderly population and the young and those without families.

The age factor intensifies the demand for private rented dwellings in inner London in two ways. First, many households regard their London home as only temporary and therefore look to the private rented market to satisfy their needs. This is confirmed by the disproportionately large

57

in-migration of single households and out-migration of young married couples. The Francis Committee (1971) found that this mobility was particularly high in furnished tenancies where 61 per cent of tenants had moved into their home within the 18 months prior to the Committee reporting. The high mobility was the result partly of dissatisfaction with former but similar accommodation. Secondly, although population has decreased in the inner London area, this has been offset by an increase in the number of households.

On the demand side, the Milner Holland Report (p.205) summarised the problem as follows:

We think that the main factors which aggravate the stresses caused by the shortage of housing in London are:

1. The rapid growth of employment in London (in the 1950s and 1960s), leading to an exceptionally high proportion of young people and single people and to a high consequent demand for separate accommodation.

2. The division of the population of London into numerous and smaller households and the consequent increase in demand for housing.

3. The accentuation of this demand by the growing number of old people who continue to maintain separate accommodation.

4. The additional demands caused by the process of slum clearance, which results in the need to cater for more households than the number of dwellings demolished.

5. The increasing competition for living space by those with increased wealth caused by higher standards of prosperity, and the consequent upward movement of house prices.

6. The national demand for higher standards of housing (then) in an era of rapid economic growth and rising prosperity.

The inability of London to satisfy the high level of demand for private rented accommodation is due to several factors on the supply side. Muth referred to the high cost of housing in relation to income and this factor is important in London where house prices are high and have increased rapidly in recent years. The GLC's Annual Abstract of Statistics (1976) recorded that in Greater London in 1969 an old house cost on average £6,059 and a new house cost on average £7,588. By 1976 the respective prices had risen respectively to £15,432 and £19,551. The high cost of inner area redevelopment has limited the supply of new private accommodation. Most new housing in London is built by the councils the proportion being 59 per cent in 1973 and 70 per cent in 1976. This has consequently increased the importance of the institutional restrictions in entering either of the favoured housing classes. The single person, the student, the unmarried mother, the young married couple, the elderly and the tenant of furnished property must all find homes in the private market. The Central Housing Advisory Committee (1969) drew attention to the tendency for many local housing departments to allocate council houses only to tenants of unfurnished property in slum clearance areas and to families who have resided in the borough for a period of time. Although owner occupation is the most desirable form of tenure in terms of tax allowances, security and capital accumulation, only for example 10 per cent of households in Westminster and 15.9 per cent in Kensington and Chelsea in 1971 owned their own homes compared

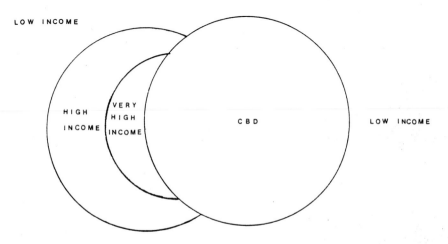

Figure 3.4   The geographical distribution of income groups
in the inner area of the city

with 50.1 per cent in Great Britain as a whole.

In the 1960s, the private rented market decreased in London at a rate of about 3 per cent per annum (Rose, 1968). The Milner Holland Report recorded that between 1960 and 1964 the number of lettings in the London conurbation fell from one and a quarter million to slightly more than a million, and the Francis Report (1971) stated that it was found that 75 per cent of landlords would continue to let furnished tenancies while only 25 per cent of the landlords of registered (unfurnished) tenancies would re-let them unfurnished if they obtained vacant possession. The 1971 Census showed that the number of private rented lettings in London had fallen to 904,445. There were three principal reasons for this decline. First, there were the fiscal arrangements for property owners. As Stone (1970) stated:

> In the absence of depreciation allowances landlords need to charge rents at a considerably higher level than they would need to meet as owner-occupiers. In terms of the capital they borrow, they need to charge interest of 12.5 to 15 per cent in order to obtain a return on their money no better than they could obtain if they invested in a building society (p.490).

The Milner Holland Report also argued that fiscal arrangements deterred a landlord from investing new capital in his property, stating that:

> it is one of the most important reasons why landlords have not been improving their property (p.56).

Secondly, private tenants were the one housing class (until the Housing Finance Act of 1972) that did not receive a direct government subsidy. Whereas in 1969-70 the government provided £215 million in tax allowances on mortgage interest payments and £126 million in council house subsidies (rates contributing an additional £48 million towards the cost of council housing), private tenants below a certain level of income could only obtain a rate rebate. Nevitt (1966) suggested that the result of this process was that it was always cheaper to buy a dwelling than to rent it. The main reason why property is rented is that families have insufficient savings (for a deposit and fee) and mortgage finance for house purchase. Thirdly, by setting rents below their market level, rent control or regulation encourages many landlords to withdraw rented accommodation from the low income market.

Finally on the supply side, there are the effects of the Green Belt. The transport cost gradient of moving further from the city centre becomes discontinuous, and the extra cost in both monetary terms and time of living beyond the Green Belt acts as a disincentive to out migration. This increases the price of residential property in the Greater London area and further results in higher densities, which in turn raises development costs. The Green Belt aggravates the problems of inner London in at least two ways. First, it increases the pressure of demand by restricting the supply of housing in the Greater London area, and it has therefore made the older dwellings in inner London more attractive to higher income groups. Secondly, by raising the cost of housing, the Green Belt reduces the ability of moderate and low income households to become owner occupiers.

The demand for housing in different areas of the city depends on the distribution of employment, accessibility, housing expenditure and income elasticity of demand for space. Social considerations also influence demand and supply. Low quality housing results from low income demand

and institutional factors which reduce the household's ability to realise their aspirations of becoming a member of a more privileged housing class. The function of low quality areas of housing is to provide a home for low income groups who have been unable to acquire a council house and for low income transient households. Property in these areas is suitable for conversion to low price units. There may however be pressure on low quality areas for high income households, and as property is consequently improved the supply of inexpensive units will be reduced without affecting the level of demand of low income households. The demand of these two housing classes is likely to produce conflict within many inner urban areas. It is therefore demand, rather than supply, which is mainly responsible for reducing the amount of private rented housing services available to the low income groups.

NOTES

(1) Group A boroughs comprise: City of London, Camden, Hackney, Hammersmith, Haringey, Islington, Kensington and Chelsea, Lambeth, Lewisham, Newham, Southwark, Tower Hamlets, Wandsworth and Westminster, City of.

(2) Inner London comprises: Group A boroughs (except Haringey and Newham) and Greenwich.

(3) Outer London comprises: Group B boroughs (except Greenwich) and Haringey and Newham.

Group B boroughs comprise: Barking, Barnet, Bexley, Brent, Bromley, Croyden, Ealing, Enfield, Greenwich, Harrow, Havering, Hillingdon, Hounslow, Kingston-upon-Thames, Merton, Redbridge, Richmond upon Thames, Sutton and Waltham Forest.

(4) As defined in the Census for 1951, 1961 and 1966, the five social classes were as follows: Social Class I, Professional; II, Intermediate; III, Skilled; IV, Partly skilled and V, Unskilled.

(5) As defined in the Census for 1971, the SEGs are as follows: 1, 2 and 13, Employers and managers in central and local government, industry and commerce, etc., including farmers; 3 and 4, Professional workers; 5 and 6, Intermediate non-manual workers and junior non-manual workers; 7, 10 and 15, Personal service workers, semi-skilled workers and agricultural workers; 8 and 9, Foremen and supervisors (manual), skilled manual workers; 11, 16 and 17, Unskilled manual workers, members of the armed forces, and persons whose occupations were inadequately described.

4 Housing rehabilitation in inner London

From 1945 until the late 1950s London had a substantial housing shortage,
numerous and large bombed sites and extensive areas of unfit housing.
An emphasis was placed on new housebuilding but the problems of relocation
and providing adequate facilities for new householders brought a reaction
against slum clearance and redevelopment schemes. At the 1968 London
Borough elections the Conservative Party made considerable gains. The
party recognised that due to high cost, large scale redevelopment could
only be undertaken publicly, but this would have involved an extension
of the municipalised housing stock with the probability of an increase
in the Labour share of the poll - as Muchnick (1970) stated:

> although a political party is committed to the provision of
> housing it is unlikely to accept the construction of a housing
> project in a ward if the new residents will mean the loss of
> that ward politically (p.24).

Rehabilitation would retain or expand the private or market sector. The
Greater London Council (GLC) saw rehabilitation and especially the
declaration of improvement areas as a means of avoiding social polarisation
and attracting back or retaining the middle classes in inner London:

> we do not aim to have a city of rich and poor alone. We want
> to retain all groups of the community, not because of some
> theoretical 'social balance' but because the good functioning
> of government and society demands that we should prevent
> extreme polarisation (GLC 1970c, p.52).

This was increasingly desirable moreover because of the rising rate burden
of the inner areas. Some years before the major shift of emphasis in
official policy in 1969 from new housebuilding to rehabilitation, certain
areas of inner London were already witnessing the process of gentrification.

> Glass (1963) explained how gentrification increased in pace:

> it goes on rapidly until all or most of the original working
> class occupiers are displaced, and the whole social character
> of the district is changed. There is very little left of the
> poorer enclaves of Hampstead or Chelsea: in those boroughs,
> the upper middle class takeover was consolidated some time ago.
> The invasion has since spread to Islington, Paddington, North
> Kensington - even to the 'shady' parts of Notting Hill - to
> Battersea, and to several other districts north and south of
> the river (p.xviii).

One of the areas of inner London to be rehabilitated in the post war
period on a major scale was Barnsbury; a district once in a semi-slum
condition located in the south west of the borough of Islington and
between high council flats in the south and unregenerated lower middle
income housing in the north. After the Rent Act of 1957, the major
private landlords - the Church Commissioners - disposed of most of its
properties in the area, and new landlords evicting their tenants to sell
with vacant possession -

often used extremely dubious and now illegal methods of
obtaining possession.   The upshot was that many properties
became available for owner-occupation (Counter Information
Services, 1973, p.62).

Between 1961 and 1966 the number of residents in the professional and
managerial socio-economic groups doubled and many became members of the
newly formed Barnsbury Association - the initial aim of which was to
counter the extension of London County Council housing in the area by
objecting to compulsory purchase orders placed on private tenancies.   A
further factor in the gentrification of the Barnsbury area was the
Barnsbury Housing Association which had strong connections with the
Barnsbury Association.   Its declared objectives were: first, to
preserve buildings of architectural merit - most of the houses being
Georgian and Victorian in character, spaciously laid out - and secondly,
to provide homes for 'middle income people' at economic rents of £12 per
week - well in excess of the prevailing local authority rents.

   In the 1960s property developers became increasingly important in this
process of gentrification.   Rent decontrol after 1957, inflation and the
easier availability of mortgages encouraged the property companies to
acquire old multi-occupied terraced houses in parts of inner London,
improve or convert them and either sell them off or let them at high rents
to middle and high income families - a sequence involving the dislodgment
of low income households.

   In 1965 the Milner Holland Committee described the processes of renewal
in three specific areas of inner London - Shepherds Bush, Canonbury and
North Kensington, the most extensive example being Canonbury - an area
where most of the houses were built between 1780 and 1850.   Its original
qualities of design and layout were there and public appreciation for
the 'period' house and its proximity to central London made improvement
feasible.   Houses previously subdivided and shared by low income households were becoming reoccupied as single houses by persons of high income.
Although each of the three areas examined were very different, there was
one common result of renewal, the housing created would -

   be occupied by different people from those who originally lived
   on these sites - and people of a generally different class of
   income.   In each of these cases there was a desperate need for
   something to be done.   What has been done and is being done
   produced and is producing housing of good quality and amenity
   by present day standards.   Desirable though that is, it has
   left the rehousing of the original occupants as a problem to be
   solved by others - probably we suspect in older unimproved
   rented housing, the section in shortest general supply and where
   the worst conditions appear to obtain (The Milner Holland Report,
   1965, p.199).

The initial effects of the Housing Act of 1969

Although in the 1960s rehabilitation had often proceeded rapidly it was
confined to a small number of areas.   Even after the 1969 Act, larger
grants with relaxed conditions attached to them did not immediately
encourage improvement on an extensive scale, nor were grants increasingly
taken up in the largest sector - privately rented housing.   Morton (1971)
described how private landlords who:

house close on 40 per cent of .... London's .... households
.... account for a minute proportion of the paltry 6,000
improvement grants given annually in the London area or the
2,500 new dwellings created by conversion (p.56).

Most improvement was being done by owner occupiers with some grants being
taken up by local authorities and housing associations for both improvement and conversion.   To speed up the improvement of private housing, the
GLC proposed that it would take seven year leases on property,
rehabilitate them, raise their rents (and provide rent rebates for tenants)
and then return them to the private landlords who would gain the benefit
of higher rents.   The idea floundered as there was no way of compelling
landlords to co-operate nor could it be guaranteed that the properties
would remain in good condition throughout their leases.

The following explanations are given for the sluggish increase in the
number of improvement grants awarded in inner London in the period
1969-71.

(1)   The 1969 Act permitted landlords to raise rents of controlled
tenancies (of which there were still 350,000 in London in 1970) up
to regulated levels after improvement, but the increase would have
to be phased over 3 to 5 years - a deterrent to investment.   Some
councils, however, such as Lambeth, by rehousing private tenants
at the outset of renovation encouraged landlords to take up grants.
On completion of the work new tenants would be nominated by the
council allowing landlords to charge fair rents immediately.

(2)   Landlords may not have had the financial resources available
to afford their proportion of improvement costs.   Although loans
could be obtained from the local authority for this purpose,
interest payments reduced the additional net rent return.

(3)   Many landlords may not have been interested in using
improvement grants to increase the capital value of their property.
The Milner Holland Report had shown there was a high proportion of
landlords owning only one house and letting part of it.   The
dwelling was first and foremost a home, and only secondly an
investment.   It would be wrong however to assume, as was suggested
by Morton (1971) that much of the private rented sector was owned
by elderly women - the Milner Holland Report had shown that women
over 60 were the landlords of only 12.5 per cent of all private
lettings.

(4)   Tenants were often reluctant to compel landlords to
rehabilitate their properties due to the undesirable repercussions
which might have resulted.   Compulsion, suggested 'Argus' of the
Municipal Engineering (1970) might involve:

attacking the landlord (with whom tenants like to keep
on amicable terms) by the off-putting methods of paper
work, officials and even the courts;   eventual installation of amenities designed by a hostile landlord
without concern for the user and probably of minimum
standard;   great disruption and possibly removal of the
tenant's whole household over a long period while works
are in progress;   and finally a series of increasing
rents for property which may be personally unsatisfactory
but no longer cheap (p.1670).

(5)   Demand may have been generally insufficient to permit increases

in rents or house prices up to a level which would have justified improvement, the GLC (1970c, p.59) stating that:

> we have now arrived at a state of affairs where the minimum rental for a 700 (square) foot family dwelling in London based on current building costs, increased rates and costs of maintenance has to be something in the order of £10 to £12 per week, and even this can only be achieved by non-profit making housing associations.

They also stated that according to the Family Expenditure Survey (1967), 79 per cent of all Greater London male workers earned less than £30 per week and that one quarter of all households had incomes of under £20 per week. The former sum was the practical minimum at which a mortgage became feasible in London in the late 1960s taking into account that very little (if any) housing was available at a price less than £5,000.

(6) Many of the larger building societies, banks and insurance companies were unwilling to make any loans at all for house purchase in much of inner London. Williams (1975), referring to Islington in the 1960s, explained the reasons for this as follows:

a) The societies were concerned that their investments should be liquid. Large houses represented to the societies the possibility of subletting and all the consequent difficulties that this would bring in the event of foreclosure.

b) Skilled workers (often highly paid and interested in becoming owner occupiers) were unlikely to acquire loans as they would generally fail to meet the stringent requirements of the larger societies.

c) The societies often lacked knowledge of the Islington area establishing offices in the borough for the first time in the 1970s.

d) Large areas of the borough were blighted as many sites were subject to proposed clearance schemes.

e) The societies thought there were far better investment opportunities in the outer London boroughs.

Similar reasons to these probably accounted for (and in some cases still account for) building society reluctance to grant mortgages for house purchase in much of inner London.

REHABILITATION IN THE PERIOD OF THE 'PROPERTY BOOM', 1971-73

By 1971 an acceleration of house prices occurred which in aggregate was due to increased incomes (statutory incomes policy lapsing in 1970), increased lending by building societies and banks, and interest on new mortgages falling from 8½% to 8% in November 1971. These factors were compounded in inner London by an increased number of people working in the City and the West End, resulting from further office development after the 'Brown Ban' was lifted and Office Development Permit restrictions were relaxed in 1970. Lomas (1974) suggested that:

> the skyscraper offices in the West End (have) strongly influenced

the inner London housing market, have encouraged gentrification
(seen perhaps as an alternative to long distance and/or costly
commuting), led to a demand for less skilled workers too, who
cannot so easily find homes .... the rapid shifts of population
make some long term residents scarcely able to recognise
their own streets, and they feel increasingly isolated (p.11).

The fixed or diminishing supply of properties in inner London further
exacerbated demand pressures. Williams (1975, pp.6-7) calculating
prices from the sales data of one estate agent in Islington showed that
average house prices increased as follows:

1959	1963	1966	1967	1969	1970	1971	1972
£s - 2,750	4,000	5,000	4,196	7,154	8,743	10,241	17,392

indicating an increase of nearly 70 per cent between 1971-72. Williams
cited an example of where a house purchased in the borough for £1,700 in
1958 was comparable to properties selling for £60,000 in 1975. He also
obtained from one agent figures showing how house sales had increased
from 45 in 1965, to 114 in 1969, to 323 in 1973. The Nationwide
Building Society reported that the price of old houses in London and the
South East increased from £4,949 in 1969 to £8,689 in 1972, a 75.6 per
cent increase compared with a 143.1 per cent increase in Islington during
the same period.

The main entrepreneurs at work in the inner areas of London were the
property speculators. The Counter Information Services (1973)
described how:

taking advantage of these low cost areas, government provided
financial inducement and the socio-economic polarisation of
London's population (the speculators) are transforming whole
areas of London. The neighbourhoods are destroyed, people
lose their homes, the stock of low rented housing is reduced.
'Improvements' simply reduce the supply of inexpensive units
in London without reducing demands ... Property developers
and speculators have been attracted by the high return on
investment to be won in rundown areas. Initially the
availability of mortgages, and the willingness to sell of the
private landlord letting in 'twilight areas' encouraged the
property companies to buy up .... old multi-occupied terraced
houses .... convert them into spacious homes and sell them
off to the well-to-do. This process is generally accompanied
by an influx of middle income families, unable to afford the
high prices in already established middle class areas (p.40).

Kilroy (1972b) indicated much the same when he stated unequivocably that:

all that has happened is that the stock of housing available
to the lower income groups has diminished and that attractive
to the middle classes has increased.

The effects of improvement upon tenants would at first be variable but
ultimately would be generally the same. In giving evidence to the
Greater London Development Plan Inquiry, Holmes (1972) argued that tenants:

will be pushed out. If they are furnished tenants they will
get notices to quit. If they are overcrowded the legal
enforcement will be applied. If they are timid or ill informed,

66

they can be harassed.   If they are stubborn the landlord may
have to wait... But in the end the conversion will go through:
the poor will be pushed out by the rich, the stock of cheap
rented housing grows scarcer and scarcer, rents, overcrowding
and homelessness are forced up and up (E 11/24).

By 1972 there were 3,000 families homeless and 200,000 on council waiting
lists in Greater London.   It is probable that a high proportion of the
numbers within the inner areas were attributable to the process of
gentrification aided by improvement grants.   Rehabilitation often became
more destructive of local communities than slum clearance schemes - where
at least the local authorities had an immediate responsibility for
rehousing the affected households.   Although local authorities have a
duty to rehouse the homeless (albeit in temporary accommodation), Coward
(1972) pointed out the irony of councils:

   paying heavy grants to well-off people to push out poor people -
   and are then having to pay again to accommodate them.

Yet the total amount of homelessness is greater than the number of
persons registered by local authorities as 'homeless'.   It is very
probable that a sizeable proportion of the 'unregistered' homeless were
also sufferers of the process of gentrification.

  There were additionally some very indirect effects of improvement upon
tenants.   New middle class residents very quickly formed themselves into
local pressure groups often for the purpose of conservation.   The
Barnsbury Association, for example, was successful in 1970 in encouraging
the GLC and Islington Borough Council to introduce an environmental
traffic scheme which eliminated through traffic from the area of
gentrified housing.   The Barnsbury Action Group (comprising private and
council tenants and local shopkeepers) in contrast pleaded unsuccessfully
against the scheme - arguing that it would divert traffic into areas of
low income housing or congest still further shopping streets in the
vicinity.

  Although the news media often publicised the adverse social effects of
rehabilitation, it sometimes took a neutral stance or indeed encouraged
the middle classes to move into areas ripe for improvement with
considerable 'profit potential' - Waroff (1973) in an article in the
Financial Times stating that the:

   concept of slum clearance is very nearly obsolete today, at
   least so far as inner London is concerned.   Planners no
   longer need to raze whole neighbourhoods and replace them
   with concrete blocks of flats in order to eradicate derelict
   housing.   All the planners have to do now is wait for a
   run-down area to be discovered - by investors, or more often
   by middle class families, happy to move into a marginal
   neighbourhood to save a few thousand pounds on the price of a
   house.   And many people are also enthusiastic about the
   creative side of doing up a house to reflect their own
   personalities.

The movement of middle class families into these 'marginal neighbourhoods'
was mainly preceded however by the activity of the developers.   Although
Mr Julian Amery, then Minister of Housing and Construction (1972b) stated
that most improvement grants were going to owner occupiers, evidence
relating to inner London did not substantiate this claim.   In 1972

private landlords and developers in Westminster were awarded 75 per cent of all grants, in Hammersmith 65 per cent and in Kensington and Chelsea 71 per cent. These were percentages of a much larger number of grants than those which had been approved in 1969-70. Many grants went to the same developers operating through different companies, and one group of companies received £120,000 between 1969 and 1972, their tenants not benefitting due to being dispossessed (Sunday Times, 29 October 1972).

In a report on rehabilitation, Shelter (1972, p.8) asked the questions:

> does improvement have to happen as it does? Should families be made homeless in the name of home improvement? Should the Government give tacit approval to the increased pressure upon private tenants?

Shelter thought not, and made the following proposals to safeguard tenants:

(1)   All families displaced by improvement should be rehoused by the council or landlord. Since furnished tenants were particularly susceptible to eviction they should be given full security of tenure.

(2)   The rent officer or Rent Tribunal should fix the rents of improved properties.

(3)   Councils should nominate the tenants of improved properties.

(4)   If the improved property is sold (within say 3 years) the grant should be repaid - if need be on a sliding scale.

(5)   A code of practice should be drawn up by the London Boroughs Association to constrain the activities of speculators.

LOCAL AND CENTRAL GOVERNMENT RESPONSE TO THE ADVERSE EFFECTS OF REHABILITATION

Spiralling property prices jeopardised local authority plans to acquire and improve twilight housing for the benefit of existing tenants. Inflated rents of improved housing were greatly in excess of the ability to pay of those in need. It was reported in 1972 that Camden bought two houses in Camden Town for £8,000 and £6,800 but after conversion rents per flat would have to have been about £21 per week. If sold, the buyers would have to have had an annual income of £3,500 to qualify for a 100 per cent council mortgage. In Lambeth the gap between the economic rent on improved council properties and the rent paid was on average £300 and was widening. Even with rent rebates available under the 1972 Housing Finance Act the gap could not be bridged.

Apart from the rising cost of acquiring housing (councils being in competition with private developers) local authorities became increasingly concerned with the immediate social effects of gentrification. In 1972, Camden began to restrict grants to owners who were prepared to retain their tenants at fair rents, and in the following year made grant applicants sign declarations that if they were to sell their property they would give the council first option to buy at prevailing market prices (less the value of the improvement grant within the first five year period). If the council did not wish to buy, the grant would still have to be repaid with interest. Clearly Camden considered that as the grants were 'discretionary' they could be awarded with conditions attached.

Islington however concentrated on imposing compulsory purchase orders on properties in an attempt to protect households from eviction though by 1973 were considering pursuing the same policy as Camden.   In contrast, Westminster (at least initially) regarded improvement mainly in terms of 'bricks and mortar' - Mr David Cobbold, Chairman of the Housing Committee (1972) stating that:

> this particular measure of housing policy (improvement) has as its top priority the securing of houses which would otherwise decay.   It was not intended essentially to help the poorer tenants.   There are other means of doing that.

Hammersmith adopted a middle path.   While not going to the extremes of Camden, its policy was to freely award grants to existing and intending owner occupiers and landlords who carried out renovation for the benefit of their tenants.   Developers and speculators received little assistance. The Department of the Environment doubted however whether local authorities did have powers to impose stringent conditions on the allocation of grants, but accepted that they had powers to refuse them.

Early in 1973 the House of Commons Expenditure Committee (Environment and Home Office Sub Committee) on House Improvement Grants received a substantial amount of evidence on the effects of grant aided improvement. The London Boroughs Association (LBA) was a major witness, and it drew attention to the increasing practice of landlords (encouraged by the escalation of property prices and the sharp rise in building costs) to use improvement grants not to improve and let, but to convert and sell - especially in the more accessible and fashionable areas close to central London.   This process (so the Association reported) frequently involved pressure being applied to tenants to move out in advance of an application for an improvement grant.   The boroughs were also concerned about the increased activity of property developers who were involved in rehabilitation solely for business purposes, taking advantage of improvement grants to increase their profits.   These circumstances firstly meant:

> that the existing tenants in London (had to)... continue to seek accommodation in a shrinking pool, and secondly (provided) an incentive for the admittedly small number of bad landlords to cause tenants to vacate improvable (and particularly convertible) property by legal or illegal means.   It was thought that this (was) particularly relevant to inner London (paragraph 10).

The LBA produced evidence which showed quite clearly that although the:

> direct relationship between the wish to improve or convert on the one hand and harassment and eviction on the other only related to a small number of grant applications .... properties which had been the subject of evictions or harassment were subsequently the subject of applications for improvement grants in a proportionately large number of cases (paragraph 14).

The LBA was not certain however, that it was desirable to return to the original basis of all grants being repaid on the resale of the property as a means of deterring owners from dispossessing tenants.   This it was thought would discourage much beneficial rehabilitation.

The London boroughs argued that it was important that improvement efforts should be concentrated within the stress areas especially as the benefits of improving individual properties would be negated by the deterioration of neighbouring houses.   In many general improvement areas - especially those centred on stress areas - owners were slow in taking up improvement grants.   Nevertheless the LBA argued that if conditions were to be improved for the benefit of the existing residents, compulsory purchase would have to be undertaken on social grounds, and that the Secretary of State for the Environment should be generally willing to confirm compulsory purchase orders made to:

> protect tenants of both furnished and unfurnished accommodation who are either threatened with eviction or are under pressure and inducement from their landlords to give up possession of their accommodation (paragraph 28).

The boroughs showed concern that GIA proposals were leading to social change.   This was brought about by harassment, eviction and the payment of relatively small financial inducements to persuade tenants to leave, vacant possession then enabling owners to sell at high prices (whether this process underlined a more intensive change in occupancy than outside of the GIAs will be examined in Chapter 6 of this book).   As a result of this sort of observation one London borough called a halt to GIA programmes, and another had decided that no further GIA would be declared until there was a strengthening of local authority powers in relation to compulsory acquisition and security for existing residents.

The Expenditure Committee called in and examined representatives from firms of developers.   There was some variation of view as to whether or not improvement grants were essential for rehabilitation to be undertaken as a business activity.   One developer (paragraphs 1824-1825) felt that with rates of return of about 25 per cent on total capital outlay grants were not very significant, but admitted that this could only have been seen with the benefit of hindsight.   In contrast, a director of another firm thought that improvement grants were very necessary and very desirable and if properly used would improve the nation's housing stock.   He thought that properties:

> which are improved through the public purse should be sold to owner occupiers because they have a good built-in obligation to keep them in good order.   If we take the money (the grant) and spend it on rented accommodation, subject to a fair rent, which with respect from our point of view is not adequate to maintain the property in future, you are merely deferring the process of decay by a number of years, at which point it becomes uneconomic to make a good property of it.   We feel that by taking these units, which are reconstructed out of existing units, and selling them on long leases we are in fact relieving the public purse, not drawing on it, because the man who buys it spends his own money on maintaining and improving it (paragraph 1845).

The same developer acknowledged that if a property was converted with the aid of a grant and then let at a rent approved by the rent officer, the net yield would be only 1 or 2 per cent in contrast to the 10-12½ per cent net return on capital outlay on which he implied he normally operated - a return which was not very different in amount from the size of the grant in respect to properties with which he was mainly concerned.

Changes in improvement policy, 1973-74

The Conservative government proposed major changes to improvement grant policy in its White Paper, Better Homes, the next priorities (1973), and

70

its successor, the Labour government, introduced new measures in its
Housing Act of 1974 aimed at reducing the disadvantageous social effects
of rehabilitation, while increasing the size of improvement grants. Both
parties recognised that improvements should benefit the existing residents
of an area - the original intention of the 1969 Act.

The Layfield Committee (1973) on the Greater London Development Plan
advised the extension of rehabilitation since, where there is a choice,
economically it is more advantageous than redevelopment. In addition it
was thought that if demolition rather than rehabilitation occurred within
the housing problem area, this would destroy whatever social cohesion
existed; that as so much demolition is needed anyway - inessential
demolition should be avoided; and that rehabilitation would make it easier
for small builders to make a contribution to improving the housing stock.
The Committee believed that extensive rehabilitation would only take place
in the private sector if local authorities themselves did the work.

Announcing the GLC's Strategic Housing Plan for London, Gladys Dimson,
then Chairman of the Housing Committee (1974b), acknowledged that the rate
at which poor accommodation had been dealt with had not kept pace with the
rate at which dwellings had fallen into disrepair. She stated that the
Plan put:

> great emphasis on making good use of existing housing ....
> London's stock of privately rented accommodation must be kept
> available for renting and put into decent condition. She
> considered the conversion of rundown property into comfortable
> homes is of key importance. We can no longer let things go
> until wholesale bulldizing is the only answer. Nor is a
> switch to luxury use acceptable as this squeezes out the very
> people of moderate income who are already the least well
> provided for (p.2).

At the subsequent Town and Country Planning Association conference London
Planning and Housing, Mrs Dimson continued this theme stating that
although the GLC aimed to clear and replace 107,000 dwellings over ten
years (equal to the number of all housing defined as 'poor' and 'unfit'
by the 1967 Survey), if the demolition programme became unviable the Plan
proposed as an alternative:

> a massive programme of rehabilitation which would mean a
> doubling of current performance until 1983 and then doubling it
> again between 1984 and 1988... If we carry out these
> rehabilitation targets ... then within ten years, some 166,000
> homes will have been put in good repair and modernised and
> another 186,000 in the five years after that (1974c, p.5).

It was argued at the conference that improvement in the future would have
to be undertaken mainly by the GLC and the Inner London Boroughs who
(together with the government) were committed to the public ownership of
most of the rented accommodation in London. But one speaker suggested
that a new housing authority (in size similar to the old London County
Council) should be established to deal with the housing problems throughout inner London, but showed concern that the construction industry might
not be equipped to carry out the housing programme prescribed.

Security of furnished tenure and rehabilitation

In a report on Rent Tribunal cases, Shelter (1973) criticised the increased

activity of developers in London's furnished property market. Between
1971-73 the proportion of property companies among landlords which sought
to evict households from furnished tenancies increased from 16 to 30 per
cent. Shelter found that 36 per cent of property companies and other
landlords said that their reason for wanting to evict households from
their furnished properties was that they wished to convert or improve the
accommodation. The proportion giving this reason for eviction had
trebled since 1971 and the number had increased from 12 to 60.

Families accounted for 40 per cent of all cases dealt with by the
Tribunals, and over a quarter of tenants were in low paid jobs and 16 per
cent were people living on pensions, unemployment benefit or student
grants.

Although under the Rent Act of 1958, the Tribunals could have granted
security of tenure for up to six months, Shelter was concerned that
several Tribunals such as Brent and Harrow, and Islington were awarding
security for quite shorter periods ranging from on average 2 to 4.1
months. In the 38 Tribunal cases where landlords wanted to evict in
order to improve or sell their property it was found that conversions
would involve a replacement of tenants by owner occupiers. Whereas 72
tenants had been given notice to quit properties subject to planning
permission, only 54 new leasehold flats were proposed - a reduction of 25
per cent in the number of dwellings.

The Chairman of Shelter hoped that the Rent Act of 1974, by granting
much greater security of tenure to furnished tenants and by introducing
regulated rents (replacing free market rents) would make possible the
implementation of:

> systematic programmes for the improvement of older housing in
> stress areas with the far lower risk that this will simply
> result in the displacement of low income tenants in favour of
> well-off owner occupiers (Holmes, 1974, p.2).

Some effects of reduced public expenditure upon improvement policy

The GLC's housing programme was adversely affected by the White Paper,
Public Expenditure to 1978-79 (1975) which announced that nationally,
public spending on improvement works would be reduced from £423 million
in 1974-75 to £297 million in the year commencing 1 April 1975. This
involved local authorities using their discretionary powers more fully
(but in accordance with the Housing Act of 1974), and reducing the amount
of house improvement which they themselves undertook. The GLC reduced
the £26 million it intended spending on improving its own estates and
newly acquired property in 1975-76 to £11 million (£1 million less than
it spent in 1973-74). There was a concentration of expenditure on
improving acquired property which involved helping tenants in the
'greatest need' and avoided the further disruption of community life.
But this emphasis was reflected in high opportunity costs. The GLC had
to leave over 1,000 properties empty on its pre war estates because of
expenditure cuts, and even estates developed in the 1950s were getting
increasingly in need of modernisation and were becoming 'ghettoes' with a
high proportion of tenants in arrear with their rents.

Whereas in 1969 there was a major shift of emphasis from new housebuilding to rehabilitation - a change of policy which had profound effects
on inner London, in September 1976 a further shift of emphasis was

announced by Mr Peter Shore (Secretary of State for the Environment) who stated that the government aimed to reverse the policy of decentralisation (pursued by both main political parties over at least the past thirty years) and concentrate public resources on improving the inner areas of cities.   In July 1977 the government announced that maximum cost limits of rehabilitation and improvement grants were to be substantially increased (Chapter 2), thereby underlining the government's increasing concern with the problem of housing within the inner areas.

THE SPECIFIC EFFECTS OF IMPROVEMENT GRANTS UPON REHABILITATION

In a paper on the relationship between improvement grants and gentrification in inner London, Hamnett (1973) argued that over the period of his research 1971-72:

> the probability of the bulk of renovation being associated with improvement grants (was) emphasised by the complete lack of restrictions on them... Though this 'no strings' policy .... without doubt led to a marked improvement in the standard of part of London's housing stock, it (was) precisely that part which .... traditionally provided accommodation to the lower income groups, the diminution of which .... led to an intensification of housing stress... We may fairly assume that improvement grants (provided) a reasonably precise reflection of gentrification, its extent and distribution (p.253).

He used data drawn from the quarterly bulletin of GLC housing statistics to show that throughout 1971 and the first three quarters of 1972 there had been a general increase in the number of improvement grants awarded in Greater London with a slight levelling off in the second and third quarters of 1972.   Apart from a great deal of improvement of privately rented and owner occupied housing, it was clear that inner London was witnessing a substantial amount of conversion of privately rented property for sale or to re-let at higher rents.

It was shown that grants were very concentrated in a small number of boroughs.   In descending order, owner occupier grants were concentrated largely in Hammersmith, Wandsworth, Greenwich and Camden; and grants for privately rented conversions were concentrated in Camden, Westminster, Kensington and Chelsea and Hammersmith.   Whereas Hammersmith ranked high for both types of grants, Westminster and Kensington and Chelsea both ranked high on privately rented conversion grants but very low on grants for owner occupation.

Hamnett attempted to explain these differences by referring to the connection between housing quality, social class composition and location. Three main relationships were found to exist.   First, a large part of Westminster, Kensington and Chelsea and Camden contain (and have contained for a considerable period) a high proportion of their population in the upper social class, this population being specifically located in areas such as Bayswater, South Kensington and Hampstead.   In these localities house prices were high, ranging from at least £30,000 to over £80,000. When houses come up for sale the only way which they can attract buyers is for them to be converted into smaller but still fairly expensive units. Gentrification does not take place as the social composition of the area's population remains largely unchanged.   Second, North Kensington,

north west Westminster and the Primrose Hill area of Camden contain a
more normally distributed class structure and a poorer housing stock.
Because of centrality and potential desirability, a price shadow was cast
over these areas by their more affluent neighbours resulting in the
conversion of privately rented properties and an inflow of a higher
income population - gentrification being manifested. Third, in the
boroughs of Hammersmith and Islington, and in the Camden Town, Chalk Farm
and the Kentish Town areas of the borough of Camden, grants were awarded
mainly for owner occupation. Although the housing stock and social
composition are similar to that in the second group of areas above,
because centrality and potential desirability is less, gentrification
generally had less affect upon price levels.

Hamnett stated in his conclusion that we must not lose sight of the
overall dominance of improvement grants for privately rented property,
and that it could be inferred that its stock was diminishing as a result
of the operation of improvement grants - a large number of dwellings
being sold for owner occupation after conversion/improvement.

Dugmore and Williams (1974) questioned Hamnett's thesis that the
distribution of improvement grants provide an indicator of gentrification.
They argued that as low income owner occupiers are assisted in improving
their properties by local authorities granting loans covering the
occupier's share of improvement cost, grants are often awarded with little
or no resulting gentrification. Conversely, property developers were
ceasing to apply for, or to be awarded improvement grants - suggesting
that gentrification may be taking place in areas where very few grants
have been distributed. Property developers in the period 1971-73 were
deterred or prevented from obtaining grants for several reasons. First,
delay in processing grant applications was costly especially as house
prices and rents were rapidly rising. Secondly, some London boroughs were
beginning to use their discretionary powers to the full to prevent grants
being awarded to developers. Thirdly, during a period of inflation the
real value of the grant fell rapidly and became equivalent to a
diminishing part of profit; and fourthly, the developer was reluctant to
publicise his activities - an inevitability in applying for a grant -
but undesirable to a developer in a speculative market. Dugmore and
Williams accepted, however, that grants aided the 'pioneering' middle
classes in gentrifying areas of inner London in the 1960s (Barnsbury and
Canonbury for example) and that with the easing of conditions attached to
grants by the Housing Act of 1969, property developers and individuals
began to make great use of grants for rehabilitation in those areas which
the 'pioneers' had earlier demonstrated had potential.

Generally, Dugmore and Williams were convinced:

> that gentrification is a response to a variety of conditions
> in the housing market of which grants are simply one aspect...
> Gentrification must be appraised (they argued) in the context
> of a complex market situation. In particular it is suggested
> that the role of all institutions affecting the housing market
> should be considered in order to develop a fuller understanding
> of the changes occurring in the inner city (p.160).

Williams (1975) went on to consider this role specifically in the borough
of Islington and found that building societies in particular influenced
the pace of rehabilitation. Referring to grants, Williams argued that:

74

their effect was to heighten demand rather than cause it.
Other interventions such as the improvement of transportation
(the Victoria line) and the development of traffic schemes
also had an impact upon changes in Islington. Similarly it
has been suggested that the activities of the Rent Officer will
induce changes in the housing market as will the provision of
local authority mortgages (p.17).

The Department of the Environment undertook a survey between 1972-74
which had the aim of assessing the social effects (if any) of house
improvement in inner London. Its findings (1975) were generally
compatible with those of Hamnett. Three broad questions were posed:

(1) To what extent were existing occupants benefitting from
     house improvement?

(2) If they did not benefit, why did they move out; where did
     they go and what were the results of moving?

(3) Did inward moving households have different socio-economic
     characteristics to outward movers - was gentrification
     taking place?

To attempt to answer these questions an investigation was undertaken of
a random sample of one in four grants approved by 12 inner London boroughs
during the first quarter of 1972, a total of 424 grants. These
comprised 195 discretionary improvement grants for single dwellings, 135
discretionary grants for the conversion of two or more dwellings and 95
grants for standard improvements.

The report of the survey stated that:

in a majority of cases, and for various reasons, the improvement
of living conditions did not benefit the original residents. Of
the grant applications sampled 68 per cent had been preceded by
the outward movement of at least one household and almost three
quarters of all households had moved away. Those leaving were
to a large extent (80 per cent) tenants most of whom had left
wholly tenanted property (p.3).

It was found that this was not so much a consequence of an owner's desire
to improve his property but more part of the process of vacation, sale
and then rehabilitation (a process earlier identified by the LBA).
About 90 per cent of all conversion applications and 60 per cent of
improvement applications were preceded by households moving out, and in
the former case four fifths of applicants were absentee owners - both
property companies and private individuals.

During the investigatory period, the London Boroughs Association was
apprehensive that the method of sampling might have resulted in:

an under-estimation of the incidence of abuse of improvement
grants, because it is apparent that about one half of the
sample is of properties in owner-occupation before and after
improvement, and the number of sample cases where abuse is
likely to have occurred will consequently be small (House of
Commons, 1973, M.11, paragraph 11).

The LBA also believed that there was a strong probability that evicted
tenants would be difficult to trace and that landlords engaged in illegal
practices would either refuse interviews or give false information. It

Table 4.1

Comparison of past and present occupants of sample properties

	Past occupants						Continuing occupants		Newcomer occupants		
	Owner occupier → Owner occupier	Unfurnished tenant → Owner occupier	Furnished tenant → Furnished tenant	Unfurnished tenant → Unfurnished tenant	Furnished tenant → LA tenant	Unfurnished tenant → LA tenant	Continuing applicants	Continuing tenants	New applicants	New owners	New tenants
Average household size	2.7	2.7	2.4	2.0	3.1	2.8	3.2	2.1	3.1	1.8	2.3
Average age (head of household)	54 years	51 years	38 years	55 years	45 years	54 years	48 years	55 years	36 years	31 years	33 years
Proportion employed full-time	42%	37%	41%	55%	18%	25%	38%	41%	43%	77%	56%
Total income	£3,048	£3,416	£2,220	£2,112	£1,462	£1,400	£2,587	£1,377	£4,084	£4,032	£3,001
Proportion of household heads in manual or service occupations	41%	50%	28%	50%	72%	53%	48%	54%	25%	6%	17%
Proportion of household heads employers managers or professional	5%	30%	-	20%	-	-	16%	2%	38%	47%	28%

Source: <u>Some Social Implications of Improvement Policy</u>, Department of the Environment, 1975

was thought that the results of the survey would consequently underestimate the extent of abuse.

The LBA was correct in assuming that evicted private tenants would be difficult to trace especially if they continued to be private tenants. Most traced former owner occupiers of improved properties either remained owner occupiers or became council rehoused tenants. The survey showed that although owner occupiers paid less for their new property than they had received for their former dwellings, the average housing expenditure generally increased - by 45 per cent in the case of former furnished tenants being rehoused by local authorities, and by 176 per cent by unfurnished tenants who continued as such elsewhere. Although very few interviewed households were less satisfied with their new accommodation, it is far from certain whether those households which were not traced (432 - 81 per cent - out of a total of 534 households which moved) would have shared this view of their new accommodation.

Table 4.1 illustrates that the survey showed:

a strong contrast between the household characteristics of outward and inward movers. The newcomers on average were much younger, more affluent with less household heads in manual or service occupations and more in employer, managerial or professional ones and more household members in employment (p.4).

This can be largely attributed to the costs associated with improving housing. New tenancies (mainly furnished flats) were mostly let at high rents of about £19 per week often involving an increase of about 250 per cent above the rents paid by previous furnished tenants at the sample properties. Incoming owner occupiers either bought unimproved houses at an average price of £7,000 and then applied for a grant (one fifth converting their house and then either letting or selling part of it) or they bought already improved properties (mainly leasehold flats) for an average price of £9,500. In both cases, the average household incomes of the outward moving tenants would generally have been inadequate for many to have remained in, or to have returned to the sample property after improvement either as owner occupiers or tenants. Although market price and rent levels were influenced by factors other than improvement, for example scarcity value, the total process of rehabilitation:

acted as a social sieve, selecting particular types of households to move into improved dwellings (p.4).

The comparatively small number of households which remained in occupation throughout improvement incurred relatively low housing costs and comprised long established unfurnished tenants, owner occupiers and sitting tenants who had recently bought at a discounted price - most of whom having the same social characteristics as the outward movers. Although the survey was confined to a sample of improvement grant houses, and did not compare trends with those obtaining to a sample of unimproved houses of similar tenure and location, it is improbable that social change would have been so marked in the case of the unimproved properties.

5 The relationship between the distribution of improvement grants and socio-economic indicators in west London

The population of Inner London increased from about 675,000 in 1700 to 900,000 in 1801 and 4.5 million by 1901. In the eighteenth century population growth was associated with the speculative development of housing within the 'Great Estates' west and north of the City of London and Westminster - a process which continued up to the twentieth century (Summerson, 1969; Jenkins, 1975; Olsen, 1975). Reeder (1968) described how west London became subject to a series of out migrations, at first by the upper classes (1827-56), and then following in succession by the middle classes (1856-70s), lower middle classes and working classes (1860s-70s). Olsen described how:

> such invasions hastened the deterioration of the older suburbs. Those in the larger houses that remained took flight to more distant suburbs, and within a few years a socially homogeneous upper middle-class neighbourhood had turned itself into an equally homogeneous lower-middle class district (p.243).

The successive out migration of the social classes generally resulted in a:

> systematic sorting-out of London into single-purpose, homogeneous specialized neighbourhoods... Strict social segregation became a prerequisite for success in any new development. Older neighbourhoods that had been socially mixed became less so (Olsen, pp.18-19).

Although some areas such as Belgravia and Bayswater retained their high-class status and were little affected by the process of 'invasion', other areas such as Notting Dale, The Potteries and Kensal New Town (adjacent to predominantly upper middle class neighbourhoods of Kensington) remained low income 'rookeries' throughout the second half of the nineteenth century (Malcolmson, 1975).

The Milner Holland Report (1965) described the process of decline in two case studies in west London: Powis Terrace (Kensington) and the Shepherds Bush Estate (Hammersmith). Powis Terrace was completed in 1865, but by the 1880s the:

> social character of the respectable middle class and artisan area was already changing .... and housing conditions were causing concern... Since then dilapidation orders, basement closures and other kinds of preventive or enforcement notices have been issued in a constant stream. By the 1950s the whole area .... in which the terrace stood was characterised by short-term lettings, lodging houses and multiple-occupation (p.425).

This pattern was largely repeated in the area of the second case study. The Shepherds Bush Estate was developed during the period 1850-70 to provide housing for the middle classes. But during the succeeding generations, according to the report:

> the neighbourhood .... was becoming less attractive to middle
> class families, who moved further afield as the suburbs expanded.
> Gradually as the attractiveness of the estate deteriorated, so
> apparently did the character of the leaseholders who were the
> immediate landlords... For the most part holding a few
> properties, these landlords lacked the skill and resources
> necessary for upkeep of the houses, and they did little to
> arrest incipient obsolescence and decay. Gradually too the
> general pattern of occupation changed. Houses were let in
> rooms and floors to working-class families .... Some of
> the locally-born tenants who had lived on the estate for many
> years felt that by the end of the fifties it had sunk low;
> 'it really was down then' even when compared to its earlier
> modest status (pp.413-414).

The deterioration of housing in areas such as these occurred contempo-
raneously with the decrease in the population of Inner London from 4.9
million in 1911 to 2.8 million in 1971.

The population of the west London boroughs has declined rapidly in
recent years - more rapidly than the decline of Greater London overall
(Table 5.1). But the supply of housing in good condition is deficient
in relation to demand or 'need'. The Milner Holland Report showed that
very large areas of west London contained fairly poor dwellings, a high
proportion of which were shared. Fig.5.1 shows that these conditions
were concentrated in Hammersmith, Kensington, Paddington and Willesden.
Extensive areas of fairly poor housing with a lower amount of sharing
were found in Fulham, Kensington, Paddington, St.Marylebone and Willesden.
The Housing Problem Areas in west London together with the 10 per cent of
wards with the highest stress index (Fig.5.2) corresponded approximately
with the areas of fairly poor housing identified by the Milner Holland
Report, although they were smaller. It is notable that of the 24
Housing Problem Areas, 20 were also the wards with the highest stress
index.

Using data from the 1971 Census (set out in Table 5.2), a comparison is
made between the housing tenure, housing characteristics and social
composition of the Housing Problem Areas and the boroughs in which they
are situated. Although in Hammersmith, the proportion of owner occupied
households was neither generally more nor less than in the borough as a
whole, in Kensington and Chelsea, Westminster and Brent there was a much
lower proportion of owner occupation within the Housing Problem Areas
than in their respective boroughs in total. Except in Westminster, the
Housing Problem Areas had a higher proportion of households living in
private tenancies than the boroughs, although in Brent the distinction
was only marginal in the case of furnished tenure. Each of the Housing
Problem Areas had a higher proportion of households living at more than
1.5 persons per room and in shared dwellings than their respective
boroughs, and generally a higher proportion of dwellings without the
exclusive use of a bath/shower, hot water and an inside W.C. There were
generally lower proportions of SEGs 1, 2 and 1-4 and higher proportions
of SEGs 7-12, 14, 15 within the Housing Problem Areas than in the
boroughs.

The 1971 Census data thus confirmed that the Housing Problem Areas
(selected largely on the basis of the GLC Housing Survey, 1967) were still

79

Table 5.1

The population of the west London boroughs and Greater London, 1901-76

(000s)

	1901	1911	1921	1931	1939*	1951	1961	1971	1976	Decrease from peak year to 1976
Hammersmith	250	275	288	286	259	241	222	187	170	41.0
Kensington and Chelsea	250	239	240	240	228	219	219	188	161	32.9
Westminster	460	421	390	372	347	300	272	240	216	53.0
Brent	120	166	184	251	310	311	296	281	257	17.4
Greater London	6510	7162	7387	8110	8615	8197	7992	7452	7028	18.4

* mid-year estimate

Sources: Census data
1976 figures: Office of Population Census and Surveys

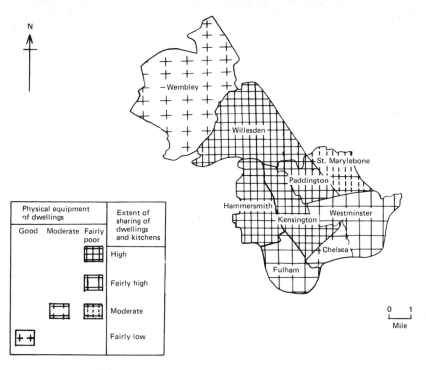

Figure 5.1   Housing conditions, west London, 1961

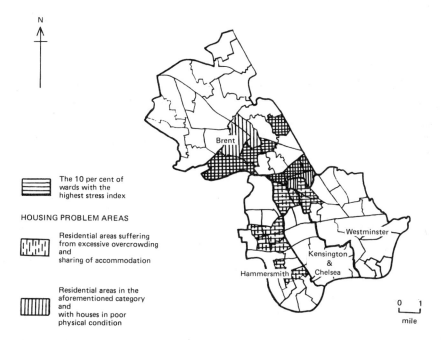

Figure 5.2   Housing Problem Areas, west London, 1966

Table 5.2

Household tenure, housing characteristics and social composition in west London boroughs, Housing Problem Areas and Housing Stress Areas, 1971

Borough and Ward	% owner-occupiers households	% private unfurnished tenancies	% private furnished tenancies	% shared dwellings	% households living at more than 1.5 persons per room	% dwellings without exclusive use of a bath/shower	% dwellings without exclusive use of hot water	% dwellings without exclusive use of an inside WC
Hammersmith	17.9	39.7	21.7	15.5	5.7	14.0	11.3	8.8
Addison	9.7	38.8	35.9	15.0	9.3	9.6	9.5	3.9
Brook Green	16.5	36.5	39.4	15.9	6.3	11.7	11.5	7.0
Coningham	18.2	41.7	26.6	24.4	10.3	21.7	18.2	9.7
Grove	18.1	46.9	23.3	19.7	7.7	25.5	19.9	19.6
Halford	16.4	43.5	18.0	20.5	4.8	22.6	15.5	6.0
Margravine	21.1	43.8	14.8	24.1	3.1	31.5	19.9	24.2
St.Stephens	11.2	41.7	26.6	24.4	10.3	21.7	18.2	9.7
Sherbrooke	25.8	48.2	13.8	20.5	4.2	33.9	24.3	17.6
Kensington & Chelsea	15.9	37.0	38.0	5.0	8.4	4.5	4.1	2.5
Golborne	6.1	44.3	25.0	22.7	15.3	8.0	8.8	8.1
Norland	15.3	35.2	29.4	9.0	6.8	7.9	8.6	5.4
St.Charles	9.8	48.0	25.6	10.3	8.7	9.1	7.1	4.4
Westminster	10.0	42.5	25.7	4.0	5.7	8.3	6.6	2.9
Harrow Road	7.8	39.2	28.7	24.0	14.9	19.2	18.3	5.8
Westbourne	7.2	23.7	37.2	10.0	10.8	11.0	11.6	4.0
Brent	55.2	21.9	16.5	11.4	5.9	4.0	4.0	2.1
Carlton*	2.5	18.0	6.0	11.4	6.4	15.3	10.6	3.6
Church End*	42.4	37.2	10.7	11.8	6.5	9.2	7.9	6.6
Cricklewood	42.8	26.7	25.1	20.0	7.7	1.4	3.4	0.9
Harlesden	28.9	42.5	25.8	33.6	10.9	12.5	12.1	4.0
Kensal Rise	34.2	38.1	21.6	33.7	11.2	15.6	14.0	10.1
Kilburn	15.7	35.6	39.1	33.1	12.0	6.4	7.6	2.3
Queens Park*	25.2	28.3	36.8	34.8	11.3	1.9	4.1	0.5
Roundwood	20.7	35.9	11.8	22.8	12.1	22.8	17.4	8.4
St.Raphael*	25.3	14.7	6.5	4.5	5.4	6.3	5.2	6.8
Stonebridge	15.6	37.8	14.5	27.0	9.6	16.6	12.8	4.8
Willesden Green	31.3	46.0	18.1	25.8	9.5	21.8	18.6	11.2

Source: Based on 1971 Census

*Housing Problems Areas only

areas which had a more than proportionate amount of private tenancies, overcrowding and sharing, and dwellings without the exclusive use of basic amenities. A further relationship existed throughout the four boroughs between tenure and the deficiency of basic amenities. Table 5.3 shows that the highest proportion of households without the exclusive use of hot water, a bath/shower and an inside W.C. was found in the private furnished sector. In contrast, a comparatively low proportion of unfurnished tenants and a very low proportion of owner occupiers were without the use of these basic amenities.

Inner West London is an example of what Medhurst and Parry Lewis (1969) defined as the 'transitional area' of decay. It provides fairly permanent homes for those households who do not qualify for a council house or are unable to obtain mortgage finance for house purchase; the large family; the 'New Commonwealth' immigrant, and others with similar demand. Alternatively it may provide inexpensive accommodation for the transient bed sitter dweller; the young married couple saving for a suburban home, and the immigrant who will return to his country of origin in a few years.

In contrast, the second type of area of decay, the 'residual area', is usually an area of nineteenth century or early twentieth century working class accommodation. Here the population is ageing rapidly, there is an absence of an inflow of new residents, the area is no longer tolerable to the younger residents, but it once contained a closely knit working class community. Decay is not associated with converted and multi-occupied property, it is the result of obsolescence of the building and the area, as well as the low income demand of the households remaining in the area. This is a situation exemplified in Deeplish, Rochdale. Except for parts of the docklands it is absent in London. Urban renewal thus has a particular relevance to the 'transitional areas' of west London, as Hall (1971) stated:

> the real weight of the London housing problem .... is no
> longer concentrated in the East End; it is in London's West
> Side (p.125).

THE SPATIAL DISTRIBUTION OF IMPROVEMENT GRANTS IN WEST LONDON

The data used to identify the spatial distribution of improvement grants is derived mainly from Tables 7 and 9 of the GLC's Annual Abstract of Statistics (1970-73) which are themselves based on the London boroughs' returns to the Department of the Environment. The returns refer to the numbers of dwellings in each tenure group likely to result from approved improvement grant applications, 1970-73. The analysis adopts a division between the Inner west London boroughs of Hammersmith, Kensington and Chelsea, and Westminster (all Group A boroughs) and Brent (a Group B borough). Although referring to all tenure categories, the analysis concentrates mainly on private tenancies and owner occupied housing which together accounted for 75.8 per cent of all improvement grants approved within the Group A boroughs and 86.3 per cent in Greater London. Grants to borough authorities and the GLC which accounted for 14.4 per cent of total grants within the Group A boroughs were largely ignored on the grounds that the improvement of local authority dwellings is not usually associated with gentrification, and grants to Housing Associations were not considered separately as they received only 9.8 per cent of the total number of grant approvals.

Figure 5.3   Improvement grants in Inner West London
and Group A boroughs, 1970-73

Fig. 5.3 shows the annual totals for improvement grants for both Inner West London and Group A boroughs. It illustrates that grants awarded in Inner West London increased substantially between 1970 and 1971 and then decreased in 1972 and 1973, while the number awarded within the Group A boroughs increased until 1972 and decreased in 1973. The relationship between the two areas remained fairly constant in 1970 and 1971 - Inner west London's percentage of the total for Group A boroughs being 39.2 and 39.3 respectively. In 1972 and 1973 the percentage diminished to 34.0 and 31.2. The difference between the peak years and the decreasing proportion of Inner West London grant approvals cannot easily be explained, although it is possible that the earlier decline in Inner west London was due to the London Borough of Hammersmith exercising its discretionary powers over grant approval (discriminating against developers and most non-resident landlords), whilst the later decline within the Grade A boroughs was attributable to changes in the underlying conditions of demand (the residential property boom reaching its peak in 1972) and uncertainty due to proposed amendments to improvement grant legislation. Because of the relatively small number of grants there is probably little significance in the increase in grant approvals in Brent between 1970 and 1973. The greatest increase between 1972 and 1973 may have been due to private landlords and developers being attracted to the borough after Hammersmith had adopted its new discretionary policy. The figures for 1970-73 are detailed in Table 5.4 and Appendix D. The total number of Inner West London grants was 13,099 and that for Group A boroughs was 41,051. Approvals in Brent numbered 1,030.

Throughout the period 1970-73 the principal recipients of grants were private landlords and developers, and owner occupiers. As shown in Table 5.4 and Fig. 5.4, private landlords and developers in Kensington and Chelsea, Westminster and Hammersmith received respectively 70.0, 67.4 and 61.9 per cent of the total grants awarded in each borough (3,019, 2,926 and 2,789 grants). Grants to owner occupiers amounted respectively to 12.0, 5.8 and 36.4 per cent (512, 350 and 1,548 grants).

In Inner West London, Group A boroughs and Brent, private landlords and developers respectively received 66.7, 50.8 and 34.4 per cent of the total grants awarded in each area. Grants to owner occupiers amounted respectively to 17.6, 25.0 and 16.4 per cent.

Changes over the period are demonstrated by the relationship between the totals for 1970, 1971 and 1973 in Inner West London, between the totals for 1970, 1972 and 1973 in the Group A boroughs, and between the totals for 1970 and 1973 in Brent (see Appendix D). In Inner West London private landlords and developers received 1,335, 2,706 and 1,988 grants and owner occupiers received 421, 611 and 590 grants. In the Group A boroughs private landlords and developers received 3,075, 6,810 and 4,843 grants and owner occupiers received 1,400, 3,139 and 3,384 grants. In Brent private landlords and developers received 68 and 442 grants and owner occupiers received 20 and 68 grants. The relationship between these and the other recipients (local authorities and housing associations) in Inner west London is shown in Fig. 5.5, from which it can be seen that grant awards to private landlords and developers were usually in excess of the grants allocated to the other recipient groups combined. Grants to this largest group exceeded the second highest group - the owner occupiers - by 214, 343, 294 and 236 per cent in the years 1970-73.

Table 5.4 indicates that the two main recipient groups varied markedly

Table 5.3

Households without exclusive use of basic amenities in the
west London parliamentary constituencies, 1971

% total households in each tenure category

Parliamentary constituency	Owner Occupied			Private Unfurnished tenancy			Private furnished tenancy		
	Hot water	Bath	Inside WC	Hot water	Bath	Inside WC	Hot water	Bath	Inside WC
Hammersmith, Fulham	13.3	22.2	20.5	34.1	48.2	33.5	37.6	61.8	60.1
Hammersmith, North	15.2	23.5	20.2	32.2	48.1	38.4	46.0	68.7	65.8
Kensington & Chelsea, Chelsea	4.4	2.6	2.3	14.7	17.1	14.7	22.5	51.3	54.1
Kensington & Chelsea, Kensington	5.6	7.2	6.3	19.3	27.8	25.1	25.0	54.2	56.7
City of London & Westminster South	4.2	4.7	3.0	15.7	21.4	12.4	24.9	46.4	47.0
City of Westminster & Paddington	9.2	12.3	8.0	20.2	25.4	18.4	31.5	61.0	60.6
City of Westminster, St.Marylebone	5.1	1.8	1.4	13.3	14.3	9.8	22.3	40.3	41.5
Brent East	9.1	13.3	9.3	30.6	40.2	26.0	41.3	67.3	65.0
Brent North	2.2	2.5	2.3	11.6	14.3	14.5	39.7	49.1	47.5
Brent South	9.0	12.1	8.6	34.0	44.2	25.3	52.5	65.4	59.8

Source: Based on 1971 Census

Table 5.4

Improvement grants awarded, 1970-73

Boroughs		Private landlords and developers C	Private landlords and developers I	Owner occupiers C	Owner occupiers I	Housing Associations C	Housing Associations I	Local Authorities C	Local Authorities I	Total C	Total I	Total C & I
Inner West London	%	56.0	10.7	6.5	11.1	8.5	0.8	4.1	2.4	75.1	25.9	
	No.	7,331	1,403	857	1,453	1,112	98	535	312	9,835	3,264	13,099
Hammersmith	%	47.8	14.1	9.2	25.2	0.4	0.2	2.7	0.4	60.2	39.8	
	No.	2,155	634	415	1,133	19	8	121	20	2,710	1,795	4,505
Kensington & Chelsea	%	66.5	3.5	7.2	4.9	14.9	0.7	0.0	0.0	91.0	9.0	
	No.	2,872	147	304	208	634	29	0	0	3,869	384	4,253
Westminster	%	53.1	14.3	3.2	2.6	10.6	1.4	8.2	6.7	75.0	25.0	
	No.	2,304	622	238	112	459	61	355	292	3,256	1,085	4,341
Group A boroughs	%	38.2	12.6	7.1	17.9	9.1	0.8	9.1	5.3	63.5	36.5	
	No.	15,683	5,157	2,921	7,333	3,731	306	3,737	2,183	26,072	14,979	41,051
Brent	%	25.6	8.7	11.4	5.1	4.4	0.3	21.9	22.6	63.3	36.7	
	No.	264	90	117	52	45	3	226	233	652	376	1,030

C   Grants for conversion

I   Grants for improvement only

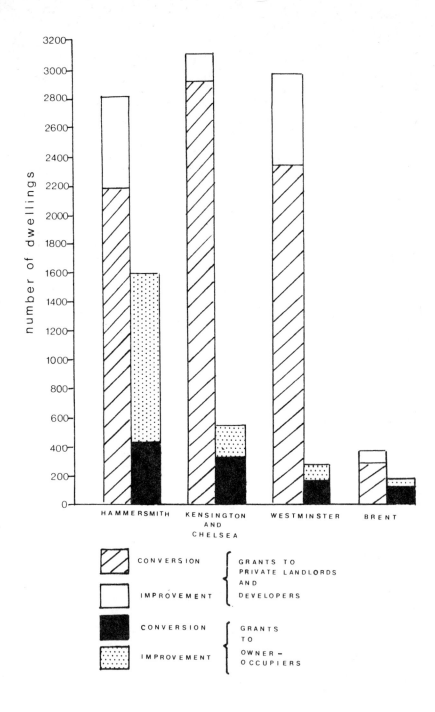

Figure 5.4   Improvement grants awarded to private landlords and developers, and owner occupiers, west London, 1970-73

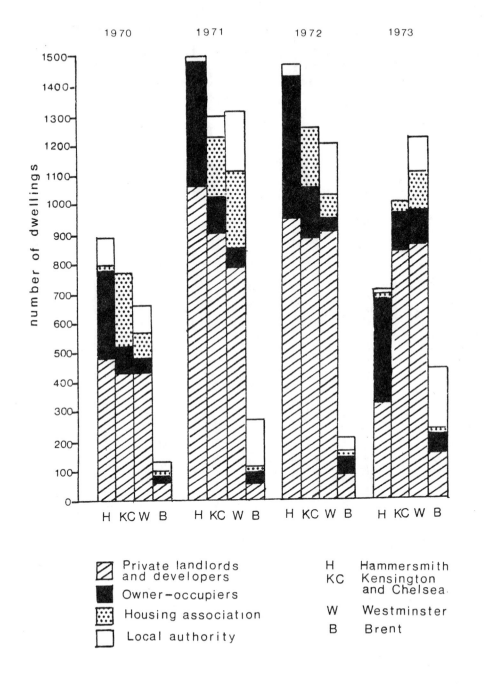

Figure 5.5   Improvement grants awarded to tenure categories, west London, 1970-73

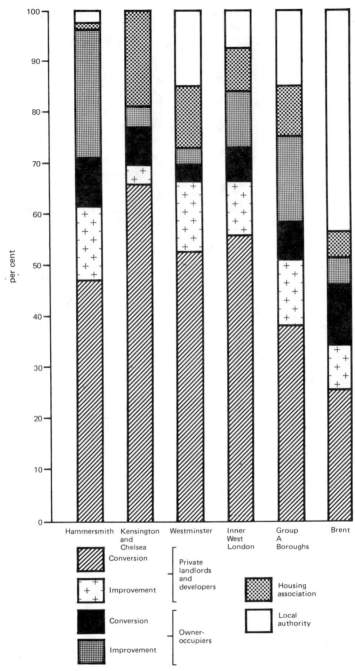

per cent

100
90
80
70
60
50
40
30
20
10
0

Hammersmith   Kensington   Westminster   Inner   Group   Brent
              and   West   A
              Chelsea   London Boroughs

Conversion ⎤
           ⎥ Private
           ⎥ landlords
Improvement⎥ and   Housing
           ⎥ developers   association
Conversion ⎤
           ⎥ Owner-
           ⎥ occupiers   Local
Improvement⎦   authority

Figure 5.6   The proportion of grants awarded for improvement
              and conversion, west London, 1970-73

90

both between the individual boroughs and between Inner West London and the Group A boroughs. The relationship of these different types of grants with each other and within these areas is shown in Fig. 5.6. Improvement grant approvals for owner occupiers as a percentage of all approvals in each borough, 1970-73, varied from 34.4 (Hammersmith) to 5.8 (Westminster) and approvals going to private landlords and developers aa a percentage of all approvals in the boroughs ranged from 71.0 (Kensington and Chelsea) to 34.4 (Brent). Grant approvals for the conversion of property owned by private landlords and developers varied from 66.5 per cent (Kensington and Chelsea) to 25.6 per cent (Brent). The relationship of these grants within Inner West London is shown in Fig. 5.7. Improvement grant approvals to owner occupiers in Inner West London as a proportion of all approvals for Inner West London, 1970-73, averaged about 18 per cent. Approvals going to private landlords and developers as a proportion of all approvals for Inner West London averaged about 67 per cent. The proportion of improvement grant approvals for conversion by private landlords and developers accounted for 56 per cent of all Inner West London grants. The importance of grants for converting property is further demonstrated in Fig. 5.8. In each of the four years under consideration and in each borough (with the exception of Hammersmith in 1973) the number of grants awarded for conversion exceeded (often by a substantial amount) the number of grants awarded for improvement. Collectively, grants for conversion exceeded grants for improvement by 85.6, 251.7, 226.4 and 233.8 per cent respectively in the four years 1970-73.

Regarding grants to owner occupiers and to private landlords and developers in Inner West London as a percentage of Group A boroughs, the disparities are again clearly shown (see Fig.5.9). Improvement grant approvals to owner occupiers in Inner West London as a proportion of grants to owner occupiers in Group A boroughs averaged about 23 per cent between 1970 and 1973. Approvals going to private landlords and developers as a proportion of approvals in Group A boroughs averaged about 41 per cent. The proportion of improvement grants for conversion by private landlords and developers accounted for 47 per cent of all Group A borough grants. Inner West London appears to have had a very large amount of conversion of privately rented property for rent or sale, greatly in excess of the considerable amount of improvement in the owner occupied and privately rented sectors of the housing market.

Analysis of the distribution of grant approvals by ward within Inner West London (its boroughs of Hammersmith, Kensington and Chelsea, and Westminster) and Brent, indicates that the pattern of rehabilitation is very localised.

Grants for both owner occupied and privately rented properties were concentrated in just a few wards (Tables 5.5, 5.6, 5.7, 5.8 and 5.9). In Inner West London, taking the first 27 (half) of the 54 ranked wards, the proportion was 78.4 per cent; in Hammersmith taking the first 11 out of the 21 ranked wards, the proportion was 72.7 per cent; in Kensington and Chelsea taking the first eight of the 15 ranked wards, the proportion was 86.3 per cent; and in Westminster taking the first nine out of the 18 ranked wards, the proportion was 82.2 per cent. In Brent taking the first 16 out of the 32 ranked wards, they accounted for 93.07 per cent of grant approvals. Separate grant information for owner occupied properties and privately rented conversion was only available in the case of Hammersmith, where the first 11 wards accounted for 72.7 and 75.6 per cent of grant approvals respectively (Table 5.6.).

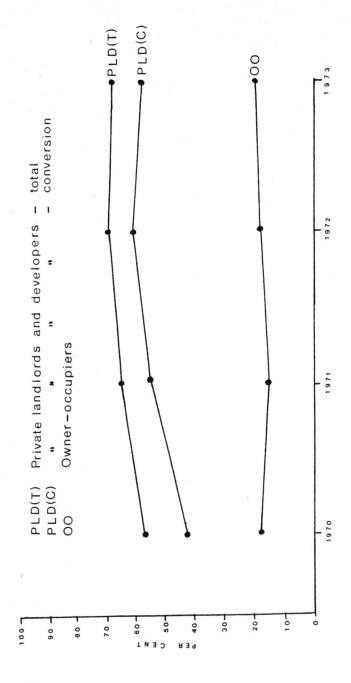

PLD(T)   Private landlords and developers — total
PLD(C)   "   "   "   — conversion
OO   Owner—occupiers

PER CENT

Figure 5.7   The relationship of different types of grants in
             Inner West London, 1970-73

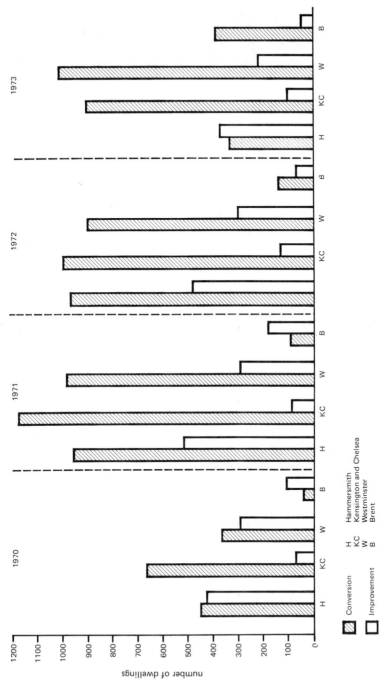

Figure 5.8   The number of grants awarded for improvement and conversion, west London, 1970-73

Conversion

Improvement

H   Hammersmith
KC   Kensington and Chelsea
W   Westminster
B   Brent

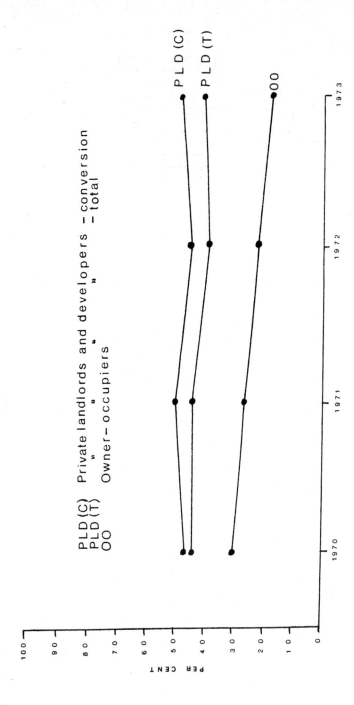

Figure 5.9 Improvement grants awarded in Inner West London as a percentage of improvement grants awarded in Group A boroughs

Table 5.5

Improvement grant - percentages and totals, Inner West London, 1970-73

Ward	Borough	Owner occupied and privately rented %	No.
Maida Vale	W	6.5	906
Harrow Road	W	5.3	744
Redcliffe	KC	5.3	743
Norland	KC	4.3	607
Brook Green	H	4.2	592
Pembridge	KC	3.5	484
Sandford	H	3.2	442
Warwick	W	3.1	429
St.Charles	KC	3.0	423
Town	H	3.0	414
Holland	KC	2.9	409
Grove	H	2.8	386
Westbourne	W	2.6	366
Sulivan	H	2.6	360
Addison	H	2.5	346
Earls Court	KC	2.4	341
Churchill	W	2.3	324
Coningham	H	2.2	311
Lords	W	2.2	309
Hyde Park	W	2.2	309
Parsons Green	H	2.1	298
Lancaster Gate	W	2.1	288
Gibbs Green	H	2.0	275
Brompton	KC	1.7	239
Sherbrooke	H	1.6	225
Halford	H	1.6	217
North Stanley	KC	1.5	211
Crabtree	H	1.5	211
Margravine	H	1.4	195
Regents Park	W	1.4	189
Regent Street	W	1.3	183
Starch Green	H	1.3	178
Baker Street	W	1.2	174
Broadway	H	1.2	169
Colehill	H	1.2	168
Queens Gate	KC	1.2	164
Cavendish	W	1.1	159
Cheyne	KC	1.0	143
Avonmore	H	0.9	132
Victoria Street	W	0.9	129
St.Stephens	H	0.8	116
White City	H	0.8	112
Royal Hospital	KC	0.8	109
Wormholt	H	0.8	106
Knightsbridge	KC	0.6	90
Church Street	W	0.6	87
College Park & Old Oak	H	0.5	71
Church	KC	0.4	55
South Stanley	KC	0.3	41
Hans Town	KC	0.3	41
Golborne	KC	0.3	35
Queens Park	W	0.1	15
Charing Cross	W	0	0
Millbank	W	0	0
Total			14,030

First 27 wards   78.4

* H Hammersmith - KC Kensington & Chelsea - W Westminster

95

Table 5.6

Improvement grant percentages and totals, Hammersmith, 1970-73

Owner occupied and privately rented			Owner occupied only			Privately rented conversions only		
Ward	%	No.	Ward	%	No.	Ward	%	No.
Brook Green	11.1	592	Sandford	9.1	166	Brook Green	13.1	372
Sandford	8.3	442	Grove	8.6	156	Addison	9.6	273
Town	7.8	414	Sulivan	8.5	155	Town	9.4	266
Grove	7.3	386	Brook Green	8.2	149	Sandford	8.1	231
Sulivan	6.8	360	Parsons Green	8.0	145	Gibbs Green	6.9	195
Addison	6.5	346	Town	6.7	122	Grove	6.7	191
Coningham	5.8	311	Crabtree	6.3	115	Coningham	6.0	172
Parsons Green	5.6	298	Sherbrooke	6.2	113	Sulivan	6.0	170
Gibbs Green	5.2	275	Coningham	5.3	96	Parsons Green	4.5	126
Sherbrooke	4.2	225	Halford	4.6	83	Halford	4.1	115
Halford	4.1	217	Starch Green	4.1	75	Avonmore	3.6	101
Crabtree	4.0	211	Margravine	3.6	64	Sherbrooke	2.9	83
Margravine	3.7	196	Colehill	3.0	63	Starch Green	2.9	82
Starch Green	3.3	178	Wormholt	3.0	54	White City	2.8	78
Broadway	3.2	169	Addison	2.9	53	St.Stephens	2.4	68
Colehill	3.2	168	Gibbs Green	2.7	49	Crabtree	2.4	67
Avonmore	2.5	132	Broadway	2.4	43	Margravine	2.3	66
St.Stephens	2.2	116	College Park & Old Oak	1.9	35	Colehill	2.2	62
White City	2.1	112	St.Stephens	1.8	32	Broadway	2.1	60
Wormholt	2.0	106	White City	1.6	29	Wormholt	1.3	37
College Park & Old Oak	1.3	71	Avonmore	1.3	23	College Park & Old Oak	0.7	21
Total		5325			1820			2836
First 11 wards	72.7			75.6			78.0	

The total numbers of wards were divided into sextiles for the purpose of mapping. Within Inner West London the 54 wards were divided into six sextiles each of nine wards. In the top sextile the wards were: Maida Vale, Harrow Road, Redcliffe, Norland, Brook Green, Pembridge, Sandford and St.Charles (Fig.5.10). Except for Warwick in south Westminster, the wards made an arc stretching from north west Westminster, to north Kensington and to central and south east Hammersmith.

It was found that within Inner West London and Brent there was an overall dominance of grants for privately rented property both for improvement and conversion. At a ward level useful information was available only in respect of Hammersmith. Table 5.10 shows the proportions of grants going to privately rented properties by ranked wards for the period 1970-73. It also shows privately rented households as a percentage of non-local authority households. From this table it is not only clear that a major proportion of Hammersmith households live in privately rented property, but that private landlords and developers do not obtain more than their proportionate share of grants to the exclusion of owner occupiers. Whereas privately rented dwellings received 65.8 per cent of grants going to both owner occupied and privately rented dwellings, privately rented dwellings alone accounted for 76.5 per cent of the households in the combined tenure category - indicating that private landlords and developers received 16.2 per cent less than their proportionate share of grants in the borough. Thus it can be inferred that given the large numbers of privately rented dwellings re-let at high rents or sold after improvement/conversion, the stock of low or medium rented accommodation in Hammersmith is diminishing as a consequence of rehabilitation assisted by improvement grants. In Kensington and Chelsea, and Westminster (where, in 1971, the proportion of privately rented households combined was 81 and 85.5 per cent respectively) the problems of the loss of inexpensive accommodation should have been an even greater cause of concern.

THE SPATIAL DISTRIBUTION OF IMPROVEMENT GRANTS AND THEIR CORRELATION WITH SELECTED SOCIO-ECONOMIC VARIABLES

In this section, an attempt is made to correlate the spatial distribution of improvement grants with a number of socio-economic variables, mainly to show the relationship between improvement grant approvals and the specific characteristics of the main areas of grant concentration. First, in 1974-75, the writer undertook a survey of the addresses or locations subject to grant approval in the period 1970-73. It was possible to inspect improvement grant registers of the London boroughs of Brent and Hammersmith and it was possible not only to identify specific dwellings but also to ascertain whether the grant was paid to landlords (resident or absentee) or to owner occupiers. Grants for improvement or conversion purposes were clearly distinguished. In the case of Westminster the writer was permitted to inspect a card index but it provided far less detailed information. Thus for example conversion grants were not distinguished from grants for improvement only. In the case of Kensington and Chelsea, it was only possible to locate the street or road etc. in which a grant had been approved, wall maps alone were made available for this purpose, registers or card indices remaining strictly confidential. There was no indication of the recipients of grants or whether the grants were for improvement or conversion. The information collected by the writer differed slightly from that published by the GLC

Table 5.7

Improvement grant percentages and totals
Kensington and Chelsea, 1970-73

Owner occupied and privately rented

Ward	%	No.
Redcliffe	18.6	743
Norland	15.2	607
Pembridge	12.1	484
St.Charles	10.6	423
Holland	10.2	409
Earls Court	8.5	341
Brompton	6.0	239
North Stanley	5.3	211
Queens Gate	4.1	164
Cheyne	3.6	143
Royal Hospital	2.7	109
Church	1.4	55
South Stanley	1.0	41
Hans Town	1.0	41
Golborne	0.9	35
Total		4004
First 8 wards	86.3	

Table 5.8

Improvement grant percentages and totals
Westminster, 1970-73

Owner occupied and privately rented

Ward	%	No.
Maida Vale	19.3	906
Harrow Road	15.8	744
Warwick	9.1	429
Westbourne	7.8	366
Churchill	6.9	324
Lords	6.6	309
Hyde Park	6.6	309
Lancaster Gate	6.1	288
Regents Park	4.0	189
Regent Street	3.9	183
Baker Street	3.7	174
Cavendish	3.4	159
Victoria Street	2.7	129
Knightsbridge	1.9	90
Church Street	1.9	87
Queens Park	0.3	15
Charing Cross	0.0	0
Millbank	0.0	0
Total		4701
First 9 wards	82.2	

Table 5.9

Improvement grant percentages and totals
Brent, 1970-73

Owner occupied and privately rented

Ward	%	No.
Church End	11.3	52
Brondesbury Park	10.6	49
Mapesbury	9.1	42
Willesden Green	8.7	40
Kilburn	8.0	37
Stonebridge	6.7	31
Roundwood	5.4	25
Carlton	5.0	23
Wembley Central	4.8	22
Queens Park	4.6	21
Barnham	4.6	21
Harlesden	3.9	18
Kensal Rise	3.0	14
Manor	3.0	14
Gladstone	2.2	10
Tokyngton	2.2	10
St.Raphael	2.0	9
Wembley Park	2.0	9
Kenton	0.9	4
Sudbury	0.9	4
Queensbury	0.4	2
Cricklewood	0.2	1
Alperton	0.2	1
Fryent	0.2	1
Roe Green	0.2	1
Brentwater	0.0	0
Chamberlayne	0.0	0
Kingsbury	0.0	0
Preston	0.0	0
Sudbury Court	0.0	0
Town Hall	0.0	0
Total		461
First 16 wards	93.0	

and Department of the Environment but this was probably inevitable as grant registers, card indices and wall maps were either not fully up to date at the time of inspection or were in an unedited or partly uncollated form.   The information was then processed and the number of grants approved in each ward was established.   Where possible and relevant the grants were further categorised into those awarded to private landlords and developers, and owner occupiers, and those awarded for improvement or conversion.   The percentage of households in each ward 'receiving' improvement grants was then calculated - 'receiving' meaning either obtaining grants directly in the case of owner occupiers or being subject to improvement grants in the case of private tenancies.

The wards in Inner West London and in each borough (see Appendix E) were then arranged in rank order, and the percentage of households receiving improvement grants was correlated with specific variables of household tenure, housing characteristics, social composition and age structure.   In this analysis standard correlation symbols are used: Rxy being the correlation coefficient, t being the student's 't' test and P being probability.   It was decided not to rank the variables in order on a ward basis, but to consider them as percentages of the number of house-holds or dwellings, or size of total population in each ward.   Census data was more relevant to this method.   This approach is customarily used in showing spatial distributions within local government areas.

In Inner West London, the highest proportion of households receiving improvement grants were within an arc from north Westminster, to north Kensington, to central and south Hammersmith, namely in the wards of Maida Vale, Harrow Road, Norland, Coningham, Grove, Brook Green, Town, Sulivan and Sandford (Fig.5.11).   In all these wards at least 9.4 per cent of households received improvement grants.   In Hammersmith, the highest proportion of non-local authority households receiving improvement grants were, in descending rank order, in the wards Brook Green, Sandford, Town and Grove, in each at least 9.9 per cent of households received improvement grants.   These wards are either situated contiguously in the central part of the borough or in two separate areas in south Hammersmith. Correlations with owner occupier households and private tenancy conversions are similarly distributed.   In Kensington and Chelsea, the highest proportion of households receiving improvement grants were in rank order in the wards of Norland, North Stanley and Redcliffe, in each of which at least 7.7 per cent of households received improvement grants. Whereas Norland is in north Kensington the other two wards are in the southern part of the borough.   In Westminster, the highest proportion of households which received improvement grants were in rank order in: Harrow Road, Maida Vale and Warwick.   In each case at least 7.0 per cent of households received improvement grants.   The first two wards formed a contiguous area in the north west of the borough and the latter ward was situated in the extreme south of Westminster.

Within Brent, in the top sextile and in rank order the highest proportion of households receiving improvement grants were in: Church End, Brondesbury Park, Stonebridge, Willesden Green and Roundwood.   In each of these wards at least 1.0 per cent of households received improvement grants.   These wards stretch from east to west across the southern part of the borough.

To identify the relationship between the approval of improvement grants and household tenure, housing characteristics, social composition and age

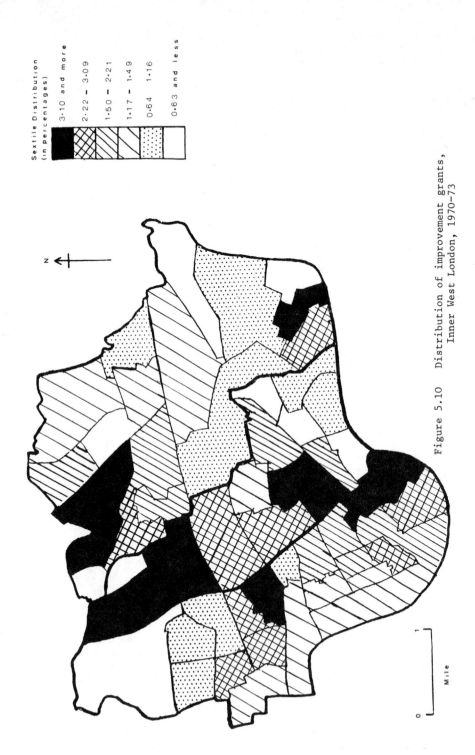

Sextile Distribution
(in percentages)

3·10 and more

2·22 — 3·09

1·50 — 2·21

1·17 — 1·49

0·64 — 1·16

0·63 and less

N

Figure 5.10   Distribution of improvement grants,
Inner West London, 1970–73

0   Mile   1

Table 5.10

Percentage of improvement grants awarded to privately rented dwellings
in Hammersmith, 1970-73
and privately rented households as a percentage of total non-local
authority households in the borough

Ward	% grants to privately rented dwellings	% privately rented households
Addison	84.9	87.1
Avonmore	82.6	91.6
Gibbs Green	82.2	90.0
Brooks Green	74.8	81.4
Broadway	74.6	81.7
White City	74.1	65.0
St.Stephens	72.4	82.6
Town	70.5	73.2
Coningham	69.1	78.0
Margravine	67.4	73.5
Colehill	62.5	69.5
Sandford	62.4	74.2
Halford	61.8	78.0
Grove	59.6	78.5
Starch Green	57.9	71.2
Sulivan	56.9	66.3
Parsons Green	51.3	71.9
College Park & Old Oak	50.7	73.7
Sherbrooke	49.8	69.7
Wormholt	49.1	61.8
Crabtree	45.5	61.5
L.B. Hammersmith	65.8	76.5

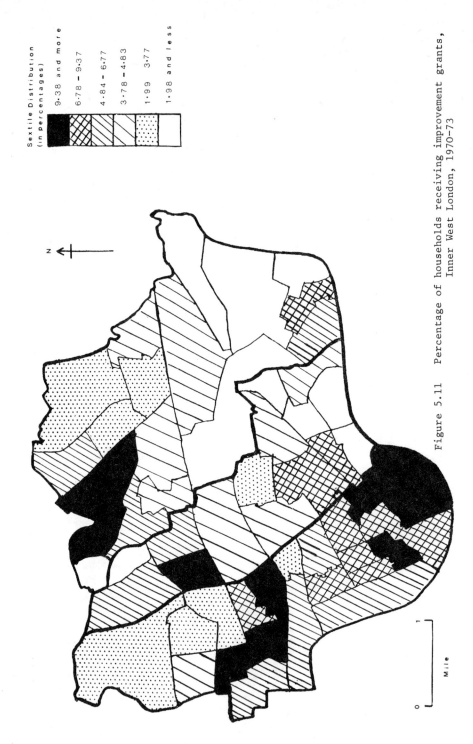

Sextile Distribution
(in percentages)

9·38 and more

6·78 – 9·37

4·84 – 6·77

3·78 – 4·83

1·99 – 3·77

1·98 and less

N

Figure 5.11   Percentage of households receiving improvement grants,
              Inner West London, 1970–73

0   1
Mile

104

structure it was decided to attempt to correlate the percentage of
households receiving improvement grants with a number of variables. Six
variables were selected for household tenure, eight variables were chosen
for housing characteristics, four variables were used for social composition and for age structure 11 variables were selected.   So as to show
the strongest relationships, and because of the method by which the data
was presented in the 1971 Census, it was considered appropriate to select
a differing number of variables, rather than to confine the analysis to a
fixed number of influences in each case.   Relationships were identified
in Inner west London and in each of the boroughs.

Inner west London

Table 5.11 shows correlations between improvement grant approvals and
selected variables.   These indicate that grants were awarded mainly in
wards where there were high percentages of private landlords and
developers;   tenants sharing (grants being concentrated in areas where
there was a severe crude net deficiency of dwellings);   a high proportion
of tenants without the use of basic amenities within their dwellings;
tenants were mainly under the age of 40 and had children under the age of
5;   and where most tenants were within the semi-skilled and unskilled
categories - socio-economic groups (SEGs) 7-12, 14-15.

Hammersmith

Table 5.12 shows correlations which indicate that most improvement grants
went to wards where there was a high percentage of private landlords and
developers specifically with furnished tenancies;   that grants were
concentrated in wards where there had been a decrease in private households, 1966-71;   where accommodation was shared;   where there was a
severe crude net deficiency of dwellings, and where tenants lacked the
provision of basic amenities.   There were no cases of correlation with
social composition variables or with any specific age group, Hammersmith
having little spatial variation in the distribution of its social and
age categories.

Kensington and Chelsea

Table 5.13 shows correlations which indicate that grant distribution
was related to the decrease in owner occupied tenure, 1966-71, and that
this was in areas where there was a severe crude net deficiency of
dwellings;   where many dwellings were shared;   and where there was a
lack of provision of basic amenities.   Grants were probably often used
for the deconversion of tenancies into owner occupied properties with
resulting doubling up of households into smaller conversions (bed sitters
or small apartments) elsewhere in the borough.   This might explain the
correlation between improvement grants and the increase in the number of
dwellings without an inside W.C.   Correlations were found with the
younger population groups, and although there was a decrease in the
population aged 20-39 in the borough as a whole, 1966-71, there was an
increase of this age group in areas of high grant concentration.   Grants
were awarded mainly to areas where a high proportion of the population
was within the semi-skilled or unskilled groups.

Westminster

Table 5.14 shows correlations which indicate that grants had been awarded

Table 5.11

Correlations between the approval of improvement grants and selected socio-economic variables within the 54 wards of the Inner West London boroughs*

	Boroughs	Ward range	Rxy	t	P
Households receiving improvement grants (1970-73)	4.96	0 - 14.3	-	-	-
Shared dwellings	9.4	0.7 - 28.8	0.52	4.38	> 0.1
Crude net deficiency	-6.2	-48.9/+ 62.2	0.47	3.87	> 0.1
Dwellings without hot water	8.4	1.4 - 27.8	0.36	2.75	1 > 0.2
Population aged under 5	5.2	1.8 - 9.9	0.32	2.47	2 > 1
Population aged under 40	57.1	37.7 - 69.0	0.28	2.09	5 > 2
Change in population aged 40-64 (1966-71)	-13.8	-41.1/+ 22.2	0.28	1.99	NS
Population aged under 15	14.8	4.4 - 29.4	0.26	1.93	NS
SEGs 7-12, 14, 15	14.4	1.8 - 27.6	0.23	1.73	NS
Dwellings without a bath/shower	10.6	1.1 - 44.0	0.23	1.70	NS
Private furnished tenancies	24.5	1.3 - 55.9	0.23	1.69	NS
Dwellings without an inside W.C.	5.6	0.2 - 36.7	0.23	1.68	NS
Population aged 40-64	30.9	22.1 - 47.9	-0.33	2.49	2 1
SEGs 1, 2	5.2	1.0 - 12.0	-0.31	2.35	5 2
SEGs 1-4	7.8	1.4 - 19.9	-0.29	2.21	5 2
Population aged 40 and over	42.9	31.0 - 62.3	-0.28	2.09	5 2
Owner occupied households	14.9	2.9 - 35.4	-0.26	1.94	NS

* Hammersmith, Kensington and Chelsea, and Westminster

Table 5.12

Correlations between the approval of improvement grants and selected socio-economic variables within the 21 wards of Hammersmith

	Borough %	Ward Range %	Rxy	t	P
Total non-local authority households					
Total non-local authority households receiving improvement grants (1970-73)	7.2	2.3 - 14.3	-	-	-
Crude net deficiency	- 18.0	-7.5/ - 31.7	0.57	3.01	1 > 0.2
Private tenancies	61.4	34.2 - 81.6	0.48	2.35	5 > 2
Change in private households (1966-71)	- 1.2	-15.1/ + 30.0	0.44	2.14	5 > 2
Shared dwellings	15.5	5.6 - 28.8	0.40	1.93	NS
Dwellings without a bath/shower	14.0	3.1 - 33.9	0.29	-	NS
Fertility ratio	32.5	13.9 - 45.9	- 0.25	-	NS
Change in dwellings without hot water (1966-71)	- 24.3	-62.4/ + 95.0	- 0.22	-	NS
Owner occupied households					
Owner occupied households receiving improvement grants as a % total households (1970-73)	2.5	0.6 - 4.4	-	-	-
Private furnished tenancies	61.4	34.2 - 81.6	0.70	4.26	1 > 0.1
Crude net deficiency	- 18.0	-7.5/ - 31.7	0.60	3.24	1 > 0.2
Shared dwellings	15.5	5.6 - 28.8	0.59	3.16	1 > 0.2
Dwellings without a bath/shower	14.0	3.1 - 33.9	0.54	2.80	2 > 1
Total private tenancies	61.4	34.2 - 81.6	0.26	-	NS
Private tenancy conversions					
Private tenancy households receiving improvement grants for conversion as a % total households (1970-73)	3.8	0.7 - 9.0	-	-	-
Crude net deficiency	- 18.0	-5.7/ - 31.7	0.60	3.27	1 > 0.2
Change in total private households (1966-71)	- 1.2	-15.1/ + 13.0	0.38	1.78	NS
Total private tenancies	61.4	34.2 - 81.5	0.26	-	NS
Fertility ratio	32.5	14.0 - 45.9	- 0.35	1.65	NS

Table 5.13

<u>Correlations between the approval of improvement grants
and selected socio-economic variables within the
15 wards of Kensington and Chelsea</u>

	Borough %	Ward %	Range	Rxy	t	P
Households receiving Improvement grants (1970-73)	5.2	0.4	-11.4	-	-	-
Dwellings without an inside W.C.	2.5	0.2	- 5.4	0.82	4.68	> 0.1
Shared dwellings	5.0	0.8	-22.7	0.69	3.20	$1 > 0$
Dwellings without hot water	4.1	1.4	- 8.8	0.66	2.94	$2 > 1$
Dwellings without a bath/shower	4.5	1.1	- 9.1	0.59	2.43	$5 > 2$
Population aged under 15	12.5	6.4	-27.4	0.53	2.06	NS
Population aged under 5	4.5	2.4	- 9.9	0.47	1.78	NS
Crude net deficiency/ surplus	- 1.3	-33.7/	+62.2	0.46	1.71	NS
SEGs 7-12, 14,15	10.0	4.3	-24.4	0.42	-	NS
Fertility ratio	15.4	6.3	-46.8	0.35	-	NS
Change in owner occupation (1966-71)	+14.0	-33.1/	+70.4	-0.61	2.56	$5 > 2$
SEGS 1.2	6.4	1.0	-12.0	-0.55	2.21	$5 > 2$
SEGs 1-4	10.0	1.4	-15.9	-0.47	1.75	NS

108

Table 5.14

Correlations between the approval of improvement grants
and selected socio-economic variables within the
18 wards of Westminster

	Borough %	Ward %	Range	Rxy	t	P
Households receiving Improvement grants (1970-73)	5.0	0	-11.1	-	-	-
Households living at more than 1.5 persons per room	5.7	1.0	-14.9	0.76	4.63	>0.1
Shared dwellings	4.0	0.7	-34.1	0.67	3.58	1>0.2
Private furnished tenancies	25.7	1.3	-49.6	0.55	2.63	2 > 1
Crude net deficiency/ surplus	- 0.5	-48.9/	+17.0	0.46	2.06	NS
Change in population aged under 20 (1968-71)*	14.0	-32.0/	+ 9.2	0.44	1.48	NS
Population aged under 5	4.1	1.8	- 9.6	0.42	1.87	NS
Population aged under 40	52.2	37.7	-62.5	0.41	1.81	NS
Population aged under 15	12.0	4.4	-26.0	0.26	1.08	NS
Change in households without an inside W.C. (1966-71)	10.9	-58.4/	+137.5	-0.92	6.99	>0.1
Population aged 40 and over	47.8	37.5	- 62.3	-0.41	1.81	NS

*Due to re-warding in Westminster in 1966, this variable was
only correlated with improvement grants in the 11 wards which
remained unchanged.

Table 5.15

Correlations between the approval of improvement grants
and selected socio-economic variables within the
31 wards of Brent

	Borough %	Ward %	Range	Rxy	t	P
Households receiving improvement grants (1970-73)	0.47	0	- 1.9	-	-	-
Private unfurnished tenancies	21.9	5.5	-46.0	0.70	4.82	> 0.1
Households without a car	55.8	32.6	-79.9	0.70	5.23	> 0.1
Households living at 1.5 persons per room	5.9	0.7	-13.6	0.63	4.30	> 0.1
Dwellings without hot water	4.0	0	-18.6	0.62	4.21	> 0.1
Total Private Tenancies	38.4	8.8	-74.8	0.62	4.27	> 0.1
Dwellings without a bath/shower	4.0	0.1	-22.8	0.59	3.90	> 0.1
Dwellings without an inside W.C.	2.1	0	-11.2	0.54	3.48	0.2 > 0.1
Population aged 20-39	29.0	20.9	-40.2	0.45	2.74	2 > 1
Private furnished tenancies	16.5	1.8	-55.7	0.45	2.72	2 > 1
Population aged under 40	57.3	48.0	-67.2	0.45	2.70	2 > 1
Shared dwellings	11.4	0.7	-34.8	0.43	2.60	2 > 1
SEGs 7-12, 14,15	17.8	6.8	-24.6	0.37	2.16	5 > 2
Population aged under 5	7.7	5.5	-10.9	0.31	1.73	NS
Owner occupied households	48.2	2.5	-90.6	-0.66	4.76	> 0.1
SEGs 1,2	4.0	0.7	- 9.3	-0.48	2.96	0.2 > 0.1
Population aged over 40	42.7	32.8	-52.0	-0.45	2.70	2 > 1
SEGs 1-4	5.7	1.2	-15.5	-0.43	2.56	2 > 1
Population aged 40-63	30.8	25.5	-37.4	-0.34	1.94	NS

110

mainly in wards where there was a high percentage of private landlords
and developers with furnished tenants; in wards where there was a severe
crude net deficiency of dwellings; and where much accommodation was
shared and overcrowded; and affecting mainly that proportion of the
population under the age of 40 including a high proportion under the age
of five. Possibly because of the poor housing condition in the areas
of high grant concentration there had been a decrease in the population
under the age of 20 between 1966-71.

Brent

Table 5.15 shows correlations which indicate that grants were awarded
mainly in wards where there was a high percentage of households living in
private unfurnished (and to a lesser extent unfurnished) tenancies; not
owning cars; living in overcrowded conditions and sharing accommodation;
lacking basic amenities; and with the head of the household generally
under 40 years of age, semi-skilled and unskilled occupationally, with
children under the age of five.

Conclusion

In general, the above correlations suggest that improvement grants were
awarded mainly in areas of poor and overcrowded housing and private
letting. The correlations do not indicate whether grants were associated
with gentrification (either mediated or unmediated) – the displacement of
low SEG, low income households by those of a higher SEG, higher income –
although in Hammersmith and Westminster correlations were found between
grant awards and furnished tenancies (the least secure tenure up to the
Rent Act of 1974). It was in this sector that landlords and developers
had the greatest opportunity to improve their properties and to sell to
owner occupiers or re-let to higher rent tenants.

THE CORRELATION OF THE SPATIAL DISTRIBUTION OF IMPROVEMENT GRANTS WITH
THE REHABILITATION-NEED INDEX

In this section the more important variables are incorporated into a
Rehabilitation-Need Index (RNI). Based on the Housing Stress Index of
the GLC, the RNI provides an overall indicator of where rehabilitation is
desirable. It is correlated with the distribution of improvement grants
over the area of Inner West London and Brent and is intended to show if
improvement grants were being approved mainly in areas of greatest need
(1970-73).

The 1971 Census provided for every ward information on household
tenure, sharing of dwellings, the provision of basic amenities (bath/
shower, hot water, an inside W.C.), socio-economic groups, car ownership
and the age of the population. Ten indicators of rehabilitation-need
were selected from the variables already considered which in turn had
been selected from the 1971 Census. They represent poor and often overcrowded housing (which is generally in need of improvement) and those
occupants least likely to be able to afford to match improvement grants
pound for pound under the terms of the Housing Act of 1969 – the lowest
socio-economic groups (often synonomous with households without a car),
families with young children (the young children being indicators) and
the elderly. The indicators are listed below:

Indicator 1	-	furnished private tenancies
Indicator 2	-	shared dwellings
Indicator 3	-	households at more than 1.5 persons per room
Indicator 4	-	dwellings without a bath/shower
Indicator 5	-	dwellings without hot water
Indicator 6	-	dwellings without an inside W.C.
Indicator 7		SEGs 7-12, 14, 15
Indicator 8	-	households without a car
Indicator 9	-	population under the age of 5
Indicator 10	-	population 65 years of age and over

The percentage of households/dwellings which fell into each category, in each ward, was found. For the purpose of comparing the rehabilitation-need between wards, the ten indicators were combined into a single index. This was done as follows:

a) The ten percentages were reduced to a common base. This was achieved by multiplying the percentage for each indicator by the sum of the Inner west London and Brent mean percentage for the other nine indicators. For example, the percentage for indicator 1 was multiplied by the sum of the Inner west London and Brent mean percentages for indicators 2-10.

b) Each of the ten percentages, as adjusted under (a) above, was then multiplied by a subjective weight, since it was considered by the writer that some indicators were more relevant than others in determining the extent of rehabilitation-need (subjective weighting had been previously used by the GLC in producing its Housing Stress Index from the 1961 Census).

c) The ten percentages were then added together. This addition resulted in an index with a range from 10 609 to 51 679 (see Appendix F). This enabled wards to be ranked, although in absolute terms the index score has no significance.

Table 5.16 sets out the means, sum of means (less indicator mean) and weights which governed the calculation of the index.

The ranked wards were divided into sextiles and mapped. Within Inner West London and Brent it was found that the 15 top sextile wards were in rank order: Kilburn, Mapesbury, Queens Park, Harrow Road, Harlesden, Kensal Rise, Coningham, Addison, Golborne, Brook Green, St.Stephens, College Park and Old Oak, Westbourne, Willesden Green and Grove (Fig.5.12). All had indices in excess of 43,100 - Kilburn having the highest index of 51,679.   The top quartile wards were concentrated in the north of Inner West London and in south east Brent with the second highest quartile wards (those with indices within the range 39,100 to 43,000) generally flanking this area: Stonebridge, Manor, Cricklewood, Roundwood and Brondesbury Park in descending rank order to the north; and Colehill, Earls Court, Sherbrooke, Gibbs Green, Pembridge, Halford, Lancaster Gate, Brompton and Redcliffe in descending rank order to the south.   Only in the case of Warwick in the extreme south east was this pattern noticeably broken.

Table 5.16

Rehabilitation-Need Index

Variables, means, sums of means and weighting

		Variable	Mean	Sum of means less indicator mean	Weight
Household tenure	1	Furnished private tenancies	20.9	166.2	3
	2	Shared dwellings	10.4	177.6	1
Housing character- istics	3	Households at more than 1.5 persons per room	5.8	181.3	1
	4	Dwellings without a bath/shower	8.4	178.7	0.33
	5	Dwellings without hot water	7.1	180.0	0.33
	6	Dwellings without an inside W.C.	4.4	182.7	0.33
Social composition	7	SEGs 7,8,9,10,11,12,14,15	46.7	140.4	2
	8	Households without a car	64.2	122.8	0.33
and age structure	9	Population under the age of 5	6.1	181.0	0.33
	10	Population 65 years of age and over	13.0	174.1	0.33

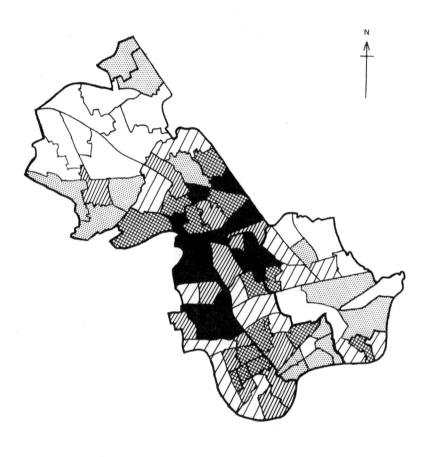

Sextile Distribution ('000s)

████	43.1 and over
▨▨	39.1-43.0
▧▧	32.9-39.0
⟋⟋	27.3-32.8
∵∵	20.0-27.2
☐	under 20.0

Figure 5.12   Rehabilitation-Need, west London, 197

Table 5.17

Correlation between the Rehabilitation-Need Index
and approval of improvement grants

	Inner West London	Brent	Brent and Inner West London
Rxy	0.65	0.71	0.48
t	2,57	2.85	2.13
P	5 > 2	5 > 2	5 > 2

The RNI was correlated with the percentage of households receiving improvement grants, 1970-73 (Table 5.17).   In Inner West London and in Brent separately there were moderate correlations (Rxy = 0.65 and 0.71 respectively) and in Inner West London and Brent together there was a low correlation (Rxy = 0.48).   In each case the correlation had the same statistical significance, P = 5 > 2.   In the case of Inner West London there were intersections in six of the nine top quartile wards (Fig.5.13):   Addison, Brook Green, Coningham, Grove, Harrow Road and Sherbrooke.   In the case of Brent, there were intersections in four of the eight top quartile wards (Fig.5.14):   Kilburn, Mapesbury, Stonebridge and Willesden Green.   In the case of Inner west London and Brent combined, there were intersections in none of the 15 top quartile wards (Fig.5.15):   Addison, Brook Green, Colehill, Coningham, Grove, Harrow Road, Sherbrooke, Warwick and Westbourne.

A SUGGESTED EXPLANATION OF THE PATTERN OF IMPROVEMENT GRANT DISTRIBUTION IN WEST LONDON

It must not be assumed that the successive westward migrations of the social classes have resulted in a concentric pattern of residential land use throughout west London, similar to that described by Burgess in Chicago (Chapter 1).   In contrast to many cities, London has a high income residential area adjacent to (or even partly within) a CBD, and in close proximity to an inner area of middle income housing.   Both areas form wedges or sectors between areas of low income housing.   Based on social and economic indicators drawn from the 1971 Census, seven broad areas of private sector housing can be identified in west London. These are: the Central Residential Area;   the West End Residential Area; the Inner, Middle and Outer Transitional Areas;   and the Inner and Outer Suburban Areas (Fig.5.16).   The Central and West End Residential Areas coincide approximately with the area of high income housing developed on the Great Estates and contain a relatively high proportion of middle class households.   The Inner, Middle and Outer Transitional Areas contain a high proportion of working class residents, often living in former high income housing converted into flats.   The Inner Suburban Areas contain a lower proportion of working class residents, many of whom are owner occupiers, and the Outer Suburban Areas again include a high proportion of middle class households, most of which are owner occupiers. It could be suggested that very generally, the processes which determined

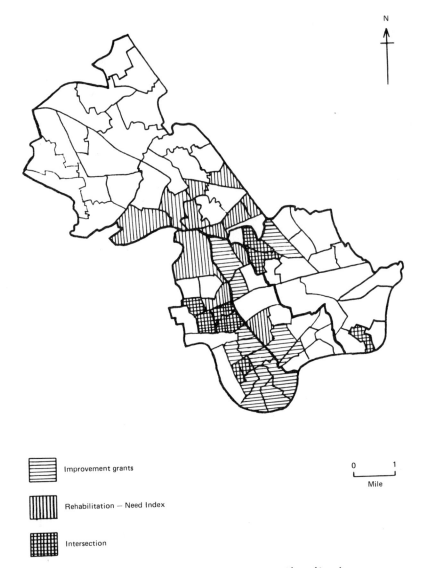

N

Improvement grants

Rehabilitation — Need Index

Intersection

0   1
Mile

Figure 5.13   Intersections of improvement grant distribution
and the Rehabilitation-Need Index,
Inner West London

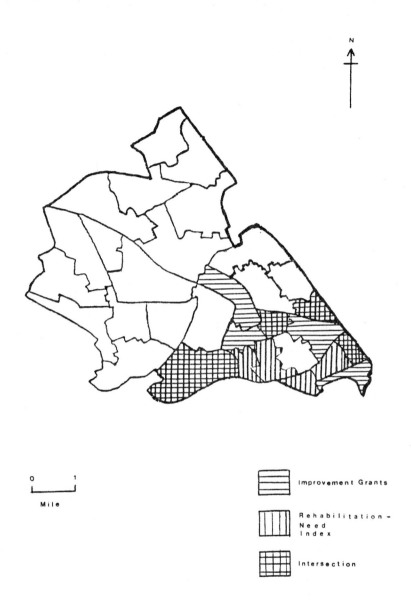

N

0 ___ 1
Mile

Improvement Grants

Rehabilitation-
Need
Index

Intersection

Figure 5.14   Intersections of improvement grant distribution
and the Rehabilitation-Need Index, Brent

117

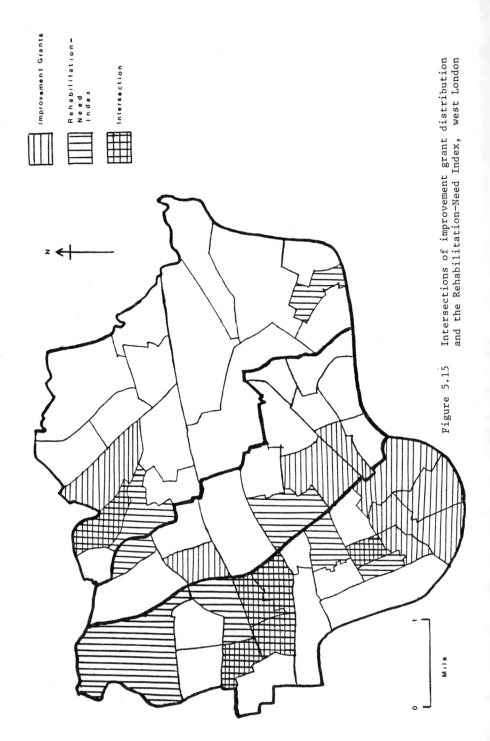

Figure 5.15   Intersections of improvement grant distribution
and the Rehabilitation-Need Index, west London

the variations in housing and occupancy outwards from the Central
Residential Area to the Outer Transitional Area are compatible with those
explained by the sector theory of Hoyt (see Chapter 1). In contrast,
the processes which formed the Inner and Outer Suburban Areas and
established the relationships both between these two areas, and between
the suburban and transitional areas, conform to Burgess' hypothesis.

In order to explain the spatial distribution of improvement grants
attention must be paid to the four factors of location, social composition,
household tenure and housing characteristics (Table 5.18). Kensington
and Chelsea and Westminster are two of the most centrally placed boroughs
in Greater London. On the basis of differences in their socio-economic
variables these boroughs consist of four residential areas: the Central
Residential Area; the West End Residential Area; the Inner Transitional
Area, and the Middle Transitional Area. The last of these areas also
includes parts of Hammersmith.

Located within the Great Estates, most of the Central and West End
Residential Areas were the first areas of housing to be extensively
developed to the west of the City of London. They have a much higher
than normal proportion of population in the highest socio-economic groups,
and have had for a considerable period. Economically active males in
SEGs 1 and 2 amounted to 7.4 and 9.9 per cent of the respective populations
of the Central and West End Residential Areas. The proportion ranged from
12 per cent (Hans Town) to 6.4 per cent (Charing Cross). With SEGs 1-4,
the proportions were 12.8 and 14.9 per cent in the Central and West End
Residential Areas respectively, and the proportions ranged from 16.2 per
cent in Knightsbridge to 9.5 per cent in Charing Cross. The principal
difference between the two areas was that in the West End Residential Area
a much higher proportion of households were owner occupiers (mainly
leaseholders), 24.4 per cent as against 6.8 per cent in the Central
Residential Area. The proportion ranged from 28.5 per cent (Hans Town)
to 2.9 per cent (Charing Cross). The Central Residential Area had the
highest proportion of households living in private unfurnished tenancies
(69.8 per cent). In both areas the proportion of households living at
more than 1.5 persons per room was small, 2.5 per cent in the Central
Residential Area and 3.3 per cent in the West End Residential Area. This
very low incidence of overcrowding and the comparatively high proportion
of the upper socio-economic classes suggest that housing quality and
residential values are also high within these areas.

The price of houses in both areas often exceeds £100,000. Therefore,
except for the very affluent, few households could afford to acquire the
freehold or leasehold of a complete property. Conversion into a large
number of smaller dwellings may be the only means of disposing of the
accommodation when it comes up for sale. Improvement grants were only
awarded to 2.5 and 3.3 per cent of households in the Central and West End
Residential Areas respectively (1970-73). Except for the Outer Suburban
Area, these proportions were the lowest in west London. It has been
shown (Table 5.4) that comparatively few improvement grants were awarded
to owner occupiers in Kensington and Chelsea, and Westminster (1970-73),
but the predominance of grant aided conversion of privately owned housing
in these areas for rent or sale cannot be termed gentrification. There
was an influx of high socio-economic class residents into areas which had
contained a relatively high proportion of this class for many generations.

The built-up area of London was extended outward from the Central and

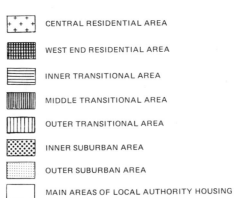

	CENTRAL RESIDENTIAL AREA
	WEST END RESIDENTIAL AREA
	INNER TRANSITIONAL AREA
	MIDDLE TRANSITIONAL AREA
	OUTER TRANSITIONAL AREA
	INNER SUBURBAN AREA
	OUTER SUBURBAN AREA
	MAIN AREAS OF LOCAL AUTHORITY HOUSING

Figure 5.16   Residential areas – west London

West End Residential Areas by residential development in the eighteenth
and particularly nineteenth century.   These extended areas of housing,
termed the Inner, Middle and Outer Transitional Areas by the author,
contain smaller proportions of the highest socio-economic groups, but
larger proportions of SEGs 7-12, 14, 15.   Economically active males in
these lower groups amounted to 10, 18 and 18.6 per cent of the populations
of the Inner, Middle and Outer Transitional Areas respectively.   The
proportions ranged from 24.4 per cent (Golborne) to 5.6 per cent (Baker
Street).   With the exception of the Central Residential Area, the
transitional areas (particularly the Middle Transitional Area) had the
lowest proportion of owner occupied households.   The principal difference
between these areas and the remainder of west London was that they
contained the highest proportion of households in private furnished
tenancies, in the Inner, Middle and Outer Transitional Areas the
proportions were 35.5, 32 and 29.6 per cent respectively.   The proportions ranged from 55.9 per cent (Brompton) to 8.9 per cent (Church).
The proportion of households living in owner occupied housing was much
smaller, and amounted to only 13.1, 7.2 and 16.7 per cent in the Inner,
Middle and Outer Transitional Areas respectively.   The transitional areas
contained the highest proportion of households living at more than 1.5
persons per room;   the proportions were 8.1, 10.0 and 7.8 per cent in the
Inner, Middle and Outer Transitional Areas respectively.   The proportions
ranged from 15.3 (Golborne) to 1.9 per cent (Lords).   The Inner, Middle
and Outer Transitional Areas are distinguished from each other mainly by
differences in the proportion of their population in the socio-economic
groups and differences in the degree of owner occupation.

The social composition of these transitional areas is more normally
distributed than in the Central and West End Residential Areas, and
housing is poorer.   Hamnett (1973) suggested that a price shadow was cast
on properties in these areas by rising values in the more 'desirable'
inner residential areas in the early 1970s.   The excess of demand over
supply within the highest value inner areas of London probably diffused
higher prices into the transitional areas.   Again, improvement grants
were used mainly for conversion purposes, particularly in the Inner and
Middle Transitional Areas which were mainly within the boroughs of
Kensington and Chelsea, and Westminster.   It was more viable economically
to convert properties into private tenancies or for sale than for owner
occupiers to improve whole houses.   In these areas, conversion was
synonymous with mediated gentrification (see Chapter 2).   The in-
migration of high socio-economic classes into predominantly lower class
areas was generally associated with the previous households moving out.
A greater proportion of households were directly affected by improvement
grants in these areas than elsewhere in west London.   Within the Inner,
Middle and Outer Transitional Areas the proportions were 5.2, 6.6 and 6.7
per cent respectively.   Chapters 2 and 4 dealt extensively with the
economic and social aspects of gentrification, most of which are
particularly relevant to the transitional areas.

In the late nineteenth and early twentieth centuries new modes of travel
such as suburban railways, the extended underground system and later the
motor car facilitated the development of housing on the periphery of the
built-up area of London.   These new suburbs can be divided into the Inner
Suburban Areas and Outer Suburban Areas.   In the Inner Suburban Areas,
economically active males in SEGs 1 and 2, and 1-4 amounted to 2.8 and 4.1
per cent of the population respectively.   The proportion of the population
in SEGs 1 and 2 ranged from 5.9 per cent (Crabtree) to 0.9 per cent

Table 5.18

Suggested residential areas in west London

	% population economically active males in SEGs			% Owner occupied households	% Private unfurnished tenancies	% Private furnished tenancies	% Private tenancies (total)	% households living at more than 1.5 persons per room	% households receiving improvement grants
	1,2	1-4	7-12 14,15						
1.Central Residential Area									
Regent Street	8.3	10.6	6.4	7.8	56.9	20.8	77.8	3.7	4.7
Victoria Street	7.7	11.1	10.3	7.4	69.6	17.1	86.7	1.8	1.3
Cavendish	7.2	19.9	1.8	9.2	64.4	18.2	82.6	4.1	3.9
Charing Cross	6.4	9.5	13.2	2.9	72.4	9.6	82.0	1.3	0
2.West End Residential Area									
Knightsbridge	12.1	16.2	6.6	21.4	47.8	16.0	63.8	1.8	1.8
Hans Town	12.0	15.9	6.4	28.5	41.3	21.8	63.1	2.9	1.3
Regents Park	10.8	15.4	4.5	25.0	49.6	21.9	71.5	1.9	3.6
Holland	10.5	15.4	4.4	25.0	35.6	37.8	73.4	6.2	4.6
Royal Hospital	9.8	15.5	5.5	24.6	46.1	26.0	72.1	2.5	3.9
Queens Gate	7.1	11.0	4.3	22.9	33.6	42.0	75.6	7.2	3.6
Cheyne	6.7	15.0	9.6	22.5	44.4	22.5	66.9	2.4	4.6
3.Inner transitional Areas									
Baker Street	9.6	13.8	5.6	11.0	51.3	31.8	83.1	3.9	2.7
Lords	8.7	14.2	6.2	17.3	56.0	14.4	70.4	1.9	5.3
Hyde Park	8.6	12.2	9.6	15.6	36.3	34.2	70.6	8.0	3.8
Warwick	7.8	11.1	14.5	9.5	31.4	49.3	81.7	9.5	7.0
Brompton	7.5	12.7	7.4	14.6	27.2	55.9	83.1	11.3	4.3
North Stanley	7.3	10.4	8.3	19.4	33.2	18.8	52.0	3.0	8.3
Lancaster Gate	6.9	10.7	9.7	8.5	29.4	49.6	79.0	11.2	4.6
Redcliffe	6.6	10.6	6.6	13.0	28.6	54.6	83.2	10.2	7.7
Earls Court	6.6	10.8	8.1	12.3	29.6	54.2	83.6	13.6	4.1
Church	6.4	9.4	9.6	13.3	70.8	8.9	79.7	3.8	1.7
Pembridge	4.6	8.6	12.5	11.1	31.3	48.4	79.7	10.9	5.9
South Stanley	4.5	5.7	18.7	10.0	49.5	11.9	61.4	10.3	1.8
Norland	4.1	7.3	13.0	15.3	35.2	29.4	64.6	6.8	11.4

	% population economically active males in SEGs			% Owner occupied households	% Private unfurnished tenancies	% Private furnished tenancies	% Private tenancies (Total)	% households living at more than 1.5 persons per room	% households receiving improvement grants
	1,2	1-4	7-12 14,15						
4. Middle transitional Areas									
Avonmore	6.2	9.1	10.1	6.3	39.3	42.3	81.6	9.3	3.5
Maida Vale	4.6	6.7	13.1	4.2	48.5	27.1	75.6	5.4	9.4
Gibbs Green	4.4	6.5	17.9	6.4	46.5	34.4	80.9	7.6	7.5
Westbourne	3.1	4.5	17.6	7.2	23.7	37.2	60.9	10.8	6.4
St.Charles	2.9	3.7	18.1	9.8	48.0	25.6	73.6	8.7	6.1
Addison	2.6	4.3	20.6	9.7	38.8	35.9	74.7	9.3	8.3
Harrow Road	1.3	1.5	21.9	7.8	39.2	28.6	67.7	14.9	11.1
Golborne	1.0	1.4	24.4	6.1	44.3	25.0	69.3	15.3	0.4
5. Outer transitional Areas									
Brondesbury Park	5.8	9.0	12.3	18.3	28.2	40.1	68.2	9.0	1.5
Mapesbury	3.9	6.2	15.4	15.4	17.0	55.7	72.7	13.6	0.9
Brook Green	3.9	6.0	17.7	16.5	36.5	39.4	75.9	6.3	14.3
Broadway	3.7	5.7	17.1	12.1	43.5	13.2	56.7	2.8	5.7
Coningham	3.5	4.4	21.5	18.2	41.7	26.6	68.3	10.3	9.6
Grove	2.9	4.1	23.5	18.1	46.9	23.3	70.2	7.7	9.4
Sandford	2.2	2.8	18.8	19.2	47.1	11.0	58.1	3.8	11.1
Kilburn	2.0	2.8	22.2	15.7	35.6	39.1	74.7	12.0	0.8
Halford	2.0	2.5	21.2	16.4	43.5	18.0	61.5	4.5	6.8
6. Inner suburban Areas									
Crabtree	5.9	7.1	16.7	35.4	48.0	9.1	57.1	1.7	5.7
Chamberlayne	4.8	6.1	17.7	47.6	24.1	19.7	43.8	6.3	0
Parsons Green	4.0	7.0	17.7	21.1	41.3	14.4	55.7	3.5	7.6
Starch Green	4.0	6.9	16.5	24.7	39.7	23.5	63.2	4.8	4.8
Town	3.7	4.9	14.2	23.0	37.9	26.8	64.7	3.9	11.0
Colehill	3.5	4.0	21.4	27.9	55.3	9.6	64.9	3.1	6.8

	% population economically active males in SEGs			% Owner occupied households	% Private unfurnished tenancies	% Private furnished tenancies	% Private tenancies (total)	% households living at more than 1.5 persons per room	% households receiving improvement grants
	1,2	1-4	7-12 14,15						
Queens Park	2.8	4.0	20.5	25.2	28.3	36.8	65.1	11.3	0.6
Sulivan	2.7	4.6	21.0	26.4	40.9	12.7	53.6	2.7	8.5
Manor	2.6	3.2	20.9	39.0	30.7	28.8	59.5	9.4	0.5
Wormholt	2.2	4.6	17.4	24.6	27.1	14.3	41.4	5.0	3.6
Church End	2.2	2.5	18.6	42.4	37.2	10.7	47.9	6.5	1.9
Sherbrooke	1.9	2.1	23.2	25.8	48.2	13.8	62.0	4.0	8.6
Margravine	1.7	2.6	19.1	21.1	43.8	14.8	58.6	3.8	6.8
Harlesden	1.7	2.1	24.1	28.9	42.5	25.8	68.3	10.9	0.6
Cricklewood	1.5	3.1	19.9	42.8	26.7	25.1	51.8	7.7	0.1
Willesden Green	1.5	3.0	22.9	31.3	46.0	18.7	64.7	9.5	1.2
Kensal Rise	0.9	1.4	24.6	34.2	38.1	21.6	59.7	11.2	0.5
7.Outer suburban Areas									
Kenton	9.3	15.5	6.8	83.0	8.9	3.9	12.8	0.5	0.1
Sudbury	8.6	11.2	11.2	80.5	12.2	3.8	16.0	0.8	0.1
Wembley Park	6.8	10.5	10.5	62.0	27.2	9.3	36.5	2.2	0.3
Kingsbury	6.5	9.7	14.4	66.5	10.2	3.0	13.2	0.7	0
Gladstone	6.5	9.4	16.1	71.9	10.2	15.1	25.3	3.5	0.3
Preston	6.3	8.6	8.9	90.6	6.3	2.5	8.8	2.1	0
Sudbury Court	6.1	9.1	9.7	88.6	5.5	5.1	10.7	1.0	0
Roe Green	5.7	7.4	14.7	68.1	20.2	7.5	27.7	1.6	0.1
Fryent	5.6	7.4	16.0	67.3	14.3	3.0	17.3	1.0	0.1
Queensbury	5.5	6.7	16.3	80.0	14.7	4.0	18.7	0.9	0.1
Barham	3.8	6.5	17.5	69.8	11.6	7.2	18.8	3.0	0.6
Tokyngton	3.4	4.6	19.1	78.4	11.4	7.1	18.5	3.8	0.3
Brentwater	3.0	4.3	20.4	64.7	15.3	8.9	24.2	3.5	0
Alperton	2.3	3.2	21.6	73.5	13.6	5.3	18.9	3.1	0.1
Wembley Central	2.3	3.2	23.6	52.1	18.0	13.8	31.8	6.1	2.2

	% population economically active males in SEGs			% Owner occupied households	% Private unfurnished tenancies	% Private furnished tenancies	% Private tenancies (total)	% households living at more than 1.5 persons per room	% households receiving improvement grants
	1,2	1-4	7-12 14,15						
1. Central Residential Area	7.4	12.8	7.9	6.8	65.8	16.4	82.2	2.7	2.5
2. West End Residential Area	9.9	14.9	5.9	24.4	42.6	26.9	69.5	3.6	3.3
3. Inner transitional Areas	6.9	10.5	10.0	13.1	39.3	35.5	74.8	8.1	5.2
4. Middle transitional Areas	3.3	4.7	18.0	7.2	41.0	32.0	73.0	10.0	6.6
5. Outer transitional Areas	3.3	4.8	18.6	16.7	37.8	29.6	67.4	7.8	6.7
6. Inner suburban Areas	2.8	4.1	19.8	30.7	38.6	19.2	57.8	6.2	4.1
7. Outer suburban Areas	5.4	7.8	15.1	73.1	13.3	6.6	19.9	2.3	0.3

Source: Based on 1971 Census data and London borough improvement grant registers.

125

(Kensal Rise), and the proportion in SEGs 1-4 ranged from 7.1 to 1.4 per
cent in the same wards.   In the Outer Suburban Areas, in contrast,
economically active males in SEGs 7-12, 14, 15 amounted to a higher
proportion of the population than in the Outer Suburban Areas, the
proportions being 19.8 and 15.1 per cent respectively.   In the Inner
Suburban Areas the proportions ranged from 24.6 per cent (Kensal Rise)
to 16,7 per cent (Crabtree), and in the Outer Suburban Areas from 23.6
per cent (Wembley Central) to 6.8 per cent (Kenton).

Differences in tenure were a major factor distinguishing the Inner and
Outer Suburban Areas.   In the Inner Suburban Areas 30.7 per cent of
households were owner occupiers in contrast to 73.1 per cent in the Outer
Suburban Areas.   The proportions ranged from 42.8 per cent (Cricklewood)
to 21.1 per cent (Margravine and Parsons Green) in the Inner Suburban
Areas.   Conversely in the Inner Suburban Areas, 57.8 per cent of households were private tenants, and in the Outer Suburban Areas the proportion
was only 19.9 per cent.   The proportion ranged from 68.3 per cent
(Harlesden) to 41.4 per cent (Wormholt) in the Inner Suburban Areas;   and
from 36.5 per cent (Wembley Park) to 8.8 per cent (Preston) in the Outer
Suburban Areas.   A further difference between the two groups of suburban
areas was the degree of overcrowding.   In the Inner Suburban Areas, 6.2
per cent of households were living at more than 1.5 persons per room,
whereas in the Outer Suburban Areas the proportion was 2.3 per cent.
The proportion ranged from 11.3 per cent (Queens Park) to 1.7 per cent
(Crabtree) in the Inner Suburban Area, and from 2.2 per cent (Wembley
Central) to a complete absence of overcrowding (Preston, Sudbury Court
and Brentwater) in the Outer Suburban Areas.

In the period 1970-73, 4.1 per cent of households in the Inner Suburban
Areas received grants compared with only 0.3 per cent of households in
the Outer Suburban Areas.   Although it was probably the higher socio-
economic groups in the suburban areas which benefitted from housing
improvement, gentrification (mainly unmediated in form) was confined to
the Inner Suburban Areas.   Here, compared with the Outer Suburban Areas,
a relatively high proportion of households were awarded grants and the
lower socio-economic groups amounted to a relatively high proportion of
the population.   In the Outer Suburban Areas any influx of middle or
upper middle class households occurred in wards containing a relatively
high proportion of residents of the same socio-economic group.   The
social composition of the Inner Suburban Areas and the Transitional Areas
were broadly comparable, but the Inner Suburban Areas contained a much
higher proportion of households living in owner occupied properties, and
a much lower proportion living in furnished tenancies and at more than
1.5 persons per room.   In contrast to the Transitional Areas, the Inner
Suburban Areas were probably at a sufficient distance from concentrations
of SEGs 1-4 (within the Central and West End Residential Areas) to avoid
the effects of the price shadow on property values.   Improvement grants
were thus mainly used for the rehabilitation of owner occupied dwellings
rather than for the conversion of properties into flats and bed sitters.
This does not eliminate the possibility that unmediated gentrification
may also have displaced tenants.

SOME SOCIAL AND ECONOMIC EFFECTS OF IMPROVEMENT GRANT POLICY IN THE
BOROUGHS OF WEST LONDON

The relationships between the spatial distribution of improvement grants and selected social and economic variables within the west London boroughs have already been summarised. It was suggested that grants were awarded mainly in areas where there were high proportions of private tenancies (particularly furnished lettings); high crude net deficiency rates, and high proportions of shared dwellings, dwellings without basic amenities; SEGs 7-12, 14, 15, and population in the age categories under five and under 40. A Rehabilitation-Need Index was devised to bring together a number of variables, and, its spatial distribution showed a correlation with the distribution of improvement grants. This showed that the areas of greatest need received a more than proportionate share of the distribution of improvement grants, but it is very probable that the economic and social effects of allocation (discussed in Chapters 2 and 4) were also concentrated in the area of Inner West London and Brent.

Although there has been little publication of research into the effects of improvement grant distribution in west London, some reports and other publications have provided an indication (either directly or indirectly) of these consequences.

In its memorandum to the House of Commons Expenditure Committee on Home Improvement Grants (1973) the council of the London Borough of Hammersmith stated that:

> There was a large loss of residential accommodation in many conversions where large numbers of families had previously lived in large properties. There are instances of landlords obtaining Possession Orders against tenants of furnished lettings with a view to carrying out works of improvement to the premises thus vacated. (But) few of the units created by conversion were intended for those in the greatest housing need (paragraphs 1.2. 9-10).

The memorandum suggested that the decline in relatively low rent accommodation may have been one of the reasons for accelerating the out migration of population from the borough, which had reached 4,000 a year in the early 1970s. Examined by the House of Commons Committee, Councillor Rayner quoted examples of harassment, 'winkling' and the subsequent profitability of house improvement in the ward which he represented (Brook Green). The council advocated to the committee that, in order to alleviate these consequences of improvement grant policy, the grant should be repaid if the property was sold within five years of the receipt of a grant; that rents should be fixed by the Rent Officer on grant improved properties; that the local authority should determine the types of tenancies made available following improvement; that the local authority should be able to nominate from its housing list the tenants to be accommodated in unfurnished tenancies resulting from improvement and the local authority should be able to give grants of from 50 to 100 per cent of the cost of improvement instead of the then current 50 per cent. Possibly due in part to the evidence submitted by the council, the Housing Act of 1974 implemented the first of these proposals and increased the proportion of the cost of improvement which could be covered by the grant (see Chapter 2).

North Kensington is another area in which the processes of gentrification have had substantial affects upon the lower income section of the population. Kilroy (1972b) reported that each housing and social agency in the area had evidence of many different forms of pressures being imposed on furnished tenants. These ranged from legal repossession, subtle

threats and offers of money, to harassment and illegal eviction.   He
disagreed with the belief that pressure would squeeze families out of
North Kensington, as they would be unlikely to go to Hammersmith or
Westminster where there would be similar pressures and it was improbable
that they would move further out.   He argued that:

> pressures are squeezing families more firmly within North
> Kensington... The social debilitation which is happening as a
> result of worsening housing conditions may typify inner London:
> homelessness and displacement may increase at the same time as
> the areas appear to 'improve' (p.81).

Although Anderson and Williams (1971) did not deal specifically with
improvement grants, their analysis of changes in housing in central
Westminster, 1961-66, identified some of the effects of increasing owner
occupation and the related increase in the proportion of higher socio-
economic groups.   They suggested that:

> one of the effects of these trends is lower occupancy rates...
> Generally speaking, owner-occupiers enjoy higher space standards
> than other tenure groups, so that any increase in owner-occupation
> will contribute to a lowering of occupancy rate.   Moreover in a
> situation where dwellings formerly occupied by several households
> became single family dwellings, the effect on occupancy rate will
> be clear (p.24).

They also drew attention to the loss of rented accommodation specifically
in Pimlico.   This they attributed to the increase in owner occupation
through the purchase of dwellings from private landlords.   It is
probable that in the early 1970s the effects of increased owner occupation
would have been similar to those suggested above, but may have stemmed
initially from grant assisted rehabilitation.

The City of Westminster's report, Housing in Westminster (1972)
discussed the possible social effects of improvement grants.   The report
showed that in the majority of instances existing residents did not
benefit and may have suffered from house improvement:

> Whereas over two-thirds of those in the unimproved properties
> are the same people as were living there .... in 1967, two-
> thirds of those in the fully improved dwellings are new.   We
> must assume that those people moved in after improvement took
> place (p.57).

The report largely discounted the possibility that landlords eased out
tenants to hasten the pace of improvement, and implied that generally
landlords waited until their property naturally became vacant before
rehabilitating the dwelling.   In making comparisons between the social
status of the residents of fully improved and unimproved dwellings, the
report suggested that there was a trend away from unskilled, intermediate
non-manual and personal service workers towards employers, managers and
skilled workers.   This was compatible with differences in levels of
income:

> people living in unimproved dwellings are the least well-off
> group, and at least two fifths of them could only be described
> as poor.   On the other hand, those in fully improved dwellings
> are well-off... The implication is that when an inadequate
> property is improved, poorer people leave and better-off people
> move in (p.61).

Further information about the social aspects of rehabilitation in
Westminster was published by a Joint Working Party of the Pimlico
Neighbourhood Aid Centre Housing Group and the Pimlico Tenants and
Residents Association (1973).   It reported that in October 1973 a property
investment company acquired 101 houses from a firm of property developers,
in an area of Pimlico known as the 'Triangle'.   The intention of the
purchaser was to convert the dwellings (mainly five storey early Victorian
houses) into 590, one or two bedroomed luxury flats, which in 1973 could
probably have been sold for £20,000 to £25,000 on the basis of the selling
price of comparable properties in the area.   A survey which had been
undertaken by the Housing Group in July 1973 showed that nearly 60 per cent
of the households interviewed were furnished tenants and a further 30 per
cent were unfurnished tenants.   About a third of the residents had lived
in the triangle for more than ten years.   In at least 25 per cent of the
houses, tenants had received Notices to Quit, and there were already 17
houses totally empty and 33 empty flats.   It is probable that conversion
of the properties into high priced flats would have brought about a change
in the social status of the occupants.   Largely to prevent this from
occurring, Westminster City Council refused to grant planning permission
for the proposed development, and subsequently purchased the properties.
In 1976 the properties were sold to a housing association and, where
necessary, planning permission was granted for the houses to be converted
into comparatively low rent flats.

In the period 1970-73, nearly 10,000 improvement grants were awarded in
Inner West London (mainly to private landlords and developers) for the
purpose of conversion.   This amounted to 75.1 per cent of the total
number of improvement grants - in Kensington and Chelsea the proportion
was 90.1 per cent (see Appendix E).   It is probable that many of these
conversions were preceded by the same stages of mediated gentrification
as was found in the Pimlico triangle.   Yet it is uncertain to what extent
grant assisted conversion contributed to the reduction in the number of
dwellings lacking adequate basic amenities.   Conversions could have
increased the proportion of dwellings without exclusive use of basic
facilities, for example, since they might have reduced the total number
of units, those still unimproved would amount to a higher proportion of
the total stock, and they might also have involved the replacement of
single family houses by flats or bed sitters with a resulting sharing of
amenities.   Many conversions, moreover, take place within buildings
already possessing satisfactory amenities.   Of the remaining 24.9 per
cent of grants (those awarded for improvement only), approximately equal
proportions were distributed to private landlords and developers, and
owner occupiers (43 and 44.5 per cent respectively).   It is thus probable
that there was a relatively lower incidence of mediated gentrification,
although it is not possible to compare the resulting social effects of
each process qualitatively.   'Improvement only' grants totalled 3,600
(1970-73).   This amounted to only 13 per cent of the 28,100 dwellings
which the GLCs report, The Condition of London's Housing (1970) identified
as being capable of improvement by the addition of a bath, or an inside
W.C. or both.   Table 5.19 sets out the equivalent amounts for the west
London boroughs, and it is notable that in Hammersmith, twice the
proportion of suitable dwellings were improved than in the other three
boroughs.   These figures, however, do not take into account the number
of dwellings which have become poor since the GLC Housing Survey.

Table 5.19

<u>The deficiency of basic amenities 1967</u>
<u>and improvement grant awards 1970-73</u>
<u>in the west London boroughs</u>

Borough	Number of dwellings which could be improved by the addition of a bath, inside W.C. or both 1967	Number of 'improvement only grants awarded 1970-73	% dwellings (capable of improvement) awarded grants
Brent	3,800	376	9.9
Hammersmith	8,900	1,795	20.2
Kensington & Chelsea	4,200	384	9.1
Westminster	11,200	1,085	9.7

Source: London Housing Survey (Part 1) and London Borough
Improvement grant registers.

6 The distribution of improvement grants in the General Improvement and Housing Action Areas of west London

In the first section of this analysis the spatial distribution of improvement grants in the GIAs and HAAs is shown. The data used derived mainly from the GLC Annual Abstract of Statistics and the same borough sources specified in Chapter 5. The analysis covers the GIAs of Masbro Road and Moore Park (Hammersmith), Colville-Tavistock (Kensington and Chelsea), Lanhill-Marylands and Westbourne Gardens (Westminster); the HAAs of Coningham Road (Hammersmith) and Tavistock (Kensington and Chelsea), and all of these areas in aggregate in Inner West London. Following the Housing Act of 1969, the GIAs were declared between 1969 and 1973 and in response to the Housing Act of 1974 the HAAs were declared in 1975. The relationship between improvement grants and a number of variables in areas which were subject to declaration as GIAs or HAAs after 1969 is examined. As in Chapter 5, grants to local authorities are not considered and grants to Housing Associations are not specifically identified being generally included (for convenience only) under the category 'private landlords and developers'.

The annual totals for improvement grants are shown in Fig.6.2 for the Inner West London GIAs and the Greater London GIAs. It can be seen from this that grants awarded to the Inner West London GIAs increased noticeably between 1970 and 1971, remained at about the same level between 1971 and 1972, and then decreased between 1972 and 1973. The number awarded to all the Greater London GIAs increased more markedly between 1970 and 1971 and continued to do so in 1972 before diminishing in 1973. The relationship between the two groups of GIAs changed substantially from 1970 to 1973, the Inner West London GIAs' percentage of the total for the Greater London GIAs was 75.2, 42.9, 20.2 and 15.5 in these four years in turn. The relationship between the number of grant approvals in the Inner West London GIAs and Inner West London generally, remained very constant - being 8.0, 8.8, 8.8 and 7.4 per cent in the years 1970-73, but this consistency was not manifested in the relationship between individual GIAs and their boroughs, or between individual GIAs and Inner West London generally. Changes in these relationships reflected local fluctuations, often speculative in character, in rehabilitative possibilities. The decrease in the number of grants awarded in 1972-73 in the GIAs can probably be explained by the decrease in the level of demand in this period associated with the end of the residential property boom. The decrease in the proportion of grants awarded to the Inner West London GIAs compared with the Greater London GIAs may have been due more to the Inner London boroughs being the first to declare GIAs after the Housing Act of 1969 rather than due to a greater interest being shown in area improvement in the other boroughs in 1972 and 1973. The figures for the period are given in Table 6.1 which show that the total number of Inner West London GIA grants was 1,094 and that for the Greater London GIAs was 4,153.

Only in Hammersmith was comprehensive information available concerning

N

Brent

3
2
8
1
6
Westminster

7
4
Kensington & Chelsea

Hammersmith

5

0   1
Mile

⊜ General Improvement Areas

△ Housing Action Areas

1 Colville-Tavistock GIA
2 Lanhill-Marylands GIAs
3 Malvern Road GIA
4 Masbro Road GIA
5 Moore Park GIA
6 Westbourne Gardens GIA
7 Coningham Road HAA
8 Tavistock HAA

Figure 6.1   The location of GIAs and HAAs in west London

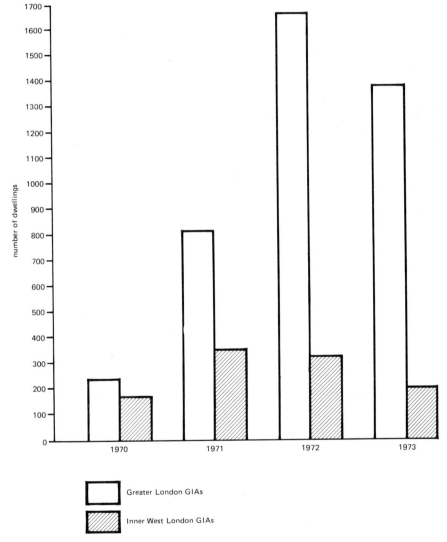

Figure 6.2   Improvement grants in the Inner West London and
Greater London GIAs

Table 6.1

Improvement grants awarded, Inner West London and Greater London GIAs, 1970-73

	1970 %	1970 No.	1971 %	1971 No.	1972 %	1972 No.	1973 %	1973 No.	Total %	Total No.	Dwellings 1971
INNER WEST LONDON											
Conversion	66.5	121	79.3	283	91.2	310	91.2	196	83.2	910	
Improvement	33.5	61	20.7	74	8.8	30	8.8	19	16.2	184	
Total:		182		357		340		215		1094	1735
% Inner West London	8.0		8.8		8.8		7.4		8.4		
% Greater London GIAs	75.2		42.9		20.2		15.5		26.3		0.75
HAMMERSMITH (Masbro Road & Moore Park)											
Conversion	36.5	35	58.0	87	72.3	68	50.0	17	55.3	207	
Improvement	63.5	61	42.0	63	27.7	26	50.0	17	44.7	167	
Total:		96		150		94		34		374	959
% Hammersmith	11.0		10.1		6.5		4.0		8.3		
% Inner West London	52.7		42.0		27.7		15.8		34.2		
% Greater London GIAs	39.7		18.0		5.6		2.4		9.0		1.52
KENSINGTON & CHELSEA (Colville-Tavistock)											
Conversion	100.0	81	97.0	97	98.7	153	97.1	68	98.1	399	
Improvement	-	-	4.0	4	1.3	2	2.9	2	2.0	8	
Total:		81		101		155		70		407	265
% Kensington & Chelsea	10.9		7.9		12.6		7.0		9.6		
% Inner West London	44.5		28.3		45.6		32.6		37.2		
% Greater London GIAs	33.5		12.1		9.2		5.0		9.8		0.34

	1970		1971		1972		1973		Total		Dwellings
	%	No.	%	No.	%	No.	%	No.	%	No.	
WESTMINSTER (Lanhill-Marylands & Westbourne Park)											
Conversion	100.0	5	93.4	99	97.8	89	100.0	111	97.1	304	
Improvement	-	-	6.6	7	2.2	2	-	-	2.9	9	
Total:		5		106		91		111		313	511
% Westminster	0.8		8.3		7.6		9.2		7.2		0.55
% Inner West London	2.8		29.7		26.8		51.6		28.6		
% Greater London GIAs	2.1		12.7		5.4		8.0		7.5		
GREATER LONDON GIAs											
Conversion	74.0	179	55.5	462	45.3	765	48.7	678	51.4	2084	
Improvement	26.0	63	44.5	371	54.7	922	51.3	713	48.6	2069	
Total:	-	242		833		1687		1391		4153	

* GIA – 1971, 2, 3 only
+ GIA – 1972, 3 only

the recipients of grants within the GIAs.   Throughout the period 1970-
73 the principal recipients of grants within the Hammersmith GIAs were
owner occupiers (see Appendix G).   Where gentrification occurred it was
thus mainly unmediated.   As is shown in Fig.6.3 owner occupiers in the
Masbro Road and Moore Park GIAs respectively received 91 and 92 grants
(63.6 and 52.0 per cent of the total grants awarded in each GIA).
Grants to private landlords and developers amounted to 52 and 85 respectively (36.4 and 48.0 per cent).   Changes over the period are demonstrated
by the relationship between the totals for 1970, 1971, 1972 and 1973, as
follows: in Masbro Road owner occupiers received 21, 32, 17 and 21
grants, and private landlords and developers received 14, 29, 13 and 6
grants;   in Moore Park owner occupiers received 41, 29, 11 and 11 grants,
and private landlords and developers received 15, 36, 23 and 11 grants.
The relationship between these recipients in Hammersmith is shown in
Fig.6.4.   Although over the whole period owner occupiers received more
grants than private landlords and developers, in the Moor Park GIA
grants to private landlords and developers just exceeded those to owner
occupiers in 1971-72 (the property boom years).

Tables 6.1 and 6.2 indicate that the proportion of the two main kinds
of grants varied markedly between the GIAs and also between the GIAs and
the boroughs.   The relationship of conversion and improvement grants to
each other and between GIAs in different boroughs is shown in Fig.6.5.
Conversion grant approvals varied from 55.3 per cent of grants approved
in the Hammersmith GIAs to 98.1 per cent in the Colville-Tavistock GIA,
the percentage within the Inner West London GIAs being 83.2 and in all
the Greater London GIAs being 51.4.   Improvement grant approvals varied
from 2.0 per cent of grants approved in the Colville-Tavistock GIA to
44.7 per cent in the Hammersmith GIAs, the percentage within the Inner
West London GIAs being 16.2 and within all of the Greater London GIAs
48.6.   Except for Hammersmith, there were higher proportions of
conversion grants awarded within the GIAs than in the boroughs.   Taking
the GIAs first and then the boroughs, the percentages of conversion
grants in Inner West London were 83.2 and 75.1, in Kensington and Chelsea
they were 98.1 and 91.0, and in Westminster 97.1 and 75.0.   In
Hammersmith by contrast the percentages were 55.3 and 60.1.

Only for Hammersmith was sufficient information available to enable the
recipients of the two kinds of grants to be broadly categorised (see
Appendix G and Fig.6.6).   Improvement grant approvals for owner occupiers
as a percentage of all approvals in each GIA, 1970-73, were 48.3 in
Masbro Road and 37.9 in Moore Park, and approvals going to private landlords and developers as a percentage of all approvals in each GIA were
14.7 in Masbro Road and 12.4 in Moore Park.   Grant approvals for the
conversion of property owned by private landlords and developers were
21.7 in Masbro Road and 35.6 in Moore Park, the approvals going to owner
occupiers as a percentage of all approvals in each GIA were 15.4 in
Masbro Road and 14.1 in Moore Park.   The relationship of these grants
within the two GIAs combined is shown in Fig.6.7.   Between 1970 and 1973
owner occupiers received 68.1, 48.4, 43.7 and 63.5 per cent of all grants
in these four years respectively.   Private landlords and developers
received in total 31.9, 51.6, 56.3 and 34.7 per cent respectively, and
received conversion grants amounting to 19.8, 38.9, 34.4 and 30.6 of the
total grants awarded.

The dominance of grants for converting property within the GIAs is
further demonstrated in Fig.6.8.   In each of the four years under

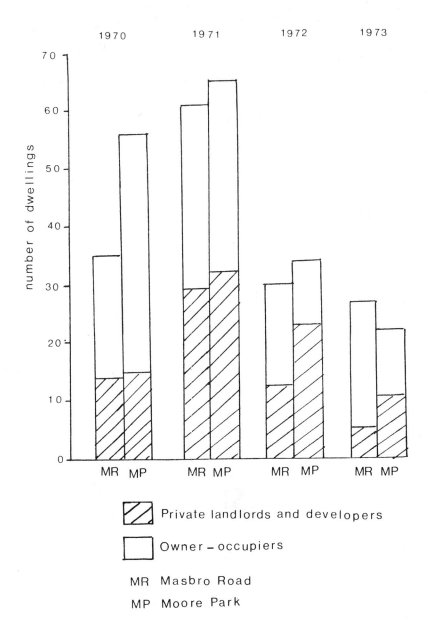

Figure 6.3   Grants awarded to private landlords and developers,
and owner occupiers for improvement and conversion,
Masbro Road and Moore Park GIAs, 1970-73

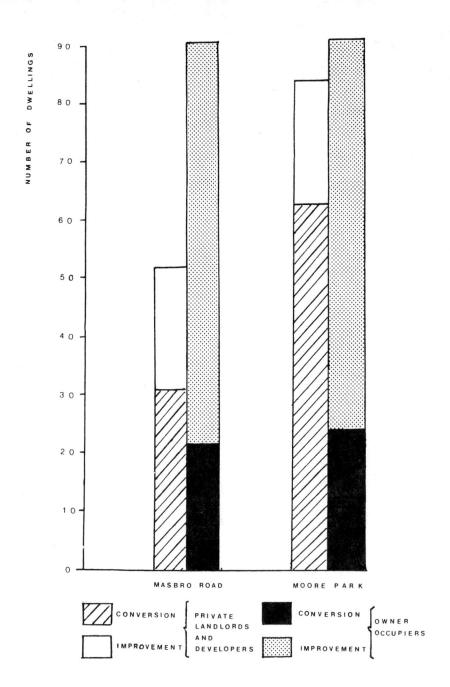

NUMBER OF DWELLINGS

MASBRO ROAD   MOORE PARK

CONVERSION {PRIVATE LANDLORDS AND DEVELOPERS

IMPROVEMENT

CONVERSION {OWNER OCCUPIERS

IMPROVEMENT

Figure 6.4   Improvement grants awarded to private landlords and developers, and owner occupiers, Masbro Road and Moore Park GIAs, 1970-73

Table 6.2

Improvement grants awarded (Conversion and Improvement)
1970-73

		Conversion		Improvement		Total
Inner West London	%	83.2		16.2		
GIAs	No.		910		184	1094
Inner W. London	%	75.1		24.9		
Masbro Road[a] &	%	55.3		44.7		
Moore Park	No.		207		167	374
Hammersmith	%	60.1		39.8		
Colville-Tavistock	%	98.1		2.0		
	No.		399		8	407
Kensington & Chelsea	%	91.0		9.0		
Lanhill-Marylands &	%	97.1		2.9		
Westbourne Gardens[b]	No.		304		9	313
Westminster	%	75.0		25.0		
Greater London GIAs	%	51.4		48.6		
	No.		2084		2069	4153

a   GIA   1971, -72, -73 only
b   GIA   1972, 73 only

139

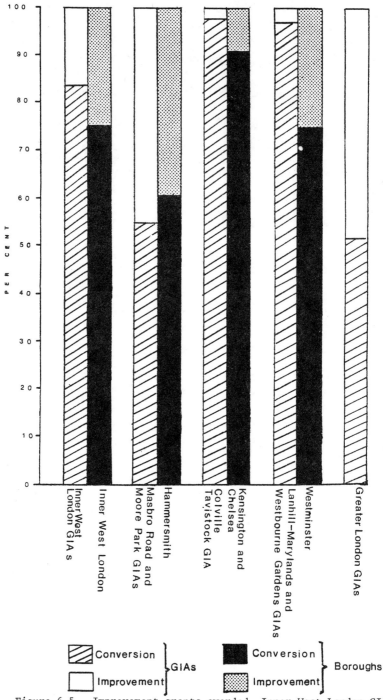

Figure 6.5   Improvement grants awarded, Inner West London GIAs
and boroughs, and Greater London, 1970-73

140

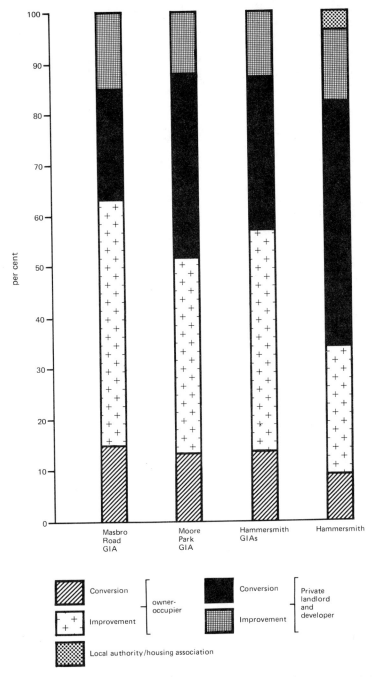

per cent

| | Masbro Road GIA | Moore Park GIA | Hammersmith GIAs | Hammersmith |

Conversion ⎫
        ⎬ owner-occupier
Improvement ⎭

Conversion ⎫
        ⎬ Private landlord and developer
Improvement ⎭

Local authority/housing association

Figure 6.6   Improvement grants awarded, Hammersmith GIAs and borough, 1970-73

141

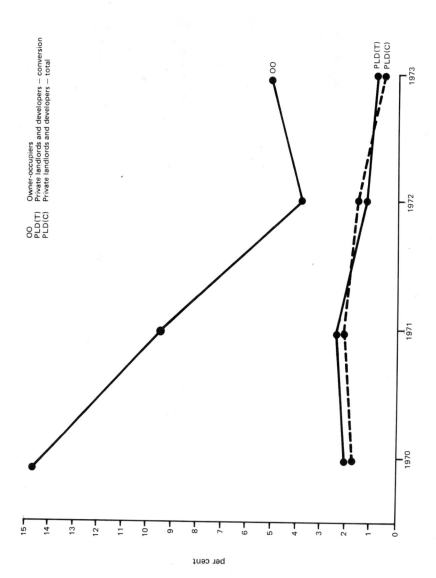

Figure 6.7   Relationship of different types of grants within the Hammersmith GIAs

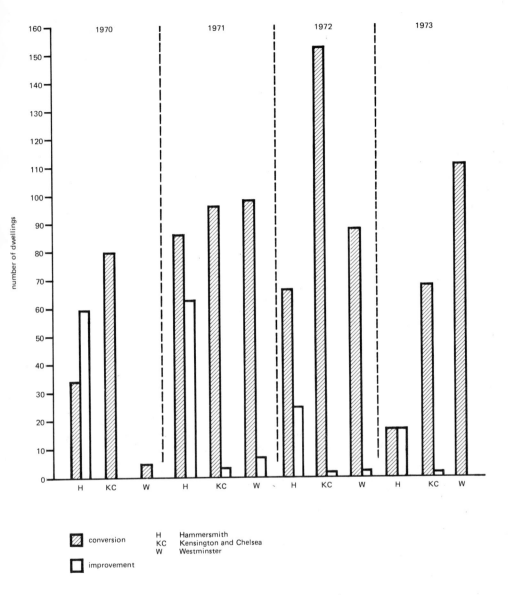

Figure 6.8   Grants for improvement and conversion,
Inner West London GIAs, 1970-73

consideration and in each group of GIAs (with the exception of the Hammersmith GIAs in 1970) the number of grants awarded for conversion exceeded – often by a very considerable amount – the number of grants awarded for improvement. Collectively, grants for conversion exceeded grants for improvement by 198.5, 382.4, 1,033.3 and 1,031.6 per cent respectively in the years 1970-73.

When examining the approval of grants to owner occupiers and to private landlords and developers in the Hammersmith GIAs as a percentage of grants awarded in Inner West London, disparities are further shown (Fig.6.9). Total grant approvals to owner occupiers within the GIAs as a proportion of grants to owner occupiers in Inner West London averaged about 7.9 per cent (1970-73), but fell rapidly from about 15.0 per cent in 1970 to about 4.0 per cent in 1972 (rising to about 5.0 per cent in 1973). Approvals going to private landlords and developers as a proportion of approvals in Inner West London averaged 1.57. The proportion of grants for conversion by private landlords and developers accounted for 1.28 per cent of all Inner West London grants. Private landlords and developers in the GIAs received a diminishing proportion of all grants awarded in Inner West London between 1971-73 from about 2.5 per cent to 1.0 per cent.

Rehabilitation brought about by improvement grants had not taken place evenly throughout inner London being concentrated in a small number of areas. Analysis of the distribution of grant approvals in the GIAs confirm this even at a very local level: improvement grants within each of the Inner West London boroughs were more heavily concentrated within the GIAs than in the rest of the borough. An Index of Improvement Grant Concentration shows that if the proportion of dwellings in each borough receiving grants is given a base index of 100, the proportions of improvement grant approvals in the GIAs greatly exceed 100 (Fig.6.10). In Hammersmith the index is 540, in Kensington and Chelsea 2810, in Westminster 1320 and in all the Inner West London GIAs, 1110.

Fig.6.11 shows the distribution of grant approvals by EDs within the GIAs and HAAs. This indicates that the pattern of rehabilitation was very localised. EDs were grouped into sextiles for the purpose of mapping. Taking the total number of EDs within the Inner London GIAs and HAAs (and the Malvern Road GIA of Brent), there were five sextiles of 11 EDs and one sextile (the lowest) of ten EDs. Within the top sextile the EDs were (in descending rank order) 3177/11, 3177/12, 3177/9, 3177/10, 3175/42, 3175/39, 3175/40, 3202/14, 3175/37, 3175/38, and 3085/8 (see Appendix H). Within the top sextile over 20.4 per cent of all households received improvement grants rising to 74.7 in 3177/11. Fig.6.12 shows that the top sextile EDs were confined to Moore Park and Masbro Road GIAs except for one ED being in Colville-Tavistock and another in Westbourne Gardens.

Within the Masbro Road GIA there were two sextiles (the highest and lowest) of two EDs and four sextiles of one ED. In the top sextile the EDs were 3175/42 and 3175/39. In this sextile over 33.3 per cent of households received improvement grants. Within the Moore Park GIA there were six sextiles of one ED each, the top sextile ED being 3177/11 with 74.8 per cent of all households receiving grants. Within the Colville-Tavistock GIA there were also six sextiles of one ED each, the top sextile ED being 3202/14 with 22.1 per cent of all households receiving grants. Within the Lanhill-Marylands GIA there were six sextiles of three EDs each, the top sextile EDs were 3062/42, 3062/53 and 3062/47

144

in descending order.   In this sextile over 10.2 per cent of households received grants rising to 13.3 per cent.   Within the Westbourne Gardens GIA there was one sextile (the highest) with two EDs, the other five sextiles comprising one ED each.   In the top sextile the EDs were 3085/8 and 3085/11.   In this sextile over 6.6 per cent of households received improvement grants rising to 20.4 per cent.   Within the Coningham Road HAA there were three sextiles the highest two and the lowest of two EDs each, the remaining sextiles having one ED each.   The top sextile EDs were 3181/20 and 3181/21.   In this sextile over 5.6 per cent of households received improvement grants rising to 7.7 per cent.   Within the Tavistock HAA there were two sextiles the highest and lowest of two EDs each, the remaining sextiles having one ED each.   The top sextile EDs were 3202/4 and 3201/26.   In this sextile over 4.8 per cent of households received improvement grants rising to 5.1 per cent.   Fig.6.12 shows the proportionate distribution of improvement grants to households within each GIA or HAA.

It was evident that much improvement occurred on adjacent sites. Table 6.3 shows that in the GIAs, and in particular Moore Park and Colville-Tavistock, adjacent rehabilitation was pronounced – both areas showing 71 per cent of improvement on adjacent sites.   In the HAAs, however, the incidence was far less, Coningham Road and Tavistock having only 20 and 16 per cent adjacent improvement.   These differences between the GIAs and HAAs reflect the earlier declaration of the former (owners having more time to improve their properties), and also suggest that the Davis and Whinston (1961) hypothesis may have had some validity – that is owners would only have found it financially rewarding to improve their housing if neighbouring improvement took place simultaneously.   Within the GIAs adjacent improvement may have been undertaken by landlords and developers owning numerous neighbouring properties, while the 'desirability' of the HAAs (prior to declaration) may not have been adequate to have attracted acquisition or stimulated extensive rehabilitation.

Table 6.3

Improvement of adjacent properties in the General Improvement and Housing Action Areas

GIA / HAA	Number of houses receiving improvement grants (1970-73)	Houses receiving improvement grants (1970-73) on adjacent sites	
		Number	Per cent
Masbro Road	116	66	57
Moore Park	132	94	71
Colville-Tavistock	79	56	71
Lanhill-Marylands	108	50	46
Westbourne Gardens	20	9	45
Coningham Road	40	8	20
Tavistock	32	5	16

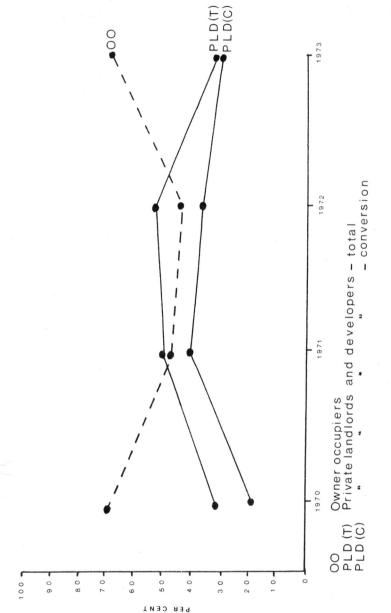

OO   Owner occupiers
PLD (T)   Private landlords and developers – total
PLD (C)   "   "   "   "   – conversion

Figure 6.9   Improvement grants awarded in Hammersmith GIAs
             as a percentage of improvement grants
             awarded in Inner West London

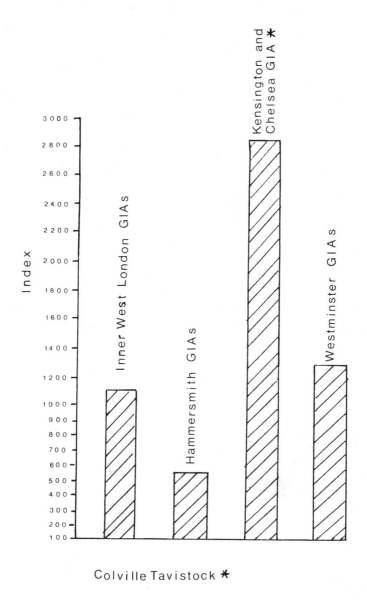

Figure 6.10   Index of Improvement Grant concentration,
Inner West London GIAs

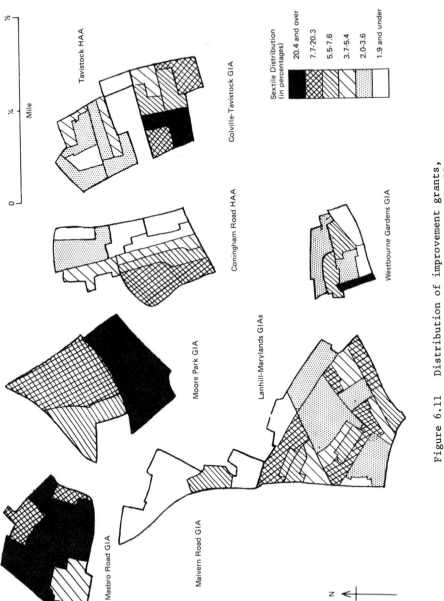

Sextile Distribution
(in percentages)

20.4 and over
7.7-20.3
5.5-7.6
3.7-5.4
2.0-3.6
1.9 and under

Tavistock HAA

Colville-Tavistock GIA

Coningham Road HAA

Westbourne Gardens GIA

Moore Park GIA

Lanhill-Marylands GIAs

Masbro Road GIA

Malvern Road GIA

Figure 6.11   Distribution of improvement grants,
west London GIAs and HAAs, 1970–73
Overall distribution

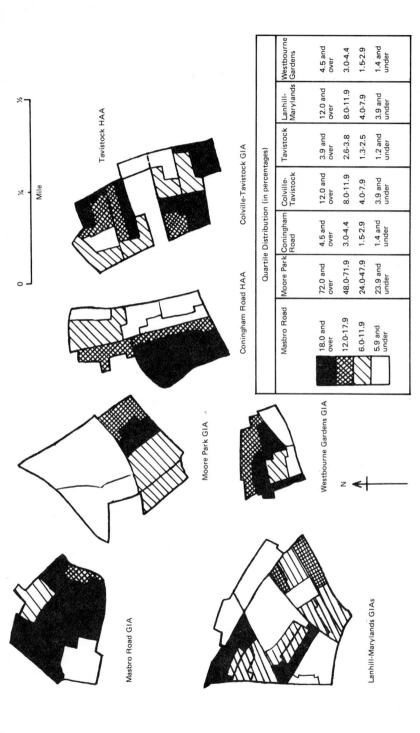

	Quartile Distribution (in percentages)						
Masbro Road	Moore Park	Coningham Road	Colville-Tavistock	Tavistock	Lanhill-Marylands	Westbourne Gardens
18.0 and over	72.0 and over	4.5 and over	12.0 and over	3.9 and over	12.0 and over	4.5 and over
12.0-17.9	48.0-71.9	3.0-4.4	8.0-11.9	2.6-3.8	8.0-11.9	3.0-4.4
6.0-11.9	24.0-47.9	1.5-2.9	4.0-7.9	1.3-2.5	4.0-7.9	1.5-2.9
5.9 and under	23.9 and under	1.4 and under	3.9 and under	1.2 and under	3.9 and under	1.4 and under

Masbro Road GIA

Moore Park GIA

Coningham Road HAA

Westbourne Gardens GIA

Colville-Tavistock GIA

Tavistock HAA

Lanhill-Marylands GIAs

0   ¼   ½
Mile

N

Figure 6.12   Distribution of improvement grants,
west London GIAs and HAAs, 1970–73,
declared area distribution

CORRELATIONS BETWEEN THE DISTRIBUTION OF IMPROVEMENT GRANTS AND SOCIO-
ECONOMIC VARIABLES

In this section an attempt is made to correlate the spatial distribution
of improvement grants with a number of housing and social variables.
The methodology is generally the same as applied in Chapter 5, although
within the GIAs and HAAs the sub areas under consideration are enumeration
districts (EDs) and not wards. These are numbered, for example 3177/11
(3177 representing the GLC Census Area and 11 being the ED number in
accordance with the 1971 Census). The location of EDs is shown in
Appendix H.

Masbro Road GIA

Table 6.4 shows all the correlations within the Masbro Road GIA. They
indicate that grants were awarded mainly in EDs with a high percentage of
dwellings lacking a bath/shower and hot water; population aged 40 and
over (especially 65 and over) and one person households (pensioners).
Correlations, however, were largely inverse and suggested that EDs with
a high percentage of private (especially furnished) tenancies, households
with only 1-2 rooms, deficient and shared dwellings, non-car owning
households, household heads in SEGs 7-12, 14,15 and populations aged
20-39 and under 40 received relatively few improvement grants. In seven
out of eight variables correlated with the distribution of improvement
grants, intersection occurred in the same ED - 3175/39, indicating a very
localised relationship between the grants and the variables.

Moore Park GIA

Table 6.5 shows all the correlations within the Moore Park GIA. They
indicate that grants were awarded mainly in EDs with a high percentage
of owner occupied households with more than four (or even seven or more)
rooms; dwellings without a bath/shower, hot water, an inside W.C., and
all three basic amenities (and shared dwellings without a bath/shower
and hot water), and in EDs where there were high fertility ratios
and a high proportion of the population under 5, 15, 20 between 20-39
and under 40. Inverse correlations indicate that EDs with a high
percentage of private tenancies, households with 1-2 rooms or with four
or less rooms, shared dwellings lacking all three basic amenities,
households without a car, and a high proportion of economically active
males in SEGs 7-12, 14, 15 received relatively few improvement grants.
In 16 out of the 24 variables correlated with the distribution of
improvement grants, intersections occurred in the same ED - 3177/11,
indicating a fairly localised relationship between the grants and the
variables.

Colville-Tavistock GIA

Table 6.6 shows all the correlations within Colville-Tavistock GIA.
They indicate that grants were awarded mainly in EDs with a high
percentage of owner occupied households, to a much lesser extent private
(and particularly unfurnished) tenancies, dwellings without bath/shower,
hot water, an inside W.C. and all three basic amenities, in EDs where
there were high proportions of economically active males and heads of
households in SEGs 7,8,9,10,11,12,14,15 and in EDs where there were high
proportions of the population aged 40 and over and one person households
(pensioners).

150

Table 6.4

Correlations between the approval of improvement grants
and selected socio-economic variables within the
eight EDs of Masbro Road GIA

	GIA %	ED range %	Rxy	t	P
Households receiving improvement grants (1970-73)	20.9	4.5 -33.7			
1 person households (pensioners)	11.9	8.0 -14.8	0.93	6.42	>0.1
Population aged 65 and over	12.7	6.6 -19.2	0.57		NS
Shared dwellings without hot water	21.1	8.1 -50.0	0.55		NS
Shared dwellings without a bath/shower	31.6	0 -50.0	0.45		NS
Population aged 40 and over	44.4	35.8 -67.9	0.35		NS
Private furnished tenancies	31.9	0 -57.3	-0.61	1.91	NS
Households with 1-2 rooms	38.7	18.5 -60.8	-0.54		NS
Population aged 20-39	35.0	18.6 -44.5	-0.52		NS
Shared dwellings	15.5	1.3 -29.1	-0.43		NS
SEGs 7-12, 14,15 (heads of households)	20.4	15.2 -30.5	-0.42		NS
Crude net deficiency/surplus	-19.4	-36.2/ + 0.7	-0.41		NS
Population aged under 40	55.6	32.1 -64.2	-0.35		NS
Households without a car	74.5	61.4 -82.4	-0.35		NS
Private tenancies (total)	67.1	0.7 -89.0	-0.31		NS

Table 6.5

Correlations between the approval of improvement grants
and selected socio-economic variables within the
six EDs of Moore Park GIA

	GIA %	ED range %	Rxy	t	P
Households receiving improvement grants (1970-73)	40.6	6.9- 74.7			
Households with 7 or more rooms	11.5	1.9- 29.6	0.89	3.86	2 > 1
Households with more than 4 rooms	32.1	9.5- 55.1	0.86	3.34	5 > 2
Shared dwellings without a bath/shower	37.4	0.0-100.0	0.82	2.82	5 > 2
Dwellings without hot water	19.3	0.6- 36.3	0.79	2.61	NS
Population under the age of 5	6.5	3.4- 11.0	0.79	2.61	NS
Shared dwellings without hot water	30.3	0.0-100.0	0.74		NS
Dwellings without a bath/shower	26.1	1.3- 54.0	0.73		NS
Owner occupied households	27.2	4.4- 47.9	0.69		NS
Dwellings without all 3 basic amenities	35.4	6.3- 68.1	0.68		NS
Population under the age of 40	55.9	33.7- 70.7	0.66		NS
Population under the age of 15	14.0	8.7- 21.0	0.62		NS
Dwellings without an inside W.C.	14.2	1.3- 29.3	0.61		NS
Fertility ratio	27.0	17.9- 40.3	0.57		NS
Population aged 20-39	37.7	17.0- 49.7	0.50		NS
Population under the age of 20	18.2	14.0- 23.4	0.49		NS
Households with 4 rooms or less	67.9	47.9- 90.6	-0.86	3.34	5 > 2
Population aged 40-64	27.7	15.5- 38.8	-0.74		NS
Population aged 40 and over	44.5	29.3- 66.3	-0.65		NS
Private tenancies (total)	62.7	42.3- 89.9	-0.63		NS
Population aged 65 and over	16.7	11.5- 27.5	-0.42		NS
SEGs 7-12, 14, 15 (economically active males)	10.4	0.0- 21.7	-0.32		NS
Households with 1-2 rooms	23.2	8.4- 48.7	-0.30		NS
Households without a car	58.7	42.3- 79.1	-0.27		NS
Shared dwellings without all 3 basic amenities	54.3	0.0-100.0	-0.27		NS

Table 6.6

Correlations between the approval of improvement grants
and selected socio-economic variables within the
six EDs of Colville-Tavistock GIA

	GIA %	ED range %	Rxy	t	P
Households receiving improvement grants (1970-73)	10.2	3.7 - 22.1			
Shared dwellings without a bath/shower			0.82	2.82	5 > 2
Dwellings without all 3 basic amenities	21.4	11.5 - 32.9	0.68		NS
Dwellings without an inside W.C.	6.4	1.2 - 23.4	0.68		NS
Owner occupied households	5.2	2.9 - 9.6	0.61		NS
Population aged 40-64	23.9	18.0 - 31.5	0.58		NS
Dwellings without a bath/shower	8.2	0.0 - 22.8	0.56		NS
Dwellings without hot water	8.6	3.7 - 17.1	0.56		NS
Population aged 40 and over	31.0	23.0 - 42.3	0.48		NS
SEGs 7-12, 14,15 (heads of households)	20.8	14.4 - 27.7	0.48		NS
SEGs 7-12, 14,15 (economically active males)	20.6	14.2 - 27.7	0.41		NS
1 person households (pensioners)	8.1	3.9 - 12.7	0.36		NS
Private unfurnished tenancies	38.9	20.9 - 64.4	0.32		NS
Private tenancies (total)	78.9	65.9 - 91.7	0.29		NS
SEGs 1-4 (heads of households	4.2	0.0 - 6.2	-0.94	5.43	1 > 0.2
SEGs 1-4 (economically active males)	4.7	0.0 - 9.0	-0.82	2.92	5 > 2
Population aged under 5	8.0	4.8 - 10.7	-0.61		NS
Fertility ratio	31.7	17.0 - 46.3	-0.48		NS
Population aged under 40	69.0	57.7 - 77.0	-0.48		NS
Population aged under 15	17.5	13.1 - 24.0	-0.45		NS
SEGs 1,2 (economically active males)	2.7	0.0 - 6.0	-0.39		NS
SEGs 1,2 (heads of households)	2.2	0.0 - 4.8	-0.35		NS
Population aged 20-39	44.0	31.9 - 43.8	-0.35		NS
Population aged under 20	25.0	19.1 - 28.3	-0.30		NS

153

Inverse correlations indicate that EDs with high percentages of economically active males and heads of households in SEGs 1, 2 or 1-4, high fertility ratios and high proportions of the population aged under 5, 15, 20 and 40, and between 20-39 received relatively few improvement grants.   In 11 out of the 23 variables correlated with the distribution of improvement grants, intersections occurred in the same ED - 3202/14, indicating that within a GIA of six EDs there was a fairly localised relationship between the grants and the variables.

Lanhill-Marylands GIA

Table 6.7 shows all the correlations within Lanhill-Marylands GIA. They indicate that grants were awarded mainly in EDs with a high percentage of households with more than four rooms; in EDs where there were high crude net deficiencies and a high proportion of shared dwellings, and in EDs where there were high fertility ratios and a high proportion of the population aged under 5 and 65 and over.

Inverse correlations indicate that EDs with a high percentage of owner occupied households, households with four rooms or less and population aged 40-64, received relatively few improvement grants.   In seven out of the nine variables correlated with the distribution of improvement grants, intersections occurred in the same two EDs - 3062/42 and 3063/53, indicating that within a GIA of 18 EDs there was a very localised relationship between the grants and the variables.

Westbourne Gardens GIA

Table 6.8 shows all the correlations within Westbourne Gardens GIA. They indicate that grants were awarded mainly in EDs with a high proportion of owner occupied households; in EDs where there was a high crude net deficiency and where there was a high proportion of shared dwellings. Within these EDs there was a high proportion of the population under the age of 5.

Inverse correlations indicate that EDs with a high proportion of households with more than 1.5 persons per room, and economically active males and heads of households in SEGs 1, 2 received relatively few improvement grants.   In five out of the seven variables correlated with the distribution of improvement grants, intersections occurred in the same ED - 3085/8, indicating that within a GIA of seven EDs there was a fairly localised relationship between the grants and the variables.

Coningham Road HAA

Table 6.9 shows all the correlations within Coningham Road HAA.   They indicate that grants were awarded mainly in EDs with a high percentage of private (especially furnished) tenancies, households with less than four rooms (especially 1-2 rooms), in EDs where there were high crude net deficiencies and a high proportion of shared dwellings, dwellings without a bath/shower, dwellings without all three basic amenities, and shared dwellings without hot water.   Grants went mainly to EDs where there were high proportions of economically active males in SEGs 1, 2 and 1-4, the heads of households in SEGs 1, 2 and to where there were high proportions of the population aged under 15, 20-39 and under 40, and where there were high fertility ratios.

Table 6.7

<u>Correlations between the approval of improvement grants</u>
<u>and selected socio-economic variables within the</u>
<u>18 EDs of Lanhill-Marylands GIA</u>

	GIA %	ED range %	Rxy	t	P
Households receiving improvement grants (1970–73)	6.0	0.6 – 13.3			
Shared dwellings	20.7	2.6 – 49.3	0.68	3.73	0.2 > 0.1
Crude net deficiency/ surplus	−24.0	−51.6/+ 2.7	0.68	3.73	0.2 > 0.1
Fertility ratio	37.5	17.3 – 58.0	0.58		NS
Population under the age of 5	8.9	5.0 – 12.1	0.46		NS
Households with more than 4 rooms	6.5	1.3 – 13.4	0.37		NS
Population aged 65 and over	10.2	5.2 – 17.5	0.28		NS
Owner occupied households	5.1	1.1 – 12.0	−0.40		NS
Households with 4 rooms or less	93.5	86.7 – 98.7	−0.37		NS
Population aged 40–64	24.9	17.7 – 31.7	−0.31		NS

155

Table 6.8

Correlations between the approval of improvement grants
and selected socio-economic variables within the
seven EDs of Westbourne Gardens GIA

	GIA %	ED range %	Rxy	t	P
Households receiving improvement grants (1970-73)	5.8	0.0 - 20.4			
Crude net deficiency/ surplus	-23.5	-67.7/+ 17.5	0.78	2.8	5 > 2
Shared dwellings	21.3	1.4 - 60.0	0.66		NS
Population aged under 5	3.6	0.0 - 6.6	0.43		NS
Owner occupied households	6.9	1.5 - 24.7	0.26		NS
SEGs 1,2 (economically active males)	4,7	0.0 - 13.0	-0.45		NS
SEGs 1,2 (heads of households)	4.4	0.0 - 13.7	-0.42		NS
Households living at more than 1.5 persons per room	6.9	0.0 - 21.3	-0.32		NS

Table 6.9

Correlations between the approval of improvement grants
and selected socio-economic variables within the
nine EDs of Coningham Road HAA

	HAA %	ED range %	Rxy	t	P
Households receiving improvement grants (1970-73)	3.2	0.5 - 7.7			
Crude net deficiency/ surplus	21.9	-43.8/+ 0.6	0.78	3.33	2 > 1
Population aged 20-39	26.9	16.4 - 39.7	0.74	2.95	5 > 2
Shared dwellings without hot water	18.4	0.0 - 42.1	0.74	2.94	5 > 2
Private tenancies (total)	51.0	0.0 - 85.9	0.74	2.90	5 > 2
SEGs 1-4 (economically active males)	3.0	0.0 - 10.8	0.74	2.89	5 > 2
Shared dwellings	25.2	0.0 - 52.1	0.72	2.74	5 > 2
Dwellings without a bath/shower	16.0	0.0 - 39.7	0.67	2.40	5 > 2
Households with 1-2 rooms	23.2	0.0 - 61.0	0.67	2.36	NS
SEGs 1,2 (economically active males)	2.3	0.0 - 8.1	0.65	2.24	NS
Dwellings without all 3 basic amenities	28.1	1.1 - 49.3	0.61	2.03	NS
Private furnished tenancies	14.0	0.0 - 39.0	0.60	1.99	NS
Population aged under 40	57.5	44.2 - 74.5	0.56		NS
Households with 4 rooms or less	74.0	52.8 - 89.0	0.52		NS
Fertility ratio	21.8	9.1 - 38.9	0.49		NS
SEGs 1,2 (heads of households)	9.5	0.0 - 27.0	0.44		NS
Population aged under 15	23.2	17.3 - 29.0	0.31		NS
Population aged 40 and over	42.5	25.5 - 55.8	-0.56		NS
Population aged 65 and over	13.2	6.7 - 20.8	-0.55		NS
Households with more than 4 rooms	26.0	11.0 - 47.2	-0.52		NS
1 Person households (pensioners)	10.9	6.7 - 16.1	-0.24		NS

157

Table 6.10

Correlations between the approval of improvement grants
and selected socio-economic variables within the
eight EDs of Tavistock HAA

	HAA %	ED range %	Rxy	t	P
Households receiving improvement grants (1970-73)	2.6	0.6 - 5.1			
Population aged 65 and over	11.1	7.7 - 15.8	0.76	2.82	5 > 2
1 person households (pensioners)	12.8	10.1 - 16.0	0.72	2.55	5 > 2
Population aged 40 and over	37.0	29.1 - 47.7	0.53		NS
Households without a car	84.2	78.1 - 93.1	0.42		NS
Dwellings without a bath/shower	7.0	0.0 - 15.3	0.41		NS
Private unfurnished tenancies	48.7	32.6 - 54.8	0.34		NS
Fertility ratio	38.8	22.2 - 55.6	0.26		NS
Population aged under 40	63.0	52.3 - 70.9	-0.53		NS
Households living at more than 1.5 persons per room	13.7	9.0 - 18.7	-0.26		NS

Inverse correlations indicate that EDs with a high percentage of households with more than four rooms, population aged 40 and over and 65 and
over, and one person households (pensioners), received relatively few
improvement grants. In the case of 12 out of the 20 variables correlated
with the distribution of improvement grants, intersections occurred in
the same ED 3181/20, indicating that within a HAA of nine EDs there was
a fairly localised relationship between the grants and the variables.

Tavistock HAA

Table 6.10 shows all the correlations within Tavistock HAA. They
indicate that grants were awarded to EDs with a high percentage of private
unfurnished tenancies and in EDs where there was a high proportion of
dwellings without a bath/shower; a high proportion of households without
a car; and a high proportion of population aged 40 and over and 65 and
over, and to EDs where there were high fertility ratios and a high
proportion of one person households (pensioners).

Inverse correlations indicated that in EDs with a high percentage of
households with over 1.5 persons per room and population under the age of
40, received relatively few improvement grants. In all nine variables
correlated with the distribution of improvement grants, intersections
occurred equally in only two EDs, 3201/26 and 3202/4, indicating that
within a HAA of only eight EDs there was a fairly localised relationship
between the grants and the variables.

Inner West London GIAs and HAAs

Table 6.11 shows all the correlations within the Inner West London GIAs
and HAAs. They indicate that grants were awarded mainly in EDs with a
high percentage of owner occupied households; households with more than
four rooms or even with seven or more rooms; in EDs with a high proportion of dwellings (shared or otherwise) without a bath/shower, hot water,
an inside W.C. and all three basic amenities, and in EDs with a high
proportion of the population aged 20-39 and 65 and over, and where there
was a high proportion of one person households (pensioners).

Inverse correlations indicate that EDs with a high percentage of private
furnished tenancies, households with 1-2 rooms or households with four
rooms or less, households with more than 1.5 persons per room, economically active males in SEGs 7-12, 14, 15, households without a car, and
population under the age of 15 or 20 received relatively few improvement
grants.

There were 18 sets of intersections of improvement grants and selected
variables.   In 17 sets, intersections occurred in ED 3177/12, in 16 sets
in ED 3177/10, in 14 sets in ED 3175/39, in 13 sets in ED 3177/11 and in
11 sets in ED 3177/9.   All of the above EDs were in Moore Park GIA,
except the third ED which was in Masbro Road GIA.   There were fewer
intersections in the other EDs.   Within a total number of 65 EDs there
was thus a highly localised relationship between the grants and the
variables.

Comparisons with Inner West London

In the case of owner occupied households, private furnished tenancies,
dwellings without a bath/shower, dwellings without hot water, dwellings

Table 6.11

Correlations between the approval of improvement grants
and selected socio-economic variables within the
65 EDs of the Inner West London GIAs and HAAs and
Malvern Road GIA

	GIAs and HAAs %	ED range %	Rxy	t	P
Households receiving improvement grants (1970-73)	10.5	0.0 - 74.7			
Shared dwellings without a bath/shower	13.6	0.0 - 100.0	0.90	6.90	>0.1
Owner occupied households	9.4	0.0 - 47.9	0.88	6.12	>0.1
Dwellings without hot water	13.6	0.0 - 42.5	0.88	6.12	>0.1
Dwellings without a bath/shower	15.2	0.0 - 54.0	0.86	5.66	>0.1
Shared dwellings without hot water	12.8	0.0 - 100.0	0.82	4.80	>0.1
Households with more than 4 rooms	14.6	1.4 - 52.1	0.81	4.63	>0.1
Shared dwellings without an inside W.C.	3.4	0.0 - 57.1	0.80	4.36	0.2>0.1
Dwellings without all 3 basic amenities	28.4	i.8 - 68.1	0.73	3.58	1.0>0.2
Dwellings without an inside W.C.	9.1	0.0 - 54.3	0.69	3.14	>0.2
Shared dwellings without all 3 basic amenities	36.9	0.0 - 100.0	0.64	2.73	2>1
Households with 7 rooms or more	3.5	0.0 - 29.6	0.62	2.55	5>2
1 person households (pensioners)	12.3	3.9 - 24.6	0.46		NS
Population aged 20-39	35.6	16.4 - 53.2	0.35		NS
Population aged 65 and over	11.7	2.1 - 27.5	0.34		NS
Households with 4 rooms or less	85.4	47.9 - 98.0	-0.81	4.63	>0.1
Households without car	75.4	42.3 - 93.1	-0.74	3.61	1.0>0.2
SEGs 7-12, 14,15 (economically active males)	20.1	0.0 - 42.7	-0.61	2.57	5>2
Households with 1-2 rooms	44.8	0.0 - 87.7	-0.61	2.52	5>2
Households living at more than 1.5 persons per room	11.8	0.0 - 30.8	-0.57	2.30	5>2
Population aged under 20	24.3	7.0 - 39.2	-0.54		NS
Private furnished tenancies	32.4	0.0 - 73.8	-0.53		NS
Population aged under 15	19.2	5.0 - 33.1	-0.49		NS

without an inside W.C., economically active males in SEGs 7, 8, 9, 10, 11, 12, 14 and 15, and population aged under 15, correlations were found in both the Inner West London GIAs and HAAs and in Inner West London generally. In the case of owner occupied households, a high direct correlation within the GIAs and HAAs   contrasted with a low inverse correlation in Inner West London.   In the case of private furnished tenancies, economically active males in SEGs 7-12, 14, 15 and population aged under 15, inverse correlations within the GIAs and HAAs contrasted with direct correlations in Inner West London.   But in the case of dwellings without a bath/shower, hot water and an inside W.C., direct correlations were found in both the GIAs and HAAs and in Inner West London, being high in the first areas and low in the second area* (Fig.6.13).

The seven variables correlated with improvement grants according to the following correlation coefficients:

	Inner West London GIAs and HAAs	Inner West London
Owner occupied households	0.88	-0.26
Private furnished tenancies	-0.53	0.23
Dwellings without a bath/shower	0.86	0.23
Dwellings without hot water	0.88	0.36
Dwellings without an inside W.C.	0.69	0.23
Economically active males in SEGs 7-12, 14, 15	-0.61	0.23
Population under the age of 15	0.49	0.26

A suggested explanation for the above differences was that, within the GIAs, improvement grants were mainly associated with unmediated gentrification.   Whenever possible, landlords obtained vacant possession and then sold their property to owner occupiers.   Grants were then obtained for improvement as the areas became up and coming middle class neighbourhoods.   In contrast, within Inner West London generally, improvement grants assisted mediated gentrification – going largely to developers/continuing landlords.   Although tenants were displaced, gentrification occurred in what remained mainly working class areas, and where private rented accommodation continued to be the principal form of tenure even though there were substantial changes taking place.

CORRELATIONS OF THE SPATIAL DISTRIBUTION OF IMPROVEMENT GRANTS WITH INDICES OF REHABILITATION-NEED AND REHABILITATION POTENTIAL

In an attempt to indicate the relationship between the spatial pattern of improvement grant approvals and an aggregate of household tenure, housing characteristics, social composition and age structure variables in the GIAs and HAAs, the Rehabilitation-Need-Index (RNI) applied initially to the wards (in Chapter 5) was used, and this was then correlated with the percentage of households receiving improvement grants.   The indicators, means, weights and methodology used in Chapter 5 are unchanged.(Table 6.12). This enables a comparison to be made between the scores for the declared areas and the wards

The ranked EDs were grouped into sextiles and mapped.   It was found that the 11 top sextile EDs comprised in rank order 3175/36, 3085/10,

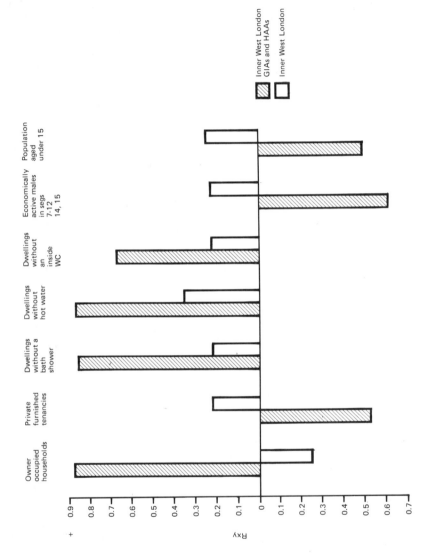

Figure 6.13   Correlation coefficients, Inner West London

3062/45, 3063/50, 3062/47, 3085/8, 3062/52, 3085/13, 3062/51, 3062/48 and
3062/57 (Fig.6.14).   All had indices in excess of 42,570, the peak index
being 52,364 (see Appendix I).   This compares with respective indices
for the boroughs of 43,100 and 51,679.   The top sextile wards were
concentrated mainly in the two Westminster GIAs of Lanhill-Marylands and
Westbourne Gardens, a very different concentration from that of improvement
grants distribution (Fig.6.11).

The RNI was correlated with the percentage of households receiving
improvement grants, 1970-73 (see Appendix I).   In the GIAs and HAAs in
aggregate there was a moderate inverse correlation (Rxy = -0.52), and
within Coningham Road and Tavistock HAAs combined there was a very low
correlation (Rxy = 0.37).   In Coningham Road HAA there was a high
correlation (Rxy = 0.67), the only one statistically significant,
P = 5 2, but in Tavistock HAA alone there was virtually no correlation
(Rxy = -0.19).   The above correlations indicate that within the GIAs
and in contrast to the wards, improvement grants were not allocated to
specific areas in greatest need in the period 1970-73 (those areas being
mainly in the Lanhill-Marylands and Westbourne Gardens GIAs), but that
within the future Coningham Road HAA, grants were awarded to specific
areas in greatest need.   A comparison between correlations in the GIAs,
HAAs and boroughs is shown in Table 6.12.

A further index was devised to show more positively that within the
GIAs and HAAs grants were awarded mainly to areas of greatest demand as
distinct from 'need'.   Using data from the 1971 Census and the same
methodology used for calculating the RNI, a Rehabilitation-Potential
Index (RPI) was compiled from the following nine indicators:

Indicator 1	Owner occupiers
Indicator 2	Non-shared dwellings
Indicator 3	Households at less than 1.5 persons per room
Indicator 4	Dwellings without a bath/shower
Indicator 5	Dwellings without hot water
Indicator 6	Dwellings without an inside W.C.
Indicator 7	SEGs 1, 2
Indicator 8	Households with a car
Indicator 9	Population aged 20-39

Six of the indicators, 1-3 and 7-9, differed from those used in the RNI,
and were included to show (in aggregate) the extent of gentrification.
Indicators 4-6 remained unchanged being prerequisites for grant approval.
The means (as in the case of the RNI) were those of the wards, and the
weights were chosen subjectively according to their relevance to gentrification.   Table 6.13 sets out the means, sum of means (less indicator
mean) and weights which governed the calculation of the index.   The nine
indicator scores were added together.   This addition resulted in an
index with a range from 44,085 to 107,917 (see Appendix J).   This
enabled EDs to be ranked, although in absolute terms the index score has
no significance.

The ranked EDs were grouped into sextiles and mapped.   It was found
that the 11 top sextile EDs were in rank order 3177/11, 3177/10, 3175/39,
3177/12, 3202/17, 3085/14, 3177/5, 3175/02, 3175/38, 3132/52 and 3175/37
(Fig.6.15).   All had RPIs in excess of 75,000, the highest being 107,917.
The top sextile EDs were concentrated mainly in the two Hammersmith GIAs
of Moore Park and Masbro Road, a very similar concentration to that of

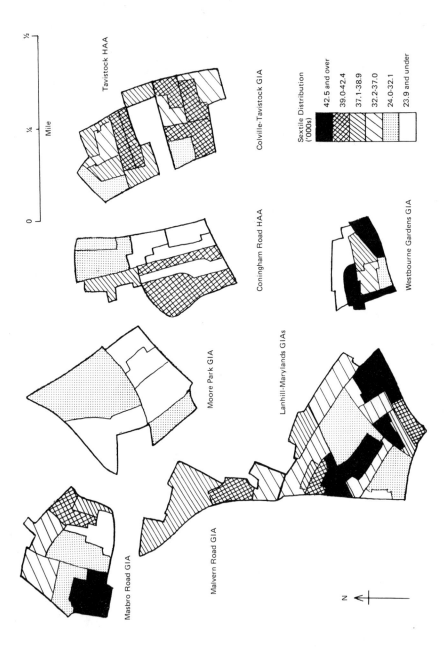

Tavistock HAA

Colville-Tavistock GIA

Coningham Road HAA

Westbourne Gardens GIA

Moore Park GIA

Lanhill-Marylands GIAs

Masbro Road GIA

Malvern Road GIA

Sextile Distribution
('000s)

42.5 and over
39.0-42.4
37.1-38.9
32.2-37.0
24.0-32.1
23.9 and under

Mile

0   ¼   ½

N

Figure 6.14   Rehabilitation–Need, west London GIAs and HAAs

Table 6.12

Correlations between Rehabilitation-Need indices, the Rehabilitation-Potential index
and the approval of improvement grants

		x	Rxy	t	f	r
	EDs in:					
Rehabilitation-Need index	Inner West London GIAs and HAAs and Malvern Road GIA	34 220	-0.52	2.04	65	NS
	Coningham Road and Tavistock HAAs	32 070	0.37	1.54	15	NS
	Coningham Road HAA	26 790	0.67	2.39	7	5 > 2
	Tavistock HAA	38 010	-0.19	–	6	NS
	Wards in:					
	Brent	31 230	0.71	2.85	8	5 > 2
	Brent and Inner West London Boroughs	30 170	0.48	2.13	15	5 > 2
	Inner West London Boroughs	32 750	0.65	2.57	9	5 > 2
	EDs in:					
Rehabilitation-Potential index	Inner West London GIAs and HAAs and Malvern Road GIA	58 685	0.89	6.44	65	> 0.1

Table 6.13

Rehabilitation-Potential Index. Variables, means, sum of means and weighting

	Variable	Mean	Sum of means less indicator means	Weight
Household tenure	1. Owner occupied	27.7	285.5	3
	2. Non-sharing households	89.6	223.6	1
	3. Households living at less than 1.5 persons per room	94.2	229.0	1
Housing character-istics	4. Dwellings without a bath/shower	8.4	304.8	0.33
	5. Dwellings without hot water	7.1	306.1	0.33
	6. Dwellings without an inside WC	4.4	308.8	0.33
Social composition and age structure	7. SEGs 1, 2	14.5	298.7	2.0
	8. Households with a car	35.8	277.5	0.5
	9. Population aged 20-39	31.5	281.7	0.5

166

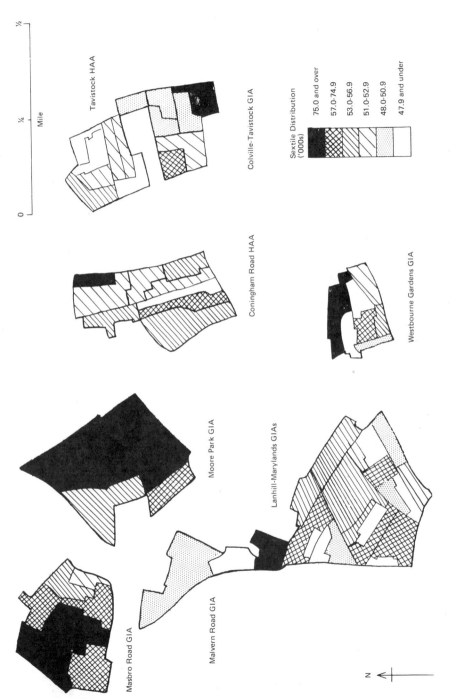

Masbro Road GIA

Moore Park GIA

Malvern Road GIA

Lanhill-Marylands GIAs

Coningham Road HAA

Westbourne Gardens GIA

Tavistock HAA

Colville-Tavistock GIA

Sextile Distribution
('000s)

75.0 and over
57.0-74.9
53.0-56.9
51.0-52.9
48.0-50.9
47.9 and under

0   ¼   ½
Mile

N ←

Figure 6.15   Rehabilitation-Potential, west London GIAs and HAAs

Table 6.14

Changes in the social composition, household tenure and housing characteristics in the
west London boroughs and selected wards, 1966-71

Borough and Ward	% population		Owner occupied house-holds %	Private furnished tenancies %	Households living at more than 1.5 persons per room %	Dwellings without exclusive use of:		
	Economically active males in SEGs 1-4	Economically active males in SEGs 7-12, 14,15				bath/shower	hot water %	inside WC %
HAMMERSMITH	+ 18.7	- 14.5	+ 11.2	+ 16.5	+ 9.8	- 14.4	- 24.3	- 12.6
Coningham (Coningham Road HAA)	+ 123.5	- 11.7	+ 30.8	- 27.3	- 20.7	- 7.8	- 15.3	+ 50.0
Grove	+ 90.5	- 8.4	+ 21.2	- 17.2	- 16.7	- 7.8	- 6.2	+ 8.9
St.Stephens	+ 62.5	+ 10.2	+ 2.1	- 16.8	- 48.8	- 25.9	- 24.6	- 3.5
Addison	+ 28.1	- 23.8	+ 62.7	+ 32.8	- 17.1	+ 9.7	+ 2.8	+ 565.0
Brook Green (Masbro Road GIA)	+ 22.2	- 14.7	+ 39.5	- 22.0	+ 43.6	+ 11.8	+ 13.0	- 26.8
Sherbrooke	NC	NC	+ 14.4	+ 114.0	- 27.3	+ 0.3	+ 6.7	+ 8.6
*Sandford (Moore Park GIA)	- 9.4	- 32.3	+ 11.4	- 17.5	+ 9.2	- 18.9	- 36.6	- 26.5
Margravine	- 16.7	- 27.0	- 3.1	- 34.6	- 47.7	- 31.2	- 26.1	- 32.4
Halford	- 35.5	- 18.1	- 1.1	- 18.6	- 19.5	- 12.8	- 24.3	- 37.6
KENSINGTON & CHELSEA	+ 4.1	- 25.7	+ 14.0	- 9.8	+ 9.0	- 15.5	- 23.6	- 10.0
Norland	+ 28.4	- 43.5	+ 6.9	- 18.8	- 28.5	- 38.1	- 35.9	- 41.6
St.Charles	+ 19.3	- 10.0	- 19.5	- 8.7	- 30.7	- 30.7	- 3.4	- 10.7
*Pembridge (Colville-Tavistock GIA)	+ 12.6	- 32.2	+ 37.7	- 15.1	- 4.6	- 1.8	- 18.1	- 19.2
Golborne (Tavistock HAA)	- 13.3	- 21.4	- 33.1	- 8.3	- 0.2	- 1.8	- 37.6	+ 94.6

| | % population | | % | % | % | Dwellings without exclusive use of: | | % |
	Economically active males in SEGs 1-4	Economically active males in SEGs 7-12 14,15	Owner occupied households	Private furnished tenancies	Households living at more than 1.5 persons per room	bath/shower	hot water	inside WC
WESTMINSTER	- 0.5	- 25.9	+ 29.7	- 4.2	- 2.6	- 15.2	- 22.9	- 110.9
Westbourne (Westbourne Gardens GIA)	+ 30.4	- 41.3	+ 10.0	- 35.2	- 28.5	+ 12.0	+ 12.8	+ 30.0
Harrow Road (Lanhill-Marylands GIA)	- 7.1	- 32.7	- 22.9	- 10.7	- 39.1	- 16.3	- 1.0	+ 137.5
BRENT (Willesden)	- 4.1	- 17.0	- 0.3	- 23.8	+ 47.9	- 66.3	- 74.5	- 72.0
Roundwood	+ 44.4	- 30.3	- 10.8	- 40.7	+ 18.2	- 59.0	- 67.8	- 71.8
Kilburn	+ 6.9	- 5.0	+ 12.3	- 20.1	+ 18.2	- 73.9	- 82.3	- 881.1
Queens Park	+ 6.3	+ 1.7	- 11.2	- 18.3	+ 65.2	+ 104.8	- 82.3	- 89.0
Willesden Green	+ 3.6	- 18.5	+ 5.9	- 23.3	+ 62.1	- 60.0	- 67.4	- 57.9
Harlesden	NC	- 11.4	+ 5.1	- 13.0	+ 3.6	- 66.6	- 76.2	- 80.7
Kensal Rise	- 20.0	- 8.8	+ 6.3	- 21.4	+ 53.8	- 59.6	- 71.2	- 65.5
St.Raphael	- 23.5	- 16.3	+ 2.2	- 44.4	+ 81.4	- 69.6	- 72.6	- 62.7
Cricklewood	- 31.8	- 10.7	+ 2.3	- 9.0	+ 72.0	+ 171.4	- 76.3	- 84.6
Carlton (Malvern Road GIA)	- 36.4	- 64.2	- 52.1	- 64.2	- 37.9	- 78.8	- 83.1	- 76.3
Stonebridge	- 43.8	- 30.3	- 14.9	- 47.0	+ 40.0	- 74.6	- 81.4	- 88.4
Church End	- 44.4	- 17.4	- 0.8	- 2.0	+ 117.5	- 59.1	- 74.0	- 67.6

NC No change
*   Wards not established as Housing Problem Areas

Source: Based on 1966 and 1971 Censuses

improvement grants distribution (Fig.6.11) and a very different concentration from that of rehabilitation-need (Fig.6.14).

The RPI was correlated with the percentage of households receiving
improvement grants 1970-73.   There was a high correlation (Rxy = 0.89)
which was statistically very significant P => 0.1 (Table 6.13).   This
showed that grants were awarded mainly to the professional and managerial
classes in the age group 20-39 who owned their homes   dwellings which
were neither overcrowded nor shared with other households but nevertheless
in need of renovation.   This only suggested gentrification as the index
did not take into account the length of residence of households prior to
grant approval.

COMPARATIVE RATES OF GENTRIFICATION

In general the results show that (in contrast to the distribution in the
west London boroughs in aggregate) EDs of greatest need have not received
the highest proportion of grants.   For example, grants were not
allocated mainly to those EDs in which there is a high proportion of
furnished rented accommodation, nor to EDs where there is a high degree
of overcrowding, a large proportion of residents in the lower socio-
economic groups, and a large proportion of the population under the age
of 15.   The analysis also shows that the relationship between the
distribution of grants and the economic and social variables is strongest
in the Moore Park and Masbro Road GIAs - both areas on the edge of
comparatively 'high status' districts of Kensington and Chelsea (see
Chapter 5).

With the exception of Colville-Tavistock and Moore Park, all the west
London GIAs and HAAs are situated in Housing Problem Areas (defined by
the GLC in 1967).   In the period 1966-71 these areas (together with
Pembridge and Sandford - the wards which contain the Colville-Tavistock
and Moore Park GIAs respectively) underwent broadly similar economic and
social changes.   These changes, set out in Table 6.14, will now be
discussed in an attempt to provide an explanation of the pattern of
rehabilitation which occurred in the period 1970-73.

In each Housing Problem Area in Hammersmith, Kensington and Chelsea,
and Westminster (with the exception of Halford) there was an increase in
the ratio of residents in the managerial and professional classes (SEGs
1-4) to those in the personal service and manual occupations (SEGs 7-12,
14, 15).   In some wards (Golborne, Harrow Road, Margravine and Sandford)
this resulted from a decrease in the number of   residents in both SEG
categories, and in one ward (St.Stephens) from an increase in both
categories.

In most of these areas in Hammersmith and Kensington and Chelsea, and
Westminster, the population in SEGs 1-4 increased at a greater rate than
in the boroughs overall - indicating a relatively greater degree of upward
transpossession.   In contrast, in Brent only five of the 12 Housing
Problem Areas showed an increase in the ratio of SEGs 1-4s to SEGs 7-12,
14, 15.   Six Housing Problem Areas showed the opposite, and the numbers
in both categories decreased.

There was a significant increase in owner occupation in most of the
areas, and in all (except Sherbrooke) there was a decrease in furnished

rented accommodation. These trends (more marked than in the boroughs overall) were clearly related to the relative increase in the proportion of residents in the higher socio-economic groups. With the exception of 11 of the 12 Housing Problem Areas in Brent, the majority of areas showed a decrease in the proportion of households living at more than 1.5 persons per room, in contrast to the trend in each borough overall, where there was an increase in the extent of overcrowding. With only a few exceptions, there was a reduction in the number of dwellings without the exclusive use of a bath/shower, hot water and an inside W.C.

These changes suggest that in general the processes of gentrification were already occurring prior to the considerable increase in improvement grant provision brought about by the Housing Act of 1969. It is notable that the greatest increase in the number of residents in SEGs 1-4 and owner occupiers, and the greatest reduction in overcrowding and dwellings without the exclusive use of basic amenities were not generally found within those wards in which GIAs and HAAs were declared in the period 1969-75.

7 Socio-economic change in the General Improvement and Housing Action Areas of west London

The data presented here derives from a recent sample survey within the GIAs, HAAs and the Wormholt ward in Hammersmith. Wormholt was chosen as a 'control area' from which comparisons were made with the GIAs and HAAs to ascertain whether changes in the declared areas were greater or smaller than (or in any other way different from) changes in a 'typical' area. Wormholt was selected as it is situated in central west London and, more importantly, 3.6 per cent of its households lived in dwellings approved for grants (1970-73), a proportion equal to the mean for the Inner West London boroughs and Brent. The survey, together with an investigation of rents, gross values and jurors, indicates the extent to which rehabilitation and social change took place in the period 1969-76.

The first section of this analysis covers a sample survey of households and dwellings in the Masbro Road, Moore Park, Colville-Tavistock, Lanhill-Marylands and Malvern Road GIAs, and in the Coningham Road and Tavistock HAAs. It was completed early in 1976 but low response in the Westbourne Gardens GIA led to the area's omission from the analysis. A questionnaire (see Appendix K) was used to record information provided by residents interviewed at addresses selected by means of random number tables (the addresses were listed and given a number 1 to x, and then paired conventionally with random numbers). Ten per cent of the addresses in the GIAs and HAAs were selected by this method, but in Wormholt, because of its greater population, only five per cent were chosen. In total, 334 addresses were visited, the response rate overall being 91 per cent (information being collected at 304 addresses). The response rate ranged from 100 per cent in Coningham and Tavistock (82 and 84 addresses) to 81.1 and 63.3 per cent (43 and 19 addresses) in Masbro Road and Colville-Tavistock. In multi occupied dwellings as many households as possible were interviewed, some of whom provided information about absent occupants and their accommodation. The results of the survey were then processed and the percentages of each selected variable were compared with the percentages of the 1971 Census. Dwellings subject to improvement grant approval were differentiated from other dwellings, and resulting variations in the 1976 percentages were clearly evident. Changes in the period 1971-76 were then compared with changes at ward level, 1966-71. The current enumeration districts were not appropriate for this purpose having only been established in 1971. As many wards had only been created in 1966, following the London Government Act of 1963, it would not have been appropriate to have attempted to have accurately traced trends back to before the mid sixties.

THE SAMPLE SURVEY AND THE CENSUSES OF 1971 AND 1966

Changes in the household tenure, housing characteristics, social composition and age structure of the GIAs and HAAs, 1971-76, are shown in Table 7.1 and Fig.7.1. Changes in the control area Wormholt are shown

172

in Table 7.2. In all these areas in aggregate there was a substantial
increase in owner occupation (and a corresponding decrease in private
tenancies). Improvement grant properties generally showed the greatest
rate of increase; although the proportion of private tenancies in total
fell within the declared areas, the reduction was less marked in the
non-improvement grant properties where there was even a slight increase
in unfurnished tenancies.

In general, there were increases in the proportion of households
sharing, and living at an occupancy rate of more than 1.5 persons per
room. This was often associated with the displacement of tenants from
improved housing and the resultant increase in overcrowding in unimproved
accommodation. Within the GIAs and HAAs together, there were large
reductions in the proportion of dwellings (especially improvement grant
dwellings) lacking all three basic amenities - hot water, bath/shower and
inside W.C. Conversely there were increases (notably in non-improvement
grant dwellings) in the deficiency of individual basic amenities (hot
water in improvement grant dwellings being an exception). This can
probably be attributable to increased sharing/conversion into bed sitters
or small apartments. Particularly in improvement grant dwellings, there
was an increase in the proportion of the population under the age of 40.
This was most notable in the 20-39 age group. The 40-64 age group showed
the greatest decline, notably in improvement grant properties.

A comparison of Tables 7.1 and 7.2 indicates the relative importance of
the GIAs, HAAs and the control area Wormholt in 1976 in terms of the
principal variables. Of the improvement grant properties, the GIAs and
HAAs still had a lower proportion of owner occupied households than
Wormholt (38.5 and 55.0 per cent respectively) despite an increase of
226.5 per cent in their number in the declared areas, 1971-76, compared
with an increase of only 47.3 per cent in Wormholt. The GIAs and HAAs
continued to have a larger proportion of private tenancies than Wormholt
(61.5 compared with 45.0 per cent) despite a slightly greater rate of
decrease in the declared areas. The GIAs and HAAs had higher proportions
of sharing households, occupancy rates in excess of 1.5 persons per room
and dwellings without hot water, bath/shower and an inside W.C., the
percentages in 1976 for the GIAs and HAAs being 46.2, 20.6, 6.5, 20.4 and
18.3 respectively - in contrast to 10.0, 5.0, 5.0, 10.0 and 7.5 per cent
in Wormholt. Over the period 1971-76 the GIAs and HAAs, unlike Wormholt,
increased their proportion of sharing households and high occupancy rates,
and there was generally an increase in the proportion of dwellings without
basic amenities both in the declared areas and in Wormholt. The GIAs
and the HAAs had higher proportions of economically active males in SEGs
1, 2, 3 and 4 - 35.4 per cent compared with 21.7 per cent in Wormholt
(although the proportion in the control area greatly increased 1971-76),
and Wormholt had the highest proportion of SEGs 5-12 and 14-15 (71.4 per
cent compared with 48.1 per cent in the GIAs and HAAs. The GIAs and HAAs had
higher proportions of population aged under 40 and 20-39, the percentages
being 72.1 and 48.8 respectively, compared with 58.3 and 25.2 per cent in
Wormholt. Conversely, Wormholt had higher proportions of population aged
40 and over, and 40-64, the percentages being 41.7 and 27.8 respectively
compared with 27.9 and 16.3 per cent in the GIAs and HAAs. In non-improvement
grant properties, the relationships between the variables within the
declared areas and Wormholt were broadly similar to those associated with
grant properties, but in the household tenure and housing characteristic
variables there are differences between the grant and non-grant properties.

Table 7.1

Household tenure, housing characteristics, social composition and age structure
West London GIAs and HAAs   1971 and 1976

Variable	Total Census 1971	Total Sample 1976	Improvement grant sample 1976	Non-improvement grant sample 1976
Household tenure				
% owner occupied	11.8	28.0	38.5	23.5
% private unfurnished tenancies	48.8	47.6	40.4	50.6
% private furnished tenancies	39.4	24.5	21.2	25.9
% private tenancies (total)	88.2	72.1	61.5	76.5
Housing characteristics				
% households sharing	20.6	47.4	46.2	47.9
% households at > 1½ persons per room	11.8	21.7	20.6	22.2
% dwellings without exclusive use of:				
hot water	13.6	15.8	6.5	19.9
bath/shower	15.2	38.8	20.4	46.9
inside W.C.	9.0	31.6	18.3	37.4
all three basic amenities	28.4	8.9	8.6	9.0
Social composition				
% economically active males (15-65) in:				
SEGs 1,2,3,4	12.1	35.4	52.0	35.3
SEGs 5-12,14,15	87.9	64.7	48.1	73.9
% households with a car	24.7	50.3	66.7	43.1
Age structure				
% population 5	7.6	7.4	7.9	7.2
% population 15	19.2	17.0	17.9	17.0
% population 20-39	35.6	40.3	48.8	36.8
% population < 40	60.2	67.3	72.1	65.3
% population 40-64	27.4	19.5	16.3	20.9
% population 64	11.7	13.2	11.7	13.9
% population 40 and over	39.0	32.7	27.9	34.7

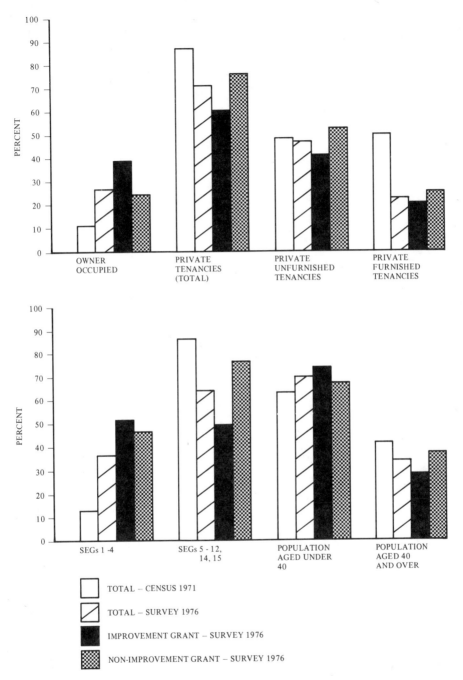

Figure 7.1   Changes in household tenure, housing characteristics,
             social composition and age structure,
             west London GIAs and HAAs, 1971-76

Table 7.2

Household tenure, housing characteristics,
social composition and age structure
Wormholt 1971 and 1976

Variable	Census 1971	Total Sample 1976	Improvement grant sample 1976	Non-improvement grant sample 1976
Household tenure				
% owner occupied	37.3	51.4	55.0	50.5
% private unfurnished tenancies	41.1	36.4	35.0	36.4
% private furnished tenancies	21.7	12.1	10.0	13.1
% private tenancies (total)	62.7	48.6	45.0	49.5
Housing characteristics				
% households sharing	10.5	5.8	10.0	4.0
% households at $> 1\frac{1}{2}$ persons per room	5.0	2.9	5.0	2.1
% dwellings without exclusive use of:				
hot water	6.1	7.2	5.0	8.1
bath/shower	6.2	13.0	10.0	14.1
inside W.C.	3.3	10.1	7.5	11.1
all three basic amenities	25.0	18.7	10.0	21.2
Social composition				
% economically active males (15-65) in:				
SEGs 1,2,3,4	4.6	21.7	28.6	18.8
SEGs 5-12,14,15	95.4	78.4	71.4	81.2
% households with a car	36.5	47.5	45.0	47.8
Age structure				
% population 5	6.6	2.9	1.7	3.5
% population 15	22.0	20.5	20.9	20.3
% population 20	28.9	28.7	33.0	26.8
% population 20-39	24.7	27.4	25.2	26.3
% population <40	53.6	56.1	58.3	53.2
% population 40-64	32.1	26.1	27.8	25.3
% population 64	14.3	17.8	13.9	19.5
% population 40 and over	46.4	43.9	41.7	44.8

It has been shown that in general, between 1971 and 1976, there were increases in (a) the proportion of owner occupied households: (b) the proportion of dwellings without basic amenities; and (c) the proportions of SEGs 1, 2, 3 and 4 and population under the age of 40. The tables also show that the proportions of privately rented accommodation were diminishing, that sharing and high occupancy rates were on the increase (accounting for the increase in dwellings without basic amenities), and that the proportions of SEGs 5-12, 14 and 15, and population aged 40 and over were on the decline. The substantial changes which occurred within the GIAs and HAAs, 1971-76, were already generally and gradually taking place between 1966-71 in the wards in which the declared areas were wholly or mainly located - Brook Green (Masbro Road GIA), Sandford (Moore Park GIA), Pembridge (Colville-Tavistock GIA), Harrow Road (Lanhill-Marylands GIA), Carlton (Malvern Road GIA), Coningham (Coningham Road GIA) and Pembridge (Tavistock HAA).

Taking Brook Green and Masbro Road as examples, and specifying firstly the percentage change for all households/dwellings 1966-71, and secondly the percentage change for improvement grant households/dwellings 1971-76, it can be seen from Table 7.3 and illustrated by Fig.7.2 that ownership of occupied households increased by 37.7 and 323.6 per cent respectively, economically active males in SEGs 1, 2, 3 and 4 increased by 38.1 and 475.0 per cent, and population aged under 40 increased by 3.6 and 27.8 per cent. It is also evident from Table 7.3 and from Fig.7.3 that households at more than 1.5 persons per room increased by 5.0 and 29.0 per cent, dwellings without exclusive use of hot water decreased by 17.3 and 67.7 per cent, and dwellings without a bath/shower decreased by 18.2 and 44.7 per cent. Although dwellings without an inside W.C. decreased by 46.2 per cent, 1966-71, there was an increase of 19.3 per cent, 1971-76, possibly due to conversion into smaller units. This was the only exception to the accelerated continuation of trends apparent in the ward, 1966-71. Other variables shown in Table 7.1 generally changed in the same direction throughout the period 1966-76. It was found that other wards, GIAs and HAAs followed much the same pattern of change as Brook Green and the Masbro Road GIA.

In most of the areas, increases and decreases (1971-76) in each variable were accentuated where improvement grant households or dwellings were involved. With owner occupier households, SEGs 1, 2, 3 and 4, and population aged under 40, proportions increased at the greatest rate in improvement grant properties. With households at more than 1.5 persons per room and dwellings lacking basic amenities, the greatest increase (or lowest decrease) was found in non-improvement grant properties.

COMPARISONS OF REHABILITATION IN THE GIAs, HAAs AND WORMHOLT, 1971-76

An attempt was made to compare the relationship between grant approvals and economic and social variables in the declared areas and Wormholt.

Table 7.4 shows that by 1976 only Moore Park and Masbro Road had greater percentages (86.7 and 78.6) of owner occupied households than Wormholt. Conversely, these GIAs were the only two areas with percentages of private tenants less than Wormholt. Fig.7.4 illustrates the comparative changes in these main forms of tenure which occurred between 1971-76. Table 7.4 indicates that by 1976 Malvern Road and Coningham Road were the two areas with the highest proportion of private unfurnished tenancies (100.0 and 67.8 per cent respectively) and Colville-Tavistock and Tavistock were the

Table 7.3

Household tenure, housing characteristics,
social composition and age structure,
Brook Green 1966 and 1971

Variable	1966	1971	% change 1966-71
Household tenure			
% owner occupied	13.0	17.9	+37.7
% private unfurnished tenancies	51.0	39.5	-22.5
% private furnished tenancies	36.0	42.6	+18.3
% private tenancies (total)	87.0	82.1	- 5.6
Housing characteristics			
% households 1½ persons per room	6.0	6.3	+ 5.0
% dwellings without exclusive use of:			
hot water	13.9	11.5	-17.3
bath/shower	14.3	11.7	-18.2
inside W.C.	13.0	7.0	-46.2
Social composition			
% economically active males (15-65) in:			
SEGs 1,2,3,4	13.9	19.2	+38.1
SEGs 5-12, 14,15	86.1	80.8	- 6.2
% households with a car	24.9	27.2	+ 9.2
Age structure			
% population 20-39	39.5	40.2	+ 1.8
% population 40	55.9	57.9	+ 3.6
% population 40-64	14.5	13.1	- 9.7
% population 40 and over	44.3	42.1	- 5.0

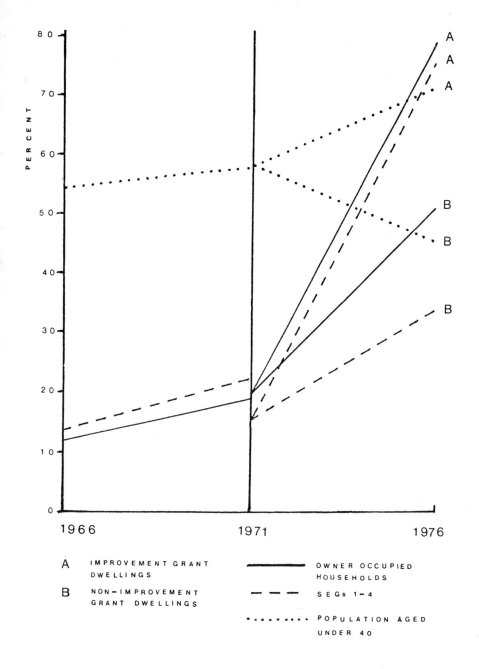

Figure 7.2   Changes in household tenure, social composition and
structure, Brook Green 1966-71 and
Masbro Road GIA, 1971-76

179

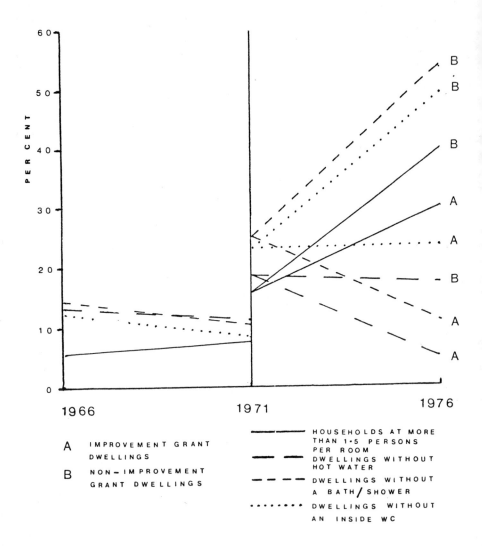

Figure 7.3   Changes in housing characteristics, Brook Green 1966-71
and Masbro Road GIA, 1971-76

Table 7.4

Household tenure, 1971 and 1976

(a) Owner occupied

	1971	1976 A	1976 B
Moore Park	30.3	86.7	47.1
Masbro Road	18.6	78.6	50.0
Wormholt*	37.3	55.0	50.5
Tavistock	6.9	38.5	36.6
Colville-Tavistock	6.2	21.4	7.4
Coningham Road	18.0	19.4	13.7
Lanhill-Marylands	5.6	12.5	12.3
Malvern Road	11.2	0.0	15.4
W.London GIAs	12.2	48.3	23.2
W.London GIAs & HAAs	11.8	38.5	23.5

Private tenancies

	1971	1976 A	1976 B
Malvern Road	88.8	100.0	83.3
Lanhill-Marylands	94.4	87.5	87.7
Coningham Road	82.0	80.7	86.3
Colville-Tavistock	93.8	78.6	92.6
Tavistock	93.1	61.5	63.5
Wormholt*	62.7	45.0	49.5
Masbro Road	81.5	21.4	50.0
Moore Park	69.7	13.3	53.0
W.London GIAs	87.8	51.7	78.8
W.London GIAs & HAAs	88.2	61.5	76.5

(b) Private unfurnished tenancies

	1971	1976 A	1976 B
Malvern Road	63.1	100.0	83.3
Coningham Road	59.7	67.8	64.7
Lanhill-Marylands	49.2	62.5	50.8
Wormholt*	41.1	35.0	36.4
Tavistock	52.0	30.8	34.2
Colville-Tavistock	46.3	28.6	63.0
Masbro Road	42.7	14.3	37.0
Moore Park	52.6	0.0	29.4
W.London GIAs	48.6	28.3	50.3
W.London GIAs & HAAs	48.8	40.4	50.6

Private furnished tenancies

	1971	1976 A	1976 B
Colville-Tavistock	47.5	50.0	29.6
Tavistock	41.1	30.8	29.3
Lanhill-Marylands	45.2	25.0	36.9
Moore Park	17.4	13.3	23.5
Coningham Road	22.3	12.9	21.6
Wormholt*	21.7	10.0	13.1
Masbro Road	38.8	7.1	13.3
Malvern Road	25.7	0.0	0.0
W.London GIAs	39.1	23.3	26.5
W.London GIAs & HAAs	39.4	21.2	25.9

A Improvement grant households   B Non-improvement grant households   * control area

Source: Census 1971, Writer's sample survey

181

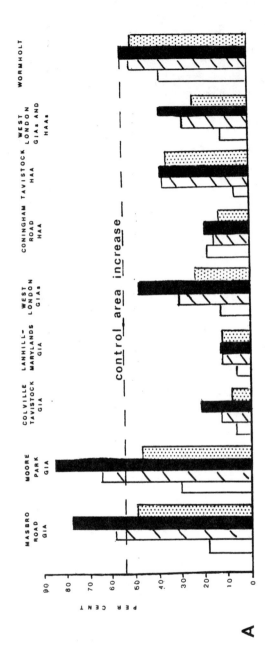

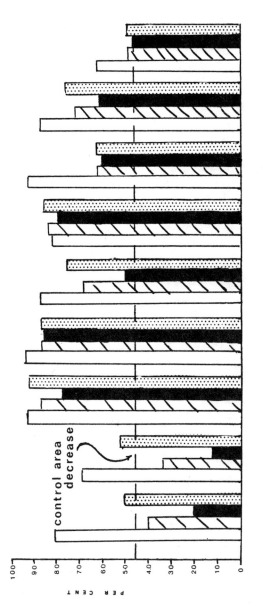

B

PER CENT

control area
decrease

Total (Census) 1971
Total (survey) 1976
Improvement grant (survey) 1976
Non–improvement grant (survey) 1976

Figure 7.4   Changes in household tenure, west London GIAs and HAAs, and Wormholt, 1971–76

183

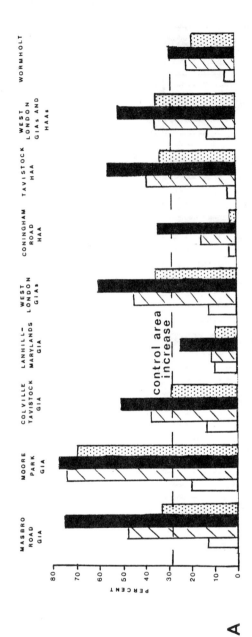

A

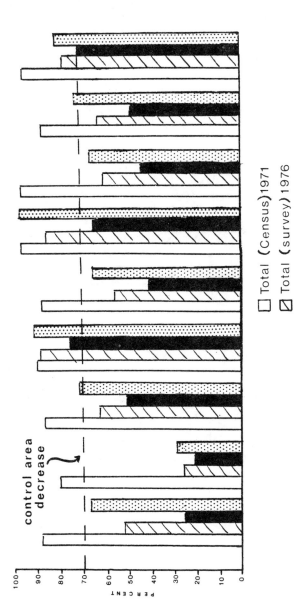

Figure 7.5   Changes in social composition, west London GIAs and HAAs, and Wormholt, 1971–76

185

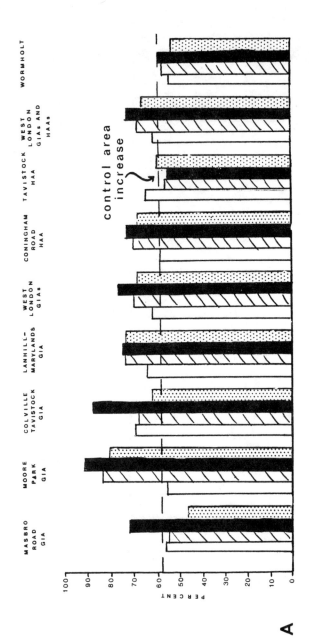

A

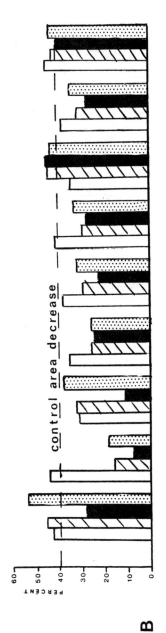

B

PERCENT

60 — 50 — 40 — 30 — 20 — 10 — 0

control area decrease

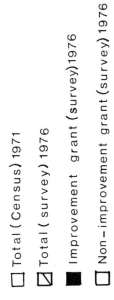

☐ Total (Census) 1971

▨ Total (survey) 1976

■ Improvement grant (survey) 1976

☐ Non-improvement grant (survey) 1976

Figure 7.6   Changes in age structure, west London GIAs and HAAs, and Wormholt, 1971–76

two areas with the highest proportion of private furnished tenancies (50.0 and 30.8 per cent).

Table 7.5 shows that by 1976 (except for Malvern Road) all the GIAs and HAAs had higher levels of households sharing and households at more than 1.5 persons per room than Wormholt; Lanhill-Marylands and Coningham Road for example having 58.3 and 27.8 and 58.1 and 27.0 per cent respectively. Approximately half of the declared areas had higher proportions of dwellings without basic amenities than Wormholt (Table 7.5). Lanhill-Marylands had the highest proportion of dwellings without hot water (16.7 per cent), bath/shower (33.4 per cent) and an inside W.C. (41.7 per cent).

It is evident from Table 7.6a that by 1971 most of the declared areas had higher proportions of economically active males in SEGs 1, 2, 3 and 4 than Wormholt; Moore Park and Masbro Road having the highest levels at 78.6 and 75.0 per cent respectively. Conversely, only Malvern Road (100.0 per cent) and Lanhill-Marylands (75.0 per cent) had higher proportions of SEGs 5-12 and 14, 15 than Wormholt. Fig.7.5 illustrates the comparative changes which occurred between 1971-76. Table 7.6b shows that by 1976 all the declared areas, except for Tavistock, exceeded Wormholt in the proportion of their population aged under 40; Malvern Road and Moore Park being the two areas with the highest levels, 100.0 and 91.7 per cent. Conversely, only Tavistock had a proportion of population – 45.2 per cent – aged 40 and over, greater than that of Wormholt. Fig.7.6 illustrates the comparative changes in these main age categories, 1971-76.

Table 7.6c shows that all the declared areas had greater proportions of population in the age group 20-39 than Wormholt; Colville-Tavistock and Moore Park having the highest levels – 75.0 and 66.7 per cent. Tavistock and Masbro Road (32.3 and 18.4 per cent) had the highest proportions of population aged 40-64.

Moore Park and Masbro Road (and particularly the former) were shown by ranking to be the principal areas in which there were the greatest absolute increases in owner occupied households, SEGs 1, 2, 3 and 4, and population aged under 40. Lanhill-Marylands was shown to be the main area of sharing households, high occupancy rates and dwellings without basic amenities, and it had the second highest proportion of private tenancies; Tavistock was notable for its high proportion of population aged 40 and over.

Table 7.7 details the percentage change of each variable in each area. Taking improvement grant properties, gentrification in the GIAs and HAAs is marked by SEGs 1, 2, 3 and 4, owner occupation and population aged under 40 increasing by 330.7, 226.5 and 19.8 per cent respectively, and by dwellings without hot water decreasing by 52.1 per cent. Conversely, shared households and dwellings without an inside W.C. and without a bath/shower increased by 124.0, 102.2 and 34.6 per cent, while SEGs 5-12, 14, 15, private tenancies and population aged 40 and over decreased by 45.4, 30.2 and 28.5 per cent.

These changes were found generally in each of the GIAs and HAAs and also, but to a different extent, in properties not subject to grant approval, for example in Colville-Tavistock, owner occupation increased less in non-grant properties than in improvement grant properties (19.1

188

Table 7.5

Housing Characteristics, 1971 and 1976

(a)

	Households sharing			1½ persons per room			Dwellings without an inside W.C.		
	1971	1976 A	1976 B	1971	1976 A	1976 B	1971	1976 A	1976 B
Lanhill-Marylands	20.7	58.3	49.0	17.0	27.8	25.0	6.2	41.7	41.2
Coningham Road	33.6	58.1	54.9	10.8	27.6	27.1			
Tavistock	28.5	46.2	41.5	13.1	23.1	19.0			
Colville-Tavistock	11.0	35.7	44.4	13.6	15.4	21.8			
Masbro Road	15.5	28.6	37.9	11.1	14.3	20.0			
Moore Park	13.5	20.0	29.4	1.8	7.1	13.3			
Wormholt*	10.5	10.0	4.0	5.0	5.0	2.2			
Malvern Road	36.3	0.0	33.3	17.5	0.0	16.7			
W.London GIAs	15.6	38.8	47.1	11.9	16.7	21.5			
W.London GIAs & HAAs	20.6	46.2	47.9	11.8	20.6	22.2			

Dwellings without an inside W.C.

	1971	1976 A	1976 B
Lanhill-Marylands	6.2	41.7	41.2
Masbro Road	18.0	21.4	48.3
Coningham Road	9.5	9.7	13.7
Wormholt*	3.3	7.5	11.1
Moore Park	14.2	6.7	27.8
Malvern Road	6.4	0.0	0.0
Colville-Tavistock	6.4	0.0	100.0
Tavistock	7.4	0.0	43.9
W.London GIAs	10.0	24.5	45.4
W.London GIAs & HAAs	9.1	18.3	37.4

(b) Dwellings without hot water

	1971	1976 A	1976 B
Lanhill-Marylands	14.7	16.7	17.6
Coningham Road	22.1	7.1	17.2
Masbro Road	19.3	6.7	16.7
Colville-Tavistock	11.2	6.5	19.6
Moore Park	6.1	5.0	8.1
Wormholt*	6.1	0.0	24.4
Tavistock	8.6	0.0	33.3
Malvern Road	29.9	0.0	11.1
W.London GIAs	16.0	8.2	18.5
W.London GIAs & HAAs	13.6	6.5	19.9

Dwellings without bath/shower

	1971	1976 A	1976 B
Lanhill-Marylands	12.7	33.4	54.9
Coningham Road	14.5	19.4	37.3
Masbro Road	25.9	14.3	51.7
Wormholt*	6.2	10.0	14.1
Moore Park	26.1	6.7	27.8
Tavistock	7.0	0.0	43.9
Colville-Tavistock	8.2	0.0	100.0
Malvern Road	40.9	0.0	22.2
W.London GIAs	18.4	22.5	52.1
W.London GIAs & HAAs	15.2	20.4	46.9

Source: Census 1971,
Writer's Sample Survey 1976

189

Table 7.6

Social composition 1971 and 1976

(a)

SEGs 1,2,3 & 4

	1971	1976 A	1976 B
Moore Park	20.4	78.6	71.4
Masbro Road	13.0	75.0	33.3
Tavistock	3.4	55.6	33.3
Colville-Tavistock	13.6	50.0	29.4
Coningham Road	3.0	34.8	2.7
Wormholt*	4.6	28.6	18.8
Lanhill-Marylands	10.5	25.0	9.1
Malvern Road	13.5	0.0	14.3
W.London GIAs	12.9	60.0	35.1
W.London GIAs & HAAs	12.1	52.0	35.3

SEGs 5-12, 14 & 15

	1971	1976 A	1976 B
Malvern Road	86.5	100.0	85.7
Lanhill-Marylands	89.5	75.0	90.0
Wormholt*	95.4	71.4	81.2
Coningham Road	97.0	65.2	97.3
Colville-Tavistock	86.4	50.0	70.6
Tavistock	96.6	44.4	66.7
Masbro Road	87.0	25.0	66.7
Moore Park	79.8	21.4	28.6
W.London GIAs	87.1	40.0	64.9
W.London GIAs & HAAs	87.9	48.1	73.9

(b) Age structure 1971 and 1976

Population < 40

	1971	1976 A	1976 B
Malvern Road	65.6	100.0	75.8
Moore Park	55.9	91.7	80.6
Colville-Tavistock	69.0	87.5	61.7
Lanhill-Marylands	63.6	74.3	73.7
Coningham Road	57.5	72.8	68.7
Masbro Road	55.6	71.1	45.1
Wormholt*	53.6	58.3	53.2
Tavistock	63.0	54.8	59.5
W.London GIAs	61.2	76.1	67.3
W.London GIAs & HAAs	60.2	72.1	65.3

Population > 40

	1971	1976 A	1976 B
Tavistock	37.0	45.2	44.9
Wormholt*	46.4	41.7	44.8
Masbro Road	43.8	28.9	54.9
Coningham Road	42.5	22.2	33.3
Lanhill-Marylands	31.0	12.5	38.3
Colville-Tavistock	31.0	12.5	38.3
Moore Park	44.5	8.3	19.4
Malvern Road	34.2	0.0	24.2
W.London GIAs	38.2	23.9	32.7
W.London GIAs & HAAs	39.6	27.9	34.7

(c) Age structure 1971 and 1976

Population 20-39

	1971	1976 A	1976 B
Colville-Tavistock	44.0	75.0	34.6
Moore Park	37.7	66.7	50.0
Masbro Road	35.0	50.0	31.0
Malvern Road	30.2	50.0	45.5
Coningham Road	26.9	47.8	29.6
Tavistock	37.9	41.9	30.3
Lanhill-Marylands	37.2	37.1	43.6
Wormholt*	24.7	25.2	26.3
W.London GIAs	37.2	51.3	40.5
W.London GIAs & HAAs	35.6	48.8	36.8

Population 40-64

	1971	1976 A	1976 B
Tavistock	25.9	32.3	33.7
Masbro Road	31.1	18.4	33.8
Coningham Road	29.4	16.3	14.8
Lanhill-Marylands	24.9	14.3	12.2
Wormholt*	14.3	13.9	19.5
Moore Park	27.7	8.3	19.4
Colville-Tavistock	33.9	4.2	24.7
Malvern Road	25.7	0.0	9.1
W.London GIAs	26.6	12.0	19.6
W.London GIAs & HAAs	11.7	11.7	13.9

Source: Census 1971
Writer's Sample Survey

Table 7.7

Changes in household tenure, housing characteristics, social composition and age structure 1971-76 (%)

Variable		Masbro Road	Moore Park	Colville-Tavistock	Lanhill-Marylands	Malvern Road	West London GIAs	Coningham Road	Tavistock	West London GIAs & HAAs	Wormholt
Household tenure											
Owner occupied	A	+323.6	+186.4	+244.5	+122.4	+100.0	+295.6	+ 7.5	+458.2	+226.5	+ 47.3
	B	+169.5	+ 55.5	+ 19.1	+118.9	+ 37.0	+ 89.7	- 23.7	+430.9	+ 99.2	+ 35.5
Private tenancies	A	- 73.7	- 80.9	- 16.2	- 7.3	+ 12.7	- 41.2	- 1.7	- 33.9	- 30.2	- 28.4
	B	- 38.9	- 24.1	- 1.3	- 7.1	- 6.1	- 12.5	+ 6.2	- 31.9	- 13.2	- 21.1
Housing characteristics											
Households sharing	A	+ 84.3	+ 48.5	+224.9	+181.9	-100.0	+120.8	+ 72.8	+ 62.2	+124.0	- 4.3
	B	+144.7	+118.8	+304.4	+136.9	- 8.2	+170.0	+ 63.4	+ 45.7	+131.9	- 61.3
Dwellings without hot water	A	- 67.7	- 65.5	-100.0	+ 13.5	-100.0	- 48.9	- 42.4	-100.0	- 52.1	- 18.0
	B	- 21.9	- 13.7	+289.4	+ 20.2	- 62.9	+ 15.6	+ 75.0	+302.5	+ 46.3	+ 32.5
Dwellings without a bath/shower	A	- 44.8	- 74.5	-100.0	+162.9	-100.0	+ 22.3	+ 55.1	-100.0	+ 34.6	+ 61.3
	B	+100.1	+ 6.4	+1125.5	+ 22.0	- 45.7	+183.9	+198.5	+526.2	+209.4	+128.1
Dwellings without an inside W.C.	A	+ 19.3	- 53.0	-100.0	+577.4	-100.0	+143.4	- 0.7	-100.0	+102.2	+127.3
	B	+168.8	- 96.0	+1469.9	+569.6	-100.0	+351.0	+ 41.0	+491.6	+313.2	+236.7
Social composition											
SEGs 1,2,3 & 4	A	+475.2	+285.0	+266.6	+138.1	-100.0	+363.7	+1047.9	+1538.6	+330.7	+521.1
	B	+155.6	+250.0	+115.6	+ 13.4	- 17.8	+170.9	- 10.9	+883.2	+192.6	+309.6
SEGs 5-12, 14,15	A	- 71.3	- 73.1	- 42.1	- 16.2	+ 15.6	- 50.1	- 32.7	- 54.0	- 45.6	- 25.1
	B	- 23.3	- 64.1	- 18.3	+ 1.6	- 22.9	- 25.4	+ 0.3	- 31.0	- 16.0	- 14.9
Age structure											
Population < 40	A	+ 27.8	+ 64.1	+ 26.8	+ 16.8	+ 52.3	+ 23.2	+ 26.7	- 13.0	+ 19.8	+ 8.7
	B	- 18.9	+ 44.2	- 10.5	+ 15.9	+ 15.4	+ 9.0	+ 19.5	- 5.5	+ 8.5	- 0.8
Population 40 and over	A	- 33.9	- 81.3	- 59.7	- 26.6	-100.0	- 37.4	- 36.1	+ 22.2	+ 28.5	- 10.0
	B	+ 25.5	- 56.3	+ 23.4	- 25.0	- 29.1	- 14.5	- 21.7	+ 21.6	- 11.0	- 3.4

A Improvement grant properties   B Non-improvement grant properties

compared with 244.5 per cent) but dwellings lacking inside W.Cs increased by 1469.9 per cent whereas in grant properties there was a decrease of 100.0 per cent.

Wormholt followed much the same pattern as the GIAs and HAAs in total. Although there was a larger percentage increase in SEGs 1, 2, 3 and 4 in Wormholt, there was a lower rate of increase in owner occupation and population under the age of 40. Although sharing diminished (in contrast to the GIAs and HAAs), there was a lower rate of decrease in dwellings without hot water and a higher rate of increase of dwellings without a bath/shower or an inside W.C. There were lower rates of decrease in the proportions of private tenancies, SEGs 5-12, 14, 15 and population aged 40 and over. In general, Wormholt was 'gentrified' to a lesser extent than the declared areas.

COMPARATIVE RATES OF GENTRIFICATION AS INDICATED BY A REHABILITATION-NEED INDEX (RNI) AND A REHABILITATION-REALISATION INDEX (RRI)

In an attempt to indicate both the relationship between the areal pattern of improvement grant approvals and selected variables within the GIAs, HAAs and Wormholt and the rate of change in these variables, 1971-76, a RNI and RRI were formulated for 1971 and 1976 and the percentage differences between the two years were calculated. The 1971 Census and 1976 sample survey provided for every enumeration district (ED) information on household tenure, sharing of dwellings, the provision of basic amenities (hot water, bath/shower, an inside W.C.), socio-economic groups, car ownership and the age of the population. The ten indicators of rehabilitation-need were the same as those used in Chapter 6, and the method of calculating the index was also, the same. The index ranged from 61,092 - 91,678 (1971) and from 43,430 - 105,936 (1976).

Table 7.8 sets out the means, sum of means (less indicator mean) and weights which governed the calculation of the index. Table 7.9 shows the RNI for 1971 and 1976, with areas arranged in rank order. It is evident that the improvement grant sample scored a lower RNI than the non-grant sample implying that in the former, grants were associated with a greater degree of rehabilitation and related social change, while in the latter the lack of grants impeded these changes. It is notable that the index of both the improvement grant and non-grant samples showed that the areas in order of greatest need were the same: Lanhill-Marylands, Colville-Tavistock, Coningham Road and Tavistock. Of the seven declared areas, five had indices higher than that of the control area.

Table 7.10 and Fig.7.7 show the percentage changes in the RNIs, 1971-76. Except for Lanhill-Marylands (where there was an increase) the indices for the improvement grant sample decreased, Masbro Road and Moore Park showing the greatest rates of decrease (55.7 and 47.7 per cent respectively). But the index for the non-grant sample generally increased - the GIAs and HAAs together showing an increase of 4.8 per cent, and Coningham Road, Lanhill-Marylands and Colville-Tavistock showing increases of 25.9, 18.5 and 17.1 per cent.

RRIs are used to show more positively that, within the GIAs, HAAs and Wormholt, there was a relationship between the approval of grants, house improvement and associated social change. Using data from the 1971

Table 7.8

Rehabilitation-Need indices, 1971 and 1976 -- Variables, means, sums of means and weighting

	Variable	Mean		Sum of means less indicator mean		Weight
		1971	1976	1971	1976	
Household tenure	1 Furnished private tenancies	32.5	20.2	256.9	274.9	3
	2 Households sharing	21.2	35.7	268.1	259.3	1
	3 Households at more than 1.5 persons per room	11.0	17.4	278.3	277.7	1
Housing characteristics	4 Dwellings without hot water	14.7	13.1	274.6	282.0	0.33
	5 Dwellings without a bath/shower	17.4	36.7	271.9	258.4	0.33
	6 Dwellings without an inside WC	8.9	30.3	280.4	264.8	0.33
	7 SEGs 5-12, 14, 15	89.7	67.4	199.6	227.7	2
Social composition and age structure	8 Households without a car	74.0	53.7	215.3	241.4	0.33
	9 Population under the age of 5	8.1	7.9	281.2	287.2	0.33
	10 Population 65 years of age and over	11.7	12.7	277.6	282.3	0.33

Table 7.9

Rehabilitation-Need indices, 1971 and 1976

Census data 1971		Total sample 1976	
Lanhill-Marylands	91,678	Lanhill-Marylands	105,936
Tavistock	91,558	Colville-Tavistock	98,830
Colville-Tavistock	87,357	Coningham Road	88,673
Masbro Road	85,063	Tavistock	82,960
Malvern Road	83,338	Malvern Road	60,897
Coningham Road	78,279	Masbro Road	60,463
Wormholt*	66,954	Wormholt*	56,766
Moore Park	61,092	Moore Park	43,430
W.London GIAs	84,742	W.London GIAs	78,471
W.London GIAs & HAAs	79,703	W.London GIAs & HAAs	76,446

Improvement grant sample 1976		Non-improvement grant sample 1976	
Lanhill-Marylands	93,415	Lanhill-Marylands	108,616
Colville-Tavistock	83,130	Colville-Tavistock	102,300
Coningham Road	72,636	Coningham Road	98,518
Tavistock	69,479	Tavistock	87,050
Malvern Road	55,870	Masbro Road	72,408
Wormholt*	52,569	Wormholt*	58,693
Masbro Road	37,723	Moore Park	53,651
Moore Park	31,979	Malvern Road	52,590
W.London GIAs	62,754	W.London GIAs	86,140
W.London GIAs & HAAs	62,278	W.London GIAs & HAAs	83,495

* Control area

Table 7.10

Changes in Rehabilitation-Need Indices, 1971-76

	% change total Index 1971-76		% change Improvement grant index 1971-76		% change Non-improvement grant index 1971-76
Masbro Road	-28.9	Masbro Road	-55.7	Malvern Road	-36.9
Moore Park	-28.9	Moore Park	-47.7	Masbro Road	-14.9
Malvern Road	-26.9	Malvern Road	-33.0	Wormholt*	-12.3
Wormholt*	-15.2	Tavistock	-24.1	Moore Park	-12.2
Tavistock	- 9.4	Wormholt*	-21.5	Tavistock	- 4.9
Colville-Tavistock	+13.1	Coningham Road	- 7.2	Colville-Tavistock	+17.1
Coningham Road	+13.3	Colville-Tavistock	- 4.8	Lanhill-Marylands	+18.5
Lanhill-Marylands	+15.6	Lanhill-Marylands	+ 1.9	Coningham Road	+25.9
W.London GIAs	- 7.4	W.London GIAs	-26.0	W.London GIAs	+ 1.7
W.London GIAs & HAAs	- 4.1	W.London GIAs & HAAs	-21.9	W.London GIAs & HAAs	+ 4.8

* Control area

Census and the 1976 sample survey, RRIs were calculated from nine indicators. These represented housing in good condition, and occupants probably able to afford to pay their share of improvement costs. The indicators are listed below:

Indicator 1	Owner occupiers
Indicator 2	Non-sharing households
Indicator 3	Households at less than 1.5 persons per room
Indicator 4	Dwellings with hot water
Indicator 5	Dwellings with bath/shower
Indicator 6	Dwellings with inside W.C.
Indicator 7	SEGs 1, 2, 3 and 4
Indicator 8	Households with a car
Indicator 9	Population aged 20-39

The subjective weightings were:

Indicator 1	3	.. ..	housing tenure
Indicator 2	1		
3	1		
4	0.33		
Indicator 5	0.33		
6	0.33	.. ..	housing characteristics
Indicator 7	2		
8	0.33		
9	0.66	.. ..	social composition and age structure

The methodology used for calculating the RRI is the same as for the RNI. Table 7.11 sets out the means, sum of means (less indicator mean) and weights which governed the calculation of the index. Table 7.12 shows the RRI for 1971 and 1976 with areas arranged in rank order. It is evident that the improvement grant sample gained a higher RRI than the non-grant sample, demonstrating that in the former sample rehabilitation and social change were causally related, while in the latter any house improvement and social change occurred without the assistance of grants. Taking the total and improvement grant samples, the areas of greatest rehabilitation by 1976 were Moore Park, Masbro Road and Wormholt. In the non-grant sample Masbro Road and Wormholt were transposed. Most GIAs and HAAs had indices lower than the control ward.

Table 7.13 and Fig.7.8 show the percentage changes in the RRIs, 1971-76. The changes of the total, improvement grant and non-grant indices all show that Moore Park, Masbro Road and Tavistock (but in a different order in each ranking) had the greatest increase in their scores, and Lanhill-Marylands, Coningham Road and Colville-Tavistock reduced their scores in the total and non-grant indices. Lanhill-Marylands also reduced its score in the grant sample. It was in the RRI of the grant sample that the GIAs and HAAs showed the greatest increase.

196

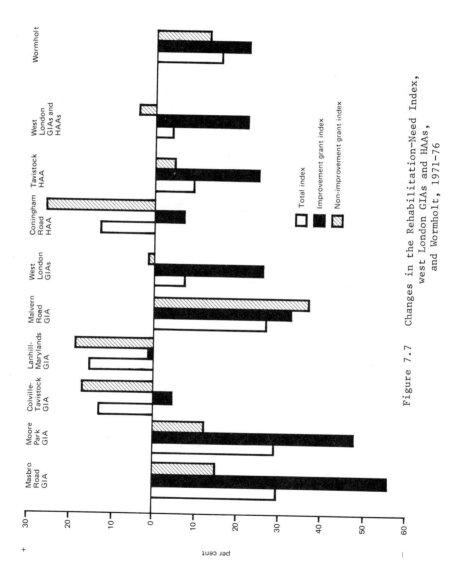

Figure 7.7   Changes in the Rehabilitation-Need Index,
west London GIAs and HAAs,
and Wormholt, 1971-76

Table 7.11

Rehabilitation-Need indices, 1971 and 1976 – Variables, means, sum of means and weighting

Variable	Mean		Sum of means less indicator mean		Weight
	1971	1976	1971	1976	
Household tenure					
1 Owner occupation	16.8	33.6	496.8	484.8	3
2 Non-sharing households	78.8	64.3	434.7	454.1	1
3 Households at less than 1.5 persons per room	88.7	82.6	424.8	435.8	1
Housing characteristics					
4 Dwellings with hot water	85.3	85.6	428.3	432.7	0.33
5 Dwellings with a bath/shower	82.6	63.4	431.0	455.0	0.33
6 Dwellings with an inside WC	91.1	69.7	442.5	448.7	0.33
Social composition and age structure					
7 SEGs 1,2,3 and 4	10.3	32.6	503.3	485.8	2
8 Households with a car	26.0	46.3	487.5	472.1	0.33
9 Population 20–39	34.1	40.3	479.5	478.0	0.66

Table 7.12

Rehabilitation-Realisation indices, 1971 and 1976

Census data 1971		Total sample 1976	
Moore Park	197,402	Moore Park	306,442
Wormholt*	191,544	Masbro Road	249,801
Masbro Road	163,458	Wormholt*	236,617
Colville-Tavistock	154,500	Tavistock	200,901
Coningham Road	148,574	Malvern Road	166,436
Lanhill-Marylands	141,061	Colville-Tavistock	150,027
Malvern Road	137,889	Coningham Road	141,262
Tavistock	135,103	Lanhill-Marylands	129,811
W.London GIAs	155,735	W.London GIAs	197,387
W.London GIAs & HAAs	150,730	W.London GIAs & HAAs	193,524

Improvement grant sample 1976		Non-improvement grant sample 1976	
Moore Park	354,045	Moore Park	266,518
Masbro Road	320,492	Wormholt*	232,958
Wormholt*	245,766	Masbro Road	213,705
Tavistock	232,413	Tavistock	191,007
Colville-Tavistock	220,679	Malvern Road	148,376
Coningham Road	172,506	Lanhill-Marylands	128,832
Malvern Road	148,575	Colville-Tavistock	123,498
Lanhill-Marylands	139,718	Coningham Road	121,237
W.London GIAs	253,315	W.London GIAs	172,438
W.London GIAs & HAAs	234,038	W.London GIAs & HAAs	182,705

* Control area

Table 7.13

Changes in Rehabilitation-Realisation indices, 1971-76

	% change total index 1971-76		% change Improvement grant index 1971-76		% change Non-improvement grant index 1971-76
Moore Park	+55.2	Masbro Road	+96.1	Tavistock	+41.4
Masbro Road	+52.8	Moore Park	+79.4	Moore Park	+35.0
Tavistock	+48.7	Tavistock	+72.0	Masbro Road	+30.7
Wormholt*	+23.5	Colville-Tavistock	+42.8	Wormholt*	+21.6
Malvern Road	+20.7	Wormholt*	+28.3	Malvern Road	+ 7.6
Colville-Tavistock	− 2.9	Coningham Road	+16.1	Lanhill-Marylands	− 8.7
Coningham Road	− 4.9	Malvern Road	+ 7.8	Coningham Road	−18.4
Lanhill-Marylands	− 8.0	Lanhill-Marylands	− 0.9	Colville-Tavistock	−20.1
W.London GIAs	+26.8	W.London GIAs	+62.7	W.London GIAs	+10.7
W.London GIAs & HAAs	+28.4	W.London GIAs & HAAs	+55.3	W.London GIAs & HAAs	+21.2

* Control area

200

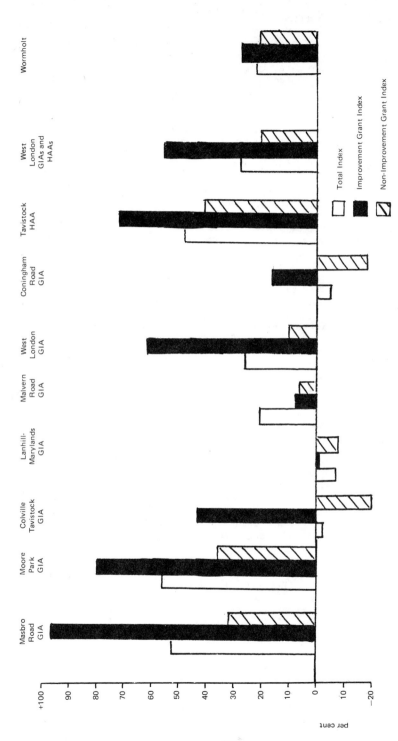

Figure 7.8   Changes in the Rehabilitation-Realisation Index, west London GIAs and HAAs, and Wormholt, 1971–76

201

LENGTH OF HOUSEHOLD RESIDENCE

In the sample survey, different numbers of residents gave information about their tenure, wages and salaries and socio-economic groups. In the GIAs and HAAs in aggregate, information was given by 340 householders regarding their tenure; 236 concerning their occupation and 167 about their wage or salary, the latter information being considered by many householders to be too confidential to divulge.

The length of household residence by tenure, gross wage or salary, and social composition in the declared areas and Wormholt are shown in Tables 7.14-15 and Fig.7.7. With minor exceptions, the highest proportion of households, wage and salary earners and economically active males who had been resident for only five years or less were found in improvement grant housing rather than in non-grant dwellings. In the GIAs and HAAs as a whole, 71.6, 83.3 and 80.5 per cent of households, wage and salary earners and economically active males respectively had moved into improvement grant housing within the five year period. In non-improvement grant housing the respective percentages were 54.6, 63.6 and 59.8 (Table 7.14).

Of the improvement grant households who had moved in during the period 1970-75, the majority were private furnished tenants followed by owner occupiers, the rest being private unfurnished tenants. Table 7.14 shows that in the GIAs and HAAs overall the respective percentages were 85.7, 73.7 and 62.8. The highest inflow of wage and salary earners were found among those earning £5,000 and over, £3,000 - £4,999 and £2,300 - £2,900, the percentages being 100.0, 87.5 and 95.0, and the highest inflow of economically active males (100.0 per cent) were those belonging to the SEGs 1, 2, 3 and 4. Within non-improvement grant housing the proportions were less in each instance.

Tables 7.14, 7.15 and 7.16 show that in general the GIAs and HAAs had a much greater proportion of new residents than the control ward, Wormholt. Within improvement grant properties, the GIAs and HAAs together, the GIAs and Wormholt had respectively 71.6, 68.9 and 52.5 per cent of households of five years or less, 83.3, 90.9 and 55.3 per cent of new wage and salary earners and 80.5, 78.3 and 65.5 per cent of new economically active males. As regards tenure, the GIAs and HAAs, GIAs and Wormholt had 85.7, 80.0 and 75.0 per cent of new households in private furnished accommodation, and 73.7, 77.8 and 59.0 per cent were owner occupied. With wages and salaries the differences were less marked, the GIAs and HAAs, GIAs and Wormholt all had 100.0 per cent of wage and salary earners of £5,000 and above becoming residents within the five year period; only in income categories below £5,000 were there lower proportions of new residents in Wormholt. Taking social composition, the GIAs and HAAs, GIAs and Wormholt had 100.0, 96.4 and 55.5 per cent of new economically active males in SEGs 1, 2, 3 and 4. Within the non-improvement grant properties, Wormholt similarly had smaller proportions of new residents, the percentages within the declared areas and Wormholt being generally lower.

Table 7.17 shows the percentages of households, wage and salary earners and economically active males beoming resident within each of the GIAs and HAAs, and Wormholt, 1970-75. The areas are ranked in descending order of the percentage of new residents in improvement grant housing. Moore Park is first in the ranking of households and economically active

Table 7.14

Length of household residence by tenure, gross wage/salary and social composition 1975-76
West London GIAs and HAAs

Variable	% Improvement grant sample — Years: 20	11-20	6-10	3-5	1-2	1	% 5 years & less	Total Nos.	% Non-improvement grant sample — Years: 20	11-20	6-10	3-5	1-2	1	% 5 years & less	Total Nos.
Household tenure																
Owner occupied	7.9	13.2	5.3	31.6	23.7	18.4	73.7	38	25.4	17.0	13.6	20.3	6.8	17.0	44.1	59
Private unfurnished tenancies	20.9	2.3	14.0	32.6	20.9	9.3	62.8	43	28.9	11.6	12.2	21.5	14.8	9.9	46.3	121
Private furnished tenancies	4.8	4.8	4.8	23.8	9.5	23.8	85.7	21	3.5	1.7	12.1	17.3	17.2	48.3	82.8	58
No. of households	13	7	9	31	25	17	71.6	102	52	25	31	48	32	50	54.6	238
Gross wage/salary £s p.a.																
5,000 & over				37.5	25.0	37.5	100.0	8				81.8	9.1	9.1	100.0	11
3,000-4,900			12.5	37.5	37.5	12.5	87.5	8	14.3		14.3	28.6	14.3	28.6	71.4	7
2,300-2,999			5.0	55.0	35.0	5.0	95.0	20	20.0	25.0	20.0	25.0	5.0	5.0	35.0	20
1,500-2,299		11.1	11.1	55.6	11.1	11.1	77.8	9	16.2	8.1	8.1	24.3	27.0	16.2	67.6	37
1,000-1,499	23.1	7.7	7.7	23.1	23.1	15.4	61.5	13	20.0	15.0	15.0	15.0	5.0	30.0	50.0	20
1,000			50.0	50.0			50.0	2	16.7			25.0	41.7	16.7	83.3	12
No. of wage/salary earners	3	2	5	21	21	8	83.3	60	17	11	11	31	19	18	63.6	107
Social composition																
SEGs 1,2,3 & 4				37.5	37.5	25.0	100.0	40	3.1	3.1	3.1	31.3	21.9	37.5	90.6	32
SEGs 5-12,14,15	13.5	13.5	10.8	32.4	21.6	8.1	62.2	37	17.3	13.4	17.3	18.9	14.2	18.9	52.0	127
No. of economically active males	5	5	5	27	23	12	80.5	77	23	18	23	34	25	36	59.8	159

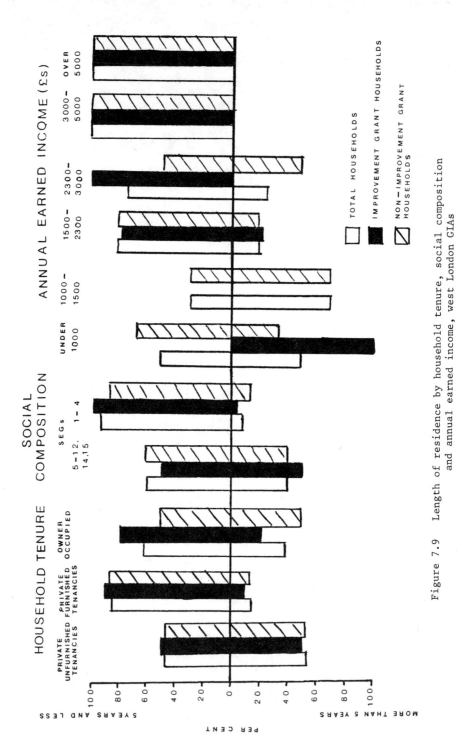

Figure 7.9   Length of residence by household tenure, social composition and annual earned income, west London GIAs

Table 7.15

Length of household residence by tenure, gross wage/salary and social composition 1975-76

West London GIAs

Variable	% Improvement grant sample								% Non-improvement grant sample							
	Years						% 5 years & less	Total Nos.	Years						% 5 years & less	Total Nos.
	20	11-20	6-10	3-5	1-2	1			20	11-20	6-10	3-5	1-2	1		
Household tenure																
Owner occupied	11.1	11.1		33.3	22.2	22.2	77.8	27	23.6	15.7	10.5	23.6	7.8	18.4	50.0	38
Private unfurnished tenancies	36.3	5.3	21.1	36.8	5.3	5.3	47.4	19	26.0	12.3	15.0	17.8	19.2	9.6	46.6	73
Private furnished tenancies	6.7	6.7	6.7	33.3	13.3	33.3	80.0	15	2.8		11.1	16.7	22.2	47.2	86.1	36
No. of households	9	5	5	21	9	12	68.9	61	29	15	19	28	25	31	57.1	147
Gross wage/salary £s p.a.																
5,000 & over				40.0	20.0	40.0	100.0	5				85.7		14.3	100.0	7
3,000-4,000				60.0	20.0	20.0	100.0	5				66.7		33.3	100.0	3
2,300-2,999				33.3	66.7		100.0	6	16.7	33.3		50.0			50.0	6
1,500-2,299			20.0	60.0		20.0	80.0	5	14.3		4.8	19.1	33.3	28.6	81.0	21
1,000-1,499									14.3	28.6	28.6			28.6	28.6	7
1,000			100.0					1	33.3			66.7			66.7	3
No. of wage/salary earners			2	10	6	4	80.9	22	6	4	3	17	7	10	72.3	47
Social composition																
SEGs 1,2,3 & 4			3.6	42.9	25.0	28.6	96.4	28	4.4	4.4	4.4	21.7	21.7	43.5	87.0	23
SEGs 5-12,14,15	11.1	22.2	16.3	33.3	5.6	11.1	50.0	18	15.8	7.9	15.8	18.4	17.1	25.0	60.5	76
No. of economically active males	2	4	4	18	8	10	78.3	46	13	7	13	19	18	29	66.7	99

Table 7.16

Length of household residence by tenure, gross wage/salary and social composition 1975-76

Wormholt

% Improvement grant sample

Variable	20	11-20	6-10 (Years)	3-5	1-2	1	% 5 years & less	Total Nos.
Household tenure								
Owner occupied	13.6	13.6	13.6	36.4	13.6	9.1	59.1	22
Private unfurnished tenancies	57.1	7.1		14.3		21.4	35.7	14
Private furnished tenancies	25.0				75.0		75.0	4
No. of households	12	4	3	10	6	5	52.5	40
Gross wage/salary £s p.a.								
5,000 & over				66.7	22.2	11.1	100.0	9
3,000-4,900			100.0				100.0	1
2,300-2,999	14.2	7.1	14.3	21.4	28.6	14.3	64.3	14
1,500-2,299	50.0		16.7			33.3	33.3	6
1,000-1,499	83.3	16.7						6
1,000	100.0							2
No. of wage/salary earners	12	2	3	10	6	5	55.3	38
Social composition								
SEGs 1,2,3 & 4			11.1	33.3	22.2	33.3	55.6	9
SEGs 5-12,14,15	25.0	10.0	10.0	30.0	10.0	15.0	55.0	20
No. of economically active males	5	2	3	9	4	6	65.5	29

% Non-improvement grant sample

Variable	20	11-20	6-10 (Years)	3-5	1-2	1	% 5 years & less	Total Nos.
Household tenure								
Owner occupied	22.9	27.1	14.6	18.8	10.4	6.3	27.1	48
Private unfurnished tenancies	42.1	26.3	18.4		7.9	5.3	13.2	38
Private furnished tenancies	9.1	9.1	27.3	9.1		45.5	54.6	11
No. of households	28	24	17	10	8	10	28.9	97
Gross wage/salary £s p.a.								
5,000 & over	10.0	20.0		30.0	20.0	20.0	70.0	10
3,000-4,900	30.0	30.0		20.0		10.0	40.0	10
2,300-2,999	15.4	30.8	38.4	7.7	7.7		15.4	13
1,500-2,299	26.1	34.8	8.7	13.0	13.0	4.4	30.4	23
1,000-1,499	52.0	20.0	12.0	4.0	4.0	8.0	16.0	25
1,000		100.0						1
No. of wage/salary earners	25	23	10	10	8	6	29.3	82
Social composition								
SEGs 1,2,3 & 4		44.4	11.1	11.1	22.2	22.2	55.6	9
SEGs 5-12,14,15	22.4	25.9	19.0	16.0	12.1	5.2	32.8	68
No. of economically active males	13	19	11	10	9	5	35.8	67

males, and second in the ranking of wage and salary earners. Coningham Road is second in the ranking of households and economically active males. Except for Malvern Road, Wormholt is last in each of the three rankings. In general, it is thus very evident that the declared areas received a much greater inflow of new residents in the period 1970-75 than the control area.

CHANGES IN RENT LEVELS, GROSS VALUES AND THE PROPORTION OF JURORS

An investigation of rents, gross values and jurors further indicates the extent to which rehabilitation and social change took place in the period following the Housing Act of 1969. Information is drawn from the Rent Officer registers, Rent Tribunal records and rating lists of the boroughs of Brent, Hammersmith, Kensington and Chelsea, and City of Westminster for the period 1969-74. In the analysis, all rents agreed or determined by the rent officers and Tribunals were recorded and used, but in the sample survey only the gross values of properties were used. The Electoral Registers for the years 1969-73 provided information about changes in the numbers of jurors in each area. By showing the letter J against their names, (and addresses) they showed those persons eligible for jury service. This practice ceased after 1973.

Rent levels

Although within the GIAs and HAAs in aggregate there had been a decrease in the proportion of private unfurnished tenancies with improvement grants (1971-76) there had been an increase in the proportion of both grant and non-grant unfurnished tenancies in Colville-Tavistock, Lanhill-Marylands, Malvern Road and Coningham, and in non-grant unfurnished tenancies in the declared areas as a whole. Demand for this accommodation remained buoyant and was only exceeded in total by the demand for owner occupied housing. Inflation raised the monetary level of this demand.

Table 7.18 shows that in the areas in which fair rents were established, improvement grant tenancies increased their mean rent level between 1969-74 at a greater rate than non-grant tenancies, in the GIAs and HAAs in aggregate the respective increases were 111.1 and 56.6 per cent. Grant tenancies in Moore Park and Masbro Road showed the greatest increase in mean fair rents, 144.0 and 134.0 per cent. There was little difference between increases in mean fair rents in the GIAs alone and GIAs and HAAs together, especially in respect of improvement grant tenancies, the increases being 111.4 and 111.1 per cent. This suggested that there was a relatively uniform level of demand throughout Inner West London. A comparison with Wormholt is difficult as information is incomplete, although the 4.4 per cent decrease, 1969-74, in the fair rents of non-grant tenancies possibly reflects a comparatively lower level of demand than in the declared areas.

In very few declared areas were the rents of furnished tenancies determined by Rent Tribunals in each year over the period 1969-74. In some areas there was an absence of Tribunal decision in 1969 and 1970. It is therefore not possible to show comparative changes in rent levels in each of the declared areas nor in Wormholt, but it is possible to calculate changes, however crudely, for the GIAs and HAAs in aggregate. Table 7.19 shows that between 1969-74 Tribunal mean rents of improvement grant furnished tenancies increased by 34.1 per cent and by 26.9 per cent

Table 7.17

The percentages of households, wage and salary earners and economically active males becoming resident within the west London GIAs and HAAs, 1970-75

Households

	A %	B %
Moore Park	85.7	80.0
Coningham Road	79.3	52.1
Masbro Road	71.4	33.3
Colville-Tavistock	69.2	60.7
Lanhill-Marylands	66.7	62.5
Tavistock	61.5	50.0
Wormholt*	52.5	28.9
Malvern Road	-	54.5
W.London GIAs	68.9	57.1
W.London GIAs & HAAs	71.6	54.6

Wage/salary earners

	A %	B %
Colville-Tavistock	100.0	86.7
Moore Park	100.0	75.0
Lanhill-Marylands	100.0	67.7
Masbro Road	88.9	50.0
Coningham Road	84.6	54.3
Tavistock	66.7	60.0
Wormholt*	55.3	29.3
Malvern Road	-	83.3
W.London GIAs	90.9	72.3
W.London GIAs & HAAs	83.3	63.0

Economically active males

	A %	B %
Moore Park	92.3	87.5
Coningham Road	86.4	48.6
Tavistock	77.8	48.0
Masbro Road	76.9	35.0
Lanhill-Marylands	75.0	66.7
Colville-Tavistock	70.0	75.0
Wormholt*	65.5	35.8
Malvern Road	-	85.7
W.London GIAs	78.3	66.7
W.London GIAs & HAAs	80.5	59.8

A - Improvement grant sample
B - Non-improvement grant sample
* Control area

Table 7.18

Changes in mean fair rents, 1969-74

Area	Types and number of tenancies and mean fair rent		1969	1970	1971	1972	1973	1974	% Change in MFR
Masbro Road	A	MFR	2.97	5.00	3.93	–	5.15	6.95	+134.0
		No.	5	1	2	–	3	5	
	B	MFR	3.88	3.25	4.58	4.06	4.76	4.75	+ 22.4
		No.	2	3	11	6	17	14	
Moore Park	A	MFR	2.00	–	–	–	5.28	4.88	+144.0
		No.	1	–	–	–	8	3	
	B	MFR	–	2.50	3.25	–	5.42	4.75	–
		No.	–	1	2	–	10	1	
Colville-Tavistock	A	MFR	3.66	1.50	4.00	5.23	5.61	6.22	+ 70.0
		No.	3	1	2	6	9	10	
	B	MFR	3.33	5.56	4.63	–	5.24	6.37	+ 91.3
		No.	3	4	3	–	19	17	
Lanhill-Marylands	A	MFR	3.75	5.25	4.06	5.88	5.63	7.23	+ 92.8
		No.	1	1	4	3	111	16	
	B	MFR	2.92	4.38	5.03	4.96	5.57	5.72	+ 95.9
		No.	3	4	6	6	154	19	
Westbourne Gardens	A	MFR	–	4.55	–	–	–	–	–
		No.	–	2	–	–	–	–	
	B	MFR	–	–	–	–	–	–	–
		No.	–	–	–	–	–	–	
Malvern Road	A	MFR	–	–	–	–	–	–	–
		No.	–	–	–	–	–	–	
	B	MFR	–	2.63	–	–	5.75	–	–
		No.	–	1	–	–	1	–	
West London GIAs	A	MFR	3.16	3.91	4.01	5.45	5.61	6.68	+111.4
		No.	10	3	8	9	131	34	
	B	MFR	3.31	4.25	4.59	4.51	5.49	5.65	+ 70.7
		No.	8	12	22	12	200	51	
Coningham Road	A	MFR	–	2.50	4.50	3.13	4.00	6.40	–
		No.	–	1	2	2	1	1	
	B	MFR	3.70	5.00	3.11	4.00	4.51	4.75	+ 28.4
		No.	6	3	9	1	18	6	
Tavistock	A	MFR	–	–	–	–	4.50	–	–
		No.	–	–	–	–	1	–	
	B	MFR	2.68	3.08	4.42	4.88	4.81	4.82	+ 79.9
		No.	2	3	3	2	15	7	
West London GIAs & HAAs	A	MFR	3.16	3.89	4.11	5.03	5.59	6.67	+111.1
		No.	10	6	10	11	133	35	
	B	MFR	3.50	4.10	4.18	4.52	5.35	5.48	+ 56.6
		No.	16	19	34	15	234	64	
Wormholt	A	MFR	–	–	–	–	4.45	5.13	–
		No.	–	–	–	–	9	2	
	B	MFR	5.00	4.56	5.30	5.15	4.84	4.78	- 4.4
		No.	2	2	5	12	98	25	

A   - Improvement grant tenancies
B   - Non-improvement grant tenancies
MFR - Mean Fair rent (£s)

Source: Rent Officers, London boroughs of Brent, Hammersmith,
Kensington & Chelsea and Westminster.

Table 7.19

Changes in mean rents, 1969-74
(as determined by Rent Tribunals)

		1969	1970	1971	1972	1973	1974	% increase in MR 1969-74
A	MR	7.64	6.77	6.93	6.34	7.00	10.24	+34.1
	No.	7	13	17	22	7	6	
B	MR	5.28	4.71	5.54	5.58	7.18	6.70	+26.9
	No.	14	26	30	52	63	20	

A Improvement grant tenancies
B Non-improvement grant tenancies
MR Mean Rent (£s)

Source: London boroughs of Brent, Hammersmith, Kensington & Chelsea and Westminster.

in cases of non-grant tenure.

Fig.7.10 illustrates that within the GIAs and HAAs rents generally increased over the period 1969-74. The mean rents of furnished accommodation were above the mean fair rents of unfurnished accommodation, and in both types of tenure rents were higher in improvement grant properties than in those not subject to grants.

Gross values

Gross values have been traditionally determined (albeit unsatisfactorily in recent years) in relation to rent levels, it was not therefore unexpected to find that, with the general increase in rents 1969-74, gross values also increased.

Table 7.20 shows that in the GIAs and HAAs in aggregate the mean gross value of improvement grant properties increased by 143.0 per cent and that of non-grant properties by 130.6 per cent. Moore Park showed the greatest increase in the mean gross value of grant properties, 200.4 per cent (although its lower valued non-grant properties increased by 207.1 per cent). Gross values in the GIAs generally increased at a greater rate than in the HAAs, and overall the GIAs and HAAs had larger percentage increases in mean gross value than Wormholt, although in Wormholt both grant and non-grant properties were more highly valued than in the GIAs overall and in the GIAs and HAAs in aggregate.

Jurors

Until 1973 most ratepayers were liable to be summoned to serve on a jury, provided that they were aged between 21 and 60, and owned and/or paid rates on property with a rateable value of at least £30 in Greater London (or £20 elsewhere). An increase in the proportion of owner occupied properties and the more expensive rented accommodation (where the tenant would probably have responsibility for rates) would increase the proportion of ratepayers eligible for jury service. Such an increase occurred in much of Inner West London between 1970-73.

Table 7.21 shows that within the GIAs in total, there was an increase in the proportion of jurors by 51.9 per cent in improvement grant properties and by 13.1 per cent in non-grant properties. The GIAs and HAAs in aggregate showed increases of 46.5 and 10.3 per cent. The three Hammersmith declared areas showed the greatest rates of increase. Taking improvement grant properties, Masbro Road, Moore Park and Coningham Road had increases of 115.4, 100.0 and 100.0 per cent, and taking non-grant properties the increases were 65.5, 62.2 and 55.3 per cent. There were large decreases in the number of jurors in Lanhill-Marylands and Colville-Tavistock which can only reflect the decrease in the proportion of ratepayers. Although, having a greater proportion of jurors than the GIAs and HAAs in aggregate, Wormholt showed a lower percentage increase in that proportion, 1970-73, reflecting a lower increase in owner occupiers and ratepaying tenants.

The relationship between the rates of increase in mean fair rents, gross values and change in the proportion of jurors is shown in Table 7.22. Moore Park and Masbro Road showed the two highest rates of increase in mean fair rents and the proportion of jurors, and Moore Park showed the greatest increase in gross values. Lanhill-Marylands and Colville-

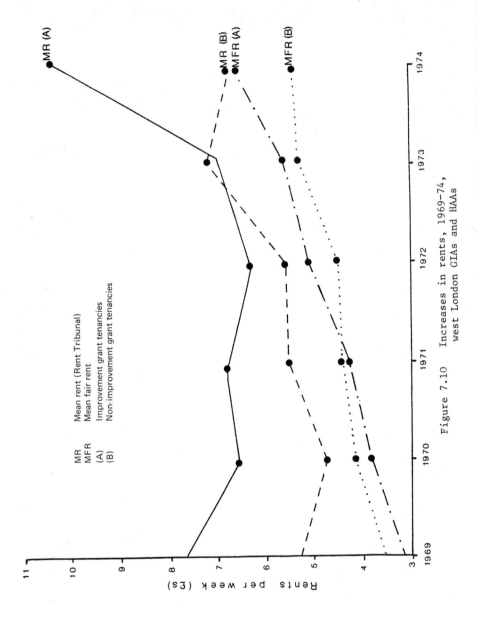

Figure 7.10 Increases in rents, 1969–74, west London GIAs and HAAs

MR   Mean rent (Rent Tribunal)
MFR   Mean fair rent
(A)   Improvement grant tenancies
(B)   Non-improvement grant tenancies

Table 7.20

Changes in mean gross values, 1969-74

Area	Types and number of dwellings and mean gross value	1969	1974	% increase in MGV 1969-74
Masbro Road	A MGV	156.66	335.33	+144.1
	No.	9	9	
	B MGV	156.05	319.80	+104.9
	No.	44	45	
Moore Park	A MGV	174.79	525.00	+200.4
	No.	14	16	
	B MGV	158.54	486.81	+207.1
	No.	37	37	
Colville-Tavistock	A MGV	208.29	486.29	+133.5
	No.	31	27	
	B MGV	196.68	380.12	+ 93.3
	No.	48	47	
Lanhill-Marylands	A MGV	104.77	265.15	+153.1
	No.	44	52	
	B MGV	116.80	279.65	+139.4
	No.	171	178	
Westbourne Gardens	A MGV	213.00	566.00	+165.7
	No.	2	4	
	B MGV	235.60	554.0	+135.1
	No.	10	16	
Malvern Road*	A MGV	83.06	197.17	+137.4
	No.	17	18	
	B MGV	121.77	288.04	+136.5
	No.	105	105	
West London GIAs	A MGV	152.32	376.98	+147.5
	No.	102	114	
	B MGV	143.17	334.25	+133.5
	No.	323	340	
Coningham Road	A MGV	200.60	479.60	+139.1
	No.	36	36	
	B MGV	177.60	358.40	+101.8
	No.	45	45	
Tavistock	A MGV	117.42	249.57	+112.5
	No.	7	7	
	B MGV	172.18	417.25	+142.3
	No.	53	55	

Table 7.20 Cont/...

Area	Types and number of dwellings and mean gross value	1969	1974	% increase in MGV 1969-74
West London GIAs & HAAs	A MGV	162.29	394.34	+143.0
	No.	145	157	
	B MGV	150.34	346.64	+130.6
	No.	421	440	
Wormholt	A MGV	191.3	421.6	+109.2
	No.	192	192	
	B MGV	173.30	394.3	+127.5
	No.	130	130	

A   - Improvement grant dwellings

B   - Non-improvement grant dwellings

MGV - Mean gross value (£s)

*   - 100% sample used.   Number divided by 10 for calculating West London data.

Source: London boroughs of Brent, Hammersmith, Kensington & Chelsea, and Westminster.

Table 7.21

Changes in the number and proportion of jurors, 1970 and 1973

Area	Types of dwelling, jurors as a % dwellings and number of jurors			1970	1973	% change in jurors 1970-73
Masbro Road	A	%		23.0	49.6	+115.4
		No.		35	56	
	B	%		13.9	23.0	+ 65.6
		No.		58	96	
Moore Park	A	%		16.7	33.3	+100.0
		No.		23	46	
	B	%		15.1	24.5	+ 62.2
		No.		45	73	
Colville-Tavistock	A	%		20.7	11.0	− 47.1
		No.		17	9	
	B	%		20.0	15.5	− 22.7
		No.		44	34	
Lanhill-Marylands	A	%		9.4	4.7	− 50.0
		No.		10	5	
	B	%		9.2	4.6	− 50.0
		No.		62	31	
Westbourne	A	%		15.0	20.0	+ 33.0
		No.		3	4	
	B	%		8.5	9.1	+ 5.9
		No.		17	18	
Malvern Road	A	%		−	−	−
		No.		−	−	
	B	%		2.6	6.0	+133.3
		No.		3	7	
West London GIAs	A	%		16.9	25.6	+ 51.9
		No.		79	120	
	B	%		12.7	14.3	+ 13.1
		No.		229	259	
Coningham Road	A	%		14.6	29.3	+100.0
		No.		6	12	
	B	%		19.5	29.9	+ 55.3
		No.		90	138	

Table 7.21 Cont/...

Area	Types of dwelling, jurors as a % dwellings and number of jurors			1970	1973	% change in jurors 1970-73
Tavistock	A	%		22.2	16.7	- 25.0
		No.		4	3	
	B	%		9.8	8.9	- 8.8
		No.		34	31	
West London	A	%		17.8	26.1	+ 46.5
		No.		99	145	
	B	%		17.6	19.4	+ 10.3
		No.		716	790	
Wormholt	A	%		22.9	31.4	+ 37.5
		No.		16	22	
	B	%		23.5	26.0	+ 10.4
		No.		453	500	

A - Improvement grant dwellings

B - Non-improvement grant dwellings

Source: Electoral Registers, London boroughs of Brent, Hammersmith, Kensington & Chelsea and Westminster.

Table 7.22

Changes in mean fair rents and gross values 1969–74 and jurors, 1970–73

Area	% increase in mean fair rents 1969–74
Moore Park	144.0
Masbro Road	134.0
Lanhill–Marylands	92.8
Colville–Tavistock	70.0
W.London GIAs	114.4
W.London GIAs & HAAs	111.1

Area	% increase in mean gross values 1969–74
Moore Park	200.4
Westbourne Gardens	165.7
Lanhill–Marylands	153.1
Masbro Road	144.1
Coningham Road	139.1
Malvern Road	137.4
Colville–Tavistock	133.5
Tavistock	112.5
Wormholt*	109.2
W.London GIAs	147.5
W.London GIAs & HAAs	143.0

Area	% change in jurors 1970–73
Masbro Road	+115.5
Moore Park	+100.0
Coningham Road	+100.0
Wormholt*	+ 37.5
Westbourne Gardens	+ 33.0
Tavistock	− 25.0
Colville–Tavistock	− 47.1
Lanhill–Marylands	− 50.0
W.London GIAs	+ 51.9
W.London GIAs & HAAs	+ 46.5

* Control area

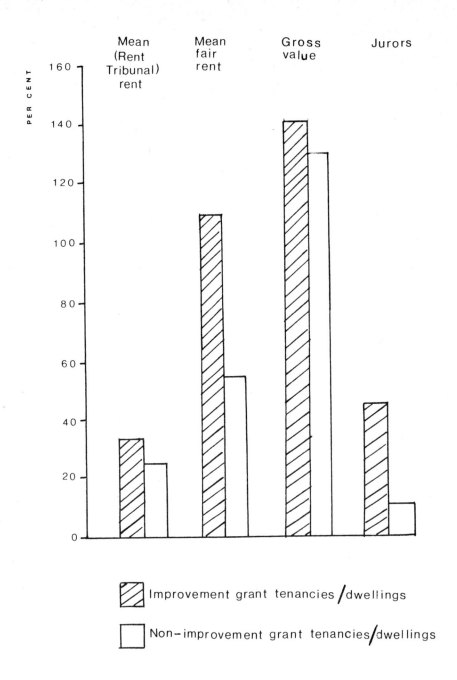

Figure 7.11   Increases in rents and gross values, 1969-74;
              and jurors, 1970-73, west London GIAs and HAAs

Tavistock showed the lowest rates of increase in mean fair rents and in reverse order showed a decrease in the percentage change in jurors. Of the declared areas, Colville-Tavistock and Tavistock showed the lowest increase in gross values. Referring to Tables 7.18, 7.19, 7.20 and 7.21 and to Fig.7.11, and taking improvement grant properties, it can be shown that in the GIAs and HAAs in aggregate, gross values, mean fair rents, the proportion of jurors and mean (Tribunal) rents increased by 143.0, 11.1, 46.5 and 34.1 per cent respectively. Taking non-grant properties the increases were less - 130.6, 56.6, 10.3 and 26.9 per cent.

FURTHER ASPECTS OF GENTRIFICATION WITHIN THE GIAs OF WEST LONDON

The foregoing suggest that the processes of gentrification (already apparent in the period 1966-71) continued into the period 1971-76, and at an accelerated rate. It was found that improvement grant housing was subject to the effects of gentrification to a considerably greater extent than those dwellings not receiving grants. Based on information derived from research undertaken within the GIAs by local authorities, other representative bodies and charities, and upon the findings of the writer's research (described earlier in this chapter), this section will deal further with some of the economic and social changes which have occurred within the GIAs, particularly Moore Park, Colville-Tavistock and Lanhill-Marylands.

Large increases in house prices and rents, and the social consequences of associated gentrification, was a major cause for concern. Contemporary evidence suggests that there were strong causal relationships between the distribution of improvement grants and economic and social change. The first example of this was in the Moore Park Road area of Hammersmith. The area was surveyed by the LCC in the 1950s and included in its Development Plan for redevelopment within the period 1960-72. Total redevelopment was to be phased as some of the area was worn out and out-moded whilst some was still of good quality. Up to May 1968, Hammersmith council had compulsorily acquired 40 per cent of the houses in the area, the purchase price probably being far lower than other similar sized properties in the vicinity, thus necessitating most of the households to move elsewhere. In 1966, the first phase of the redevelopment scheme (council housing on the western edge of the area) was commenced. Further redevelopment, however, was halted following the 1968 White Paper, Old houses into new homes and the Housing Act of 1969, which shifted the emphasis of housing policy from development or redevelopment towards the rehabilitation of the existing housing stock. In February 1970, Hammersmith council consequently declared the Moore Park area a GIA. At that time, the council owned 42 per cent of the 409 properties, the rest being privately owned.

During the 1960s, the social composition of the Moore Park area changed. Table 7.23 shows that between 1961 and 1966 the number of economically active males (as a proportion of the total population) in SEGs 1-4 decreased from 6.1 to 3.9 per cent. In the ward of Sandford (which contains the Moore Park area), the 1966 proportion was 8.0 per cent and in Hammersmith as a whole the proportion was 10.7 per cent. The Moore Park area was clearly suffering from blight and the higher socio-economic groups were leaving either compulsorily or voluntarily. The change in the policy of the council in declaring the GIA reversed this out migration. There was a sudden increase in demand from the upper income groups for

properties in the area.   This was probably not only due to the area
being declared a GIA, but also due to its 'prime' location (near Chelsea).

Table 7.23

Economically active males in the Moore Park GIA

Socio-Economic Groups	% economically active males		
	1961	1966	1971
1 - 4	6.1	3.9	20.4
5 - 17	93.9	96.1	79.6

Source: 1961, 1966 and 1971 Census

The diversion of demand away from other parts of the private housing
market (where scarcity and mortgage availability were accelerating price
increases) also contributed to an increase in demand for houses in the
GIA.   Rayner and Raynsford (1972) reported that as soon as proposals for
declaring the GIA became known, prices of houses in the Moore Park area
increased from £2,000 to £9,000, and to £12,000 by the time declaration
was made.   By January 1972 (two years later), prices had reached £16,000
for a 'two-up and two-down' property.   It is probable that the price of
four storey improved properties in the area at that time would have
greatly exceeded this amount.   As most of the residents of the area
(prior to the declaration of the GIA) consisted of the lower socio-economic
and income groups, it would have been very unlikely for them to have
purchased their dwellings from their local authority or private landlord.
The GLC's Family Expenditure Survey (1967) had shown that 79 per cent of
all employed men in Greater London had earnings of less than £30 per week
(£1,560 per annum).   On the assumption that mortgages were generally
granted at two and a half times an applicant's earnings, mortgage finance
would have been insufficient for those even at the top of that income level
to acquire the houses for sale in the GIA.   The displacement of the lower
socio-economic groups in consequence of their inability to compete for
housing within the GIA is indicated by Table 7.23.   In the period 1966-71,
SEGs 1-4 increased in proportion from 3.9 to 20.4 per cent in the Moore
Park area (compared with 10 per cent in Sandford and 14.3 per cent in the
borough), and all other SEGs decreased from 96.1 to 79.6 per cent.   In
order to reduce the pace of displacement, the newly elected Labour council
in 1971 stopped the sale of council owned houses in the GIA.   In accordance with the Housing Act of 1969, this was a decision intended to ensure
that improvement should benefit at least some of the households which were
resident in the GIA at the time of its declaration.

The Masbro Road area became Hammersmith's second GIA in March 1971.
Rayner and Raynsford estimated that house prices immediately increased in
the area from about £2,500 to £7,500 and in some cases increased fourfold
(March 1971 - January 1972).   They also reported that in both of
Hammersmith's GIAs:

    Residents of long standing .... were encouraged to quit, often
    by the dubious but legal offers of money (the going rate is

about £2000 in Moore Park Road and £1000 in Masbro for
vacant possession of a house... Occasionally there was
harassment and illegal eviction, the maximum penalties for
which are a £100 fine or six months imprisonment.   In one
case, in the Masbro Road area, a fine of £75 for harassment
was in fact obtained from the courts - even then hardly a
deterrent for someone who stood to make in excess of £2000
if the premises were vacated (p.76).

Within the GIAs, house prices continued to rise very rapidly, 1972-73,
and if the property had been rehabilitated, the increase was usually
much in excess of the cost of improvement work.   in giving evidence to
the House of Commons Expenditure Committee, 1973, Mr A.G. Babbage (House
Improvement Officer, London Borough of Hammersmith) stated that the
council was currently:

looking at cases where properties were sold in April (1972)
for £10,000; one of these has been improved .... and is
currently on the market for about £40,000.   We know that
the amount spent by the owner is not such that he is not
making a vast profit (paragraph 527).

Because of the above consequences of declaring GIAs,in November 1975 the
council used powers under the Housing Act of 1974 to declare a HAA
(rather than a GIA) in the Coningham Road area, one of the worst Housing
Problem Areas in Hammersmith.   The provisions of the Act (see Chapter 2)
made it less likely that harassment, displacement and socio-economic
change would occur in the Coningham Road HAA on the same scale as in the
GIAs in the early 1970s.

Within the Pembridge ward of North Kensington, the Colville-Tavistock
area was declared a GIA by the Kensington and Chelsea council on
28 October 1969.   A major problem of the area was the extent of multiple
occupation.   This at first deterred landlords from taking up improvement
grants.   Conversion into self contained flats (an aim of the council in
declaring the GIA) would have involved great expense and a smaller number
of rented dwellings.   To encourage owners to undertake repairs, provide
sanitary facilities and amenities and means of escape from fire, the
Housing Committee of the council approved a recommendation that (following
a systematic house-to-house inspection) appropriate notices should be
served to owners, under Section 9 of the Housing Act of 1957, and
Sections 14, 15 and 16 of the Housing Act of 1961.

The Colville Tavistock Study (1972) showed that this action, together
with the inflationary spiral of house values, resulted in the increase
in improvement and conversion works in 1971-72.   Substantial rent
increases resulted as grants covered only half the cost of improvement,
and many regulated unfurnished dwellings were converted into unregulated
furnished accommodation.   The study reported that this process:

can only be efficiently carried out with vacant possession...
Where houses have been intensively occupied by many families
sharing common facilities, a conversion into self-contained
and fully self-sufficient units must result in a reduction in
occupation (p.201).

The Notting Hill Peoples' Association Housing Group (1972) produced
further evidence of rent increases.   It showed that 40 per cent of the
study area (containing 738 houses) changed from being a 'low rent' to a
'high rent' area, and that 75 per cent of the 'high rent' dwellings were

conversions into luxury flats. Before conversion the average rents were
£4.80 and after conversion £14-£15. Some rents increased to £25. The
study reported that dwellings were also being converted into luxury leasehold and freehold properties. This not only further reduced the supply
of rented accommodation, but by being associated with rapidly rising
house prices in North Kensington, made it increasingly difficult for
housing associations to acquire properties to rehabilitate and let.
Kilroy (1972a) stated that:

> the rate of price increase of houses (in the area) is far above
> the national London or West London percentages, and threatens
> to halt housing associations' activity.

The higher rents and house prices resulting from conversion were almost
certainly beyond the means of most of the residents living in the GIA at
the time of declaration. The Colville Tavistock Study showed that 71
per cent of the incomes of heads of households were less than £30 per
week. The area contained a relatively small proportion of economically
active males in SEGs 1-4. According to the study, 13 per cent were in
this category compared with 21.1 per cent in Pembridge and 27.6 per cent
in the borough as a whole in 1971. As table 6.5 shows, however, by
1976 the proportion of this SEG in the Colville Tavistock GIA may have
increased to 37.0 per cent. As in the GIAs of Hammersmith, the result
of the influx of higher income households was the displacement of many
lower income residents.

Whilst it may have been thought in the past that North Kensington
contained a very high proportion of transient households, the study showed
that the Colville-Tavistock area:

> has a very high proportion of long standing residents. As
> long term residents, many have developed strong ties with
> the Area and should have the right to be allowed to remain
> to benefit from improvements that have been so long overdue
> (p.311).

The study's social survey was based on a 25.0 per cent property sample
(containing 1119 households) and had a response rate of 62 per cent.
When asked whether or not they would like to remain in North Kensington,
71 per cent of the respondents replied that they would like to stay and
40 per cent stated that they had relatives in the area. These findings
correspond very closely with the results of a GLC census in the Swinbrook
area of North Kensington, also taken in 1972. The area was scheduled
for redevelopment, and the GLC decided to test the importance to residents
of remaining in the area. Redpath (1974) reported that 92 per cent of
the estimated 1000 households in the area gave completed interviews, and
that the census showed that 70 per cent wanted to stay in areas of North
Kensington, partly because friends and neighbours would be missed if the
respondent had to leave the area. Redpath suggested that:

> Social ties to neighbours, friends and relatives - not, for
> example, location of work or type of house - rank highest
> of all factors (at least in a twilight area), in determining
> the choice to stay.

Partly because house owners were selling their properties to non-residents,
the Colville Tavistock Study proposed that compulsory purchase of housing
by the council was applicable, and that this would also be warranted as
the private acquisition of solitary properties would not produce the
desirable uplift of the area. Public funds could be at risk unless for

222

example a whole terrace was improved at the same time. The Housing Act
of 1974 conferred upon local authorities compulsory improvement powers
and additional powers of compulsory acquisition. Because of the extent
of improvement within the Colville Tavistock GIA, Kensington and Chelsea
council may be more likely to use these powers within the Tavistock HAA
(declared in December 1974) than within the GIA. The HAA has a very
similar composition to the GIA immediately to the south, but in the period
1969-73 received only about a fifth of the improvement grants awarded to
the GIA.

North Westminster was one of the areas of worst housing stress according
to the Milner Holland Report. The Westminster City Council's North
Westminster Study (1967) confirmed that within the area there was a high
degree of poverty, multiple occupation and overcrowding. It proposed
that 3,000 houses should be demolished, 3,000 replacement dwellings built
and 3,000 houses rehabilitated. To further part of this aim, the
Lanhill and Marylands GIAs were declared in 1969. In 1966, 63.8 per cent
of the 511 dwellings in the area were privately rented, half of which were
furnished lettings. In the Lanhill GIA, 12.5 per cent of households
lived at more than 1.5 persons per room and in Marylands, 16.4 per cent
lived above this occupancy rate. Possibly because the GIAs were on the
edge of Maida Vale (a relatively high status area) improvement became
associated with gentrification. In the period 1966-71 the proportion
of economically active males in the area in SEGs 1-4 increased from 5.0
to 10.5 per cent, of which about 35.0 per cent were probably in the
highest income category earning more than £40 per week (GLC, 1970a).

The Central London Housing Study (1972) showed that rents of improved
houses had risen from an average of £5.70 to an average of £22.39 after
conversion. There was little security for the 64 per cent of households
in the GIA who were furnished tenants, many of whom should have been
unable to have paid higher rents. Shelter (1972) reported that in
north Westminster only four per cent of tenants assisted at the Rent
Tribunal by the local tenants' association were able to return to their
improved accommodation; the rest (and other tenants displaced by
improvement) moved away mainly to the area's decaying properties.

The Report of the Decline of Low Rented Accommodation in Westminster
(1974) showed that in the GIAs the average rent of improved properties
was still about £22 (although some rents were as high as £35 per floor),
while by comparison new local authority dwellings in the area were let at
fair rents of £7.37 - £8.94 and Mulberry Housing Trust dwellings were let
at £5.95. Unimproved private rented accommodation was rented at £6.25
on average (furnished) and £4.10 on average (unfurnished). Yet in the
areas as a whole, the average working man's income was £25 - £40 per
week, insufficient even with the maximum possible rebate of £8 to pay
£20 - £25 per week in rent on an improved property. While recognising
that some displacement was a necessary consequence of rehabilitation, the
report drew attention to the harassment which often accompanied the
improvement of both furnished and unfurnished dwellings. The Paddington
Law Centre had reported to the council that in the nine months, March -
December 1973, out of 16 cases dealt with in the GIAs, 13 were Notices
to Quit and three were illegal evictions. In ten cases the reason for
eviction was 'Conversion of Property'. The report recorded that in
September - October 1973, the council undertook a 100 per cent survey of
houses in Sutherland Avenue in the Marylands GIA. It found that 62 per
cent of the households had lived in the area for more than five years,

and that 89 per cent of the households (despite some dissatisfaction with the standard of accommodation) wanted to remain in the area. This possibly reflected the wishes of the majority of the residents of the GIAs and indicated the strength of social ties in the area.

Westminster City council (1974) produced a report which reviewed improvement policy in the Lanhill and Marylands GIAs. By December 1973, 26 per cent of the property within the GIAs had been improved, mostly by housing associations (particularly the Mulberry Trust), which owned 17 per cent of the dwellings in the area. But rising house prices were making it difficult for the housing associations to acquire more property, their acquisitions diminishing from 16 houses per annum in the late 1960s to two in 1972.

Although the council considered that the rate of improvement was too low, there had been a marked increase in owner occupation and a large reduction in private unfurnished tenancies in the period 1966-71 (Table 7.24), indicative of gentrification and displacement. The report showed that 77 per cent of households living in improved dwellings did not live there before improvement, and 63 per cent were not residents of Westminster prior to improvement. Tables 7.25 a,b,c show that a very high proportion of tenants in improved properties (85 per cent) had lived in the GIA for only five years or less. This corresponds with the writer's survey which showed that 66.7 per cent of residents in improved properties had lived in these properties for five years or less.

Table 7.24

Tenure of households in the Lanhill-Marylands GIAs, 1966-71

Tenure	1966	1971
Owner occupied	6	26
Private unfurnished	42	24
Private furnished	45	50
	93	100

Source: Based on 1966 and 1971 Censuses

It is evident that the highest proportion of residents who had resided in the GIAs for five years or less were furnished tenants, and relating to this Table 7.25b shows that the highest proportion of improved dwellings were furnished (and unregulated). The council's survey showed that only 23 per cent of residents out of 64 interviewed households living in improved dwellings had lived in their dwellings prior to them being improved, the displacement rate thus being 77 per cent. Yet it was found that improvement brought higher rather than lower occupancy rates. Within the GIAs, 43.9 per cent of households in improved properties lived at more than one person per room whereas in Harrow Road in 1966 the proportion in all dwellings was 29 per cent. The report suggested that this surprising increase in the occupancy rate may have been due to high rents, tenants having to share or sub-let their improved dwellings. House prices had risen substantially - from £5,000 on average in 1965 to £12,500 on average in 1971. By the early 1970s the price of an improved

Table 7.25

(a) Length of residence of private tenants in improved property
Length of residence (years)

	Over 20	11-20	6-10	3-5	1-2	Less than 1	5 or less	Total Response
No.of households	3	4	3	5	13	38	56	66
% households	4.5	6.1	4.5	7.6	19.7	56.6	84.9	100.0

(b) Length of residence of private furnished tenants in improved property

	Over 20	11-20	6-10	3-5	1-2	Less than 1	5 or less	Total Response
No.of households	0	1	0	0	4	27	31	32
% households	7.1	0	14.3	3.6	25.0	50.0	78.6	100.0

(c) Length of residence of private unfurnished tenants in improved property

	Over 20	11-20	6-10	3-5	1-2	Less than 1	5 or less	Total Response
No.of households	3	3	3	5	9	11	25	32
% households	8.8	8.8	8.8	14.7	26.5	32.4	73.6	100.0

Source: City of Westminster Council, 1974

dwelling on one floor of a house would have been equal to the price of a four storey unimproved house the previous year. Because of potentially high profits, the conversion of properties into self contained units for sale thus became a new form of development in north Westminster.

After rehabilitation, there was an increase in the percentage of higher socio-economic cl sses and income categories and the cost of improved accommodation increased above the level which the former residents could afford. Table 7.26 shows that whereas the proportion of economically active males in SEGs 1-4 in Harrow Road was 5 per cent in 1966, according to the council's survey the proportion of these SEGs living in improved properties was 34.5 per cent in 1973. According to the writer's survey the proportion was only 25 per cent in 1976. The difference between the two figures can be partly explained by the fact that the council obtained their information entirely from respondents living in improved properties, whereas the writer extracted his information from a sample survey of all households in the GIA. The total number of respondents in the council's survey was 58 and in the writer's survey it was 50.

Table 7.26

Socio-economic groups of economically active males in the
Lanhill-Marylands GIAs (1974, 76) and in
Harrow Road (1966)

		Economically active males in SEGs		
		1-4	5-17	Total
No. of respondents	CS	20	38	58
in GIAs	WS	5	45	50
% of respondents	CS	34.5	65.5	100
in GIAs	WS	25.0	75.0	100
1966				
% economically active males in Harrow Road		5.0	95.0	100

CS — Council's survey

WS — Writer's survey

Sources: 1966 Census and surveys of Westminster City Council 1974 and author 1976

The increase in the proportion of the higher socio-economic groups corresponded with the increase in the proportion of high income households. Whereas none of the respondents who had lived in the area over ten years earned more than £3,000 per annum (£57 per week), three-quarters of those who had lived in the GIA less than one year earned this amount, and 35 per cent earned more than £5,000 per annum (£96 per week). In conclusion, the survey showed that the largest proportion of the owner occupiers of improved properties (and by implication the highest income categories) consisted of the managerial and professional classes (SEGs 1-4).

226

8 Conclusions

The results of the research presented in Chapters 5-7 add to the evidence
favouring the hypothesis that there are strong causal relationships
between the distribution of improvement grants and social and economic
change in west London. The changes in part are a reversal of trends
which had previously occurred over a period of about one hundred years.
In much of west London (and specifically within the GIAs and HAAs) houses
were converted into smaller units in the late nineteenth and early
twentieth centuries due to a high level of low income demand. The low
quality of the units, and the demand for housing in suburban locations
as incomes increased, protected these areas from high income demand.
Rent control may also have contributed to the deterioration of housing in
inner London throughout a large part of this century. But in the 1960s
and 1970s the units were under severe competition as a result of demand
from higher income groups - a demand increased by the availability of
improvement grants and stimulated by the cost and inconvenience of
commuting. It became more profitable for landlords to sell their
properties to developers or owner occupiers than to rent them to low
income tenants.

Although in west London generally, improvement grants were found to be
distributed mainly to areas with a high proportion of residents in the
lower socio-economic groups (see Chapter 5), it is suggested that these
residents failed to benefit from rehabilitation and indeed suffered due
to the loss of their accommodation. The conversion of low income
dwellings into owner occupied properties or high rent luxury accommodation
has forced the poor to consume less housing space, often within the same
borough, and homelessness and council housing waiting lists are
increasing - in part a consequence of rehabilitation. It has been shown
(see Chapters 5-7) that in the declared areas, and related to rehabilitation, there was a considerable increase in owner occupation and the
proportion of young, 'middle-class' and high income residents; conversely
there was a decrease in private rented accommodation and the proportion
of older, 'working-class' and low income residents - processes of grant
aided gentrification described by Hamnett (1973) and Merrett (1976).
Tenure and low income demand were thus two factors which were largely
ignored by improvement policy. If Muth (1969) was right and poor
housing is the result of low income, the whole basis of improvement policy
must be called into question. Yet Rothenberg (1967) saw urban renewal
as a means of attracting the middle classes back to the inner areas - a
view shared by the GLC (1970c) with regard to inner London. But
Rothenberg also saw increased employment opportunities and the mitigation
of poverty as two further goals of urban renewal policy. Improvement in
west London has not been combined with a policy of stimulating employment,
nor with a policy of raising incomes so that all households could afford
minimum standard housing.

Although the Housing Acts of 1969 and 1974 stressed that house improvement should be for the benefit of the existing residents of an area, in
the light of research reported in this book it is very questionable

whether this goal has been compatible with the goal of attracting the middle classes back to inner London. The shift of emphasis from re-development to rehabilitation was seen very largely as a physical matter, and its effects have been partly to reverse the process of low income residential zones or sectors 'invading' higher income areas - the basis of ecological theories of urban growth expounded, especially by Burgess (1923) and Hoyt (1939).

Housing improvement policy in west London clearly did not work in the first half of the 1970s and reduced public expenditure in the mid 1970s, impeding the application of the Housing Act of 1974. Since the research reported in Chapters 5-7 was completed, five further GIAs and 17 HAAs have been declared in west London (1). These areas provide local authorities with the best opportunity for ensuring that the economic and social disadvantages of improvement grant policy described in this book do not recur. Backed by the provisions of the Housing Act of 1974, the London boroughs and the GLC may now be able to bring about an improvement in the living conditions of those for whom the legislation is mainly intended.

At the time of writing it is still too soon to say for sure whether the amended improvement policies will be successful. Voices are raised against rehabilitation. It is said that a policy of improvement is a 'vast exercise in putting off the evil day'; the old age of Britain's housing will make it unsuitable for the needs of young families in AD 2000, and even the conservation argument for improvement is questioned if the enhanced external appearances and amenities are not matched by structural soundness and convenience internally.

As an increase in urban renewal expenditure in real terms is lagging behind the formation of new slums, it is essential that the allocation of resources to urban renewal programmes should be based on further investigation into the desirable mix of rehabilitation and redevelopment so as to ensure that limited expenditure produces the maximum net social benefit. Where it is advantageous to rehabilitate, compulsory improve-ment should be speedily enforced, and where this is not possible, acquisition by the local authority or housing associations should be extensively undertaken and focused on those areas in greatest need. But any loosening of the strings attached to improvement grants (especially during a period of escalating house prices) in an attempt to attract private speculative capital into housing rehabilitation would produce consequences similar to those of the Housing Act of 1969.

NOTE

(1) The GIAs declared were: Kensal Green, Queen's Park and Woodhayes Road (Brent); Willow Vale (Hammersmith) and Lots Road (Kensington and Chelsea). The HAAs declared were: Craven Park, Priory Park, South Harlesden and South West Harlesden (Brent); College Park, Devenport Road, Lindrop-Elbe Roads, Overstone Park, Richford Street, Sands End, Sherbrooke Road and Sinclair Road (Hammersmith); Colville Tavistock and Tavistock Crescent-Westbourne Park Road (Kensington and Chelsea), and Coomassie Road North, Coomassie Road South, and Star Street-St.Michael Street (Westminster).

Appendices

APPENDIX A   12-POINT STANDARD - HOUSING ACT OF 1969

After improvement, the dwelling must have at least a 30 year life and conform with the following requirements:-

(i)   be in a good state of repair and substantially free from damp;

(ii)   have each room properly lighted and ventilated;

(iii)   have an adequate supply of wholesome water laid on inside the dwelling;

(iv)   be provided with efficient and adequate means of supplying hot water for domestic purposes;

(v)   have an internal water closet if practicable, otherwise a readily accessible outside water closet;

(vi)   have a fixed bath or shower in a bathroom;

(vii)   be provided with a sink and with suitable arrangements for the disposal of waste water;

(viii) have a proper drainage system;

(ix)   be provided in each room with adequate points for gas or electric lighting (where reasonably available);

(x)   be provided with adequate facilities for heating;

(xi)   have satisfactory facilities for storing, preparing and cooking food;   and

(xii)   have proper provision for the storage of fuel (where required).

APPENDIX B   THE GRANT SYSTEM – HOUSING ACT OF 1974

		Improvement Grant	Intermediate Grant	Repair Grant	Special Grant at LA discretion	Environmental Grants
Outside GIA/HAA	LA grant[a]	50%	50%	Nil	50%	CG Contrib. — Nil
	CG contrib.[b]	75%	75%	Nil	75%	
In GIA	LA grant	60%	60%	60%	60%	CG contrib. — 50% eligible expenditure
	CG contrib.	90%	90%	90%	90%	
In HAA	LA grant	75% (90%)	75% (90%)≠	75% (90%)	75% (90%)≠	CG contrib. — 50% eligible expenditure
		90%	90%	90%	90%	
Limit of eligible expense	2 storey	£3,200	£1,500ø	£800		GIA £50 per house
	3 storey conversion	£3,700	NA	NA		HAA
	Outside 2	£1,600	£750	Nil		Nil
	3+	£1,850	NA	Nil		
	2	£1,920	£900	£480	Varies according to amenities provided	£100 x no. of dwellings
Maximum Grants	In GIA					
	In HAA 3+	£2,200	NA	NA		
	2	£2,400 (£2,800)≠	£1,125 (£1,350)	£600 (£720)≠		£25 x no. of houses
	3	£2,775 (£350)≠	NA	NA		

a LA grant = Local Authority – appropriate % of eligible expense
b CG contribution = Central Government – relevant % of LA grant
NA Not applicable
≠ 90% grant in cases of hardship
ø £1,500 = £700 for amenities + £800 for repair

After improvement, the dwelling must have at least a 30 year life and conform with the following requirements:-

    (i)   be substantially free from damp;

    (ii)   have adequate natural lighting and ventilation in each habitable room;

    (iii)   have adequate and safe provision throughout for artificial lighting and have sufficient electric socket outlets for the safe and proper functioning of domestic appliances;

    (iv)   be provided with adequate drainage facilities;

    (v)   be in a stable structural condition;

    (vi)   have satisfactory internal arrangement;

    (vii)   have satisfactory facilities for preparing and cooking food;

    (viii) be provided with adequate facilities for cooking;

    (ix)   have proper provision for the storage of fuel (where necessary) and for the storage of refuse;   and

    (x)   conform with the specifications applicable to the thermal insulation of roof spaces laid down in Part F of the Building Regulations in force at the date of the grant approval.

APPENDIX D   IMPROVEMENT GRANT APPROVALS TO DIFFERENT HOUSEHOLD
TENURE GROUPS, 1970-73

	1970		1971		1972		1973		Total	
	No.	%	No.	%	No.	%	No.	%	No.	%
BRENT										
Private landlords & developers										
Conversion	14		46		78		126		264	
Improvement	54		11		9		16		90	
Total	68	54.8	57	21.8	87	42.2	142	32.4	354	34.4
Owner occupiers										
Conversion	17		17		36		47		117	
Improvement	3		13		15		21		52	
Total	20	16.1	30	11.5	51	24.8	68	15.5	169	16.1
Housing Assocs.										
Conversion	1		12		10		22		45	
Improvement	3		0		0		0		3	
Total	4	3.2	12	4.6	10	4.9	22	10.7	48	4.7
Local Authority										
Conversion	0		13		17		196		226	
Improvement	32		150		41		10		233	
Total	32	25.8	163	62.2	58	28.2	206	47.0	459	44.6
All owners										
Conversion	32		88		141		391		652	
Improvement	92		174		65		47		378	
Total	124		262		206		438		1030	
% Greater London	1.1		1.3		1.0		1.8		1.3	
INNER WEST LONDON										
Private landlords & developers										
Conversion	986		2239		2367		1730		7331	
Improvement	349		467		329		258		1403	
Total	1335	58.1	2706	66.9	2696	69.3	1988	68.6	8734	66.7
Owner occupiers										
Conversion	121		214		268		254		857	
Improvement	300		397		418		336		1453	
Total	421	18.5	611	15.1	686	17.6	590	20.4	2310	17.6
Housing Assocs.										
Conversion	228		453		262		169		1112	
Improvement	79		1		9		9		98	
Total	307	13.5	454	11.2	271	7.0	178	6.1	1210	9.2
Local Authority										
Conversion	141		242		75		77		535	
Improvement	66		30		151		65		312	
Total	207	9.1	272	6.7	226	5.8	142	4.9	847	6.5
All owners										
Conversion	1476		3148		2981		2230		9835	
Improvement	794		895		907		668		3264	
Total	2270		4043		3888		2898		13099	
% Group A boroughs	32.7		36.8		30.3		28.2		31.9	
% Greater London	19.6		19.8		16.6		11.6		16.3	

	1970		1971		1972		1973		Total	
	No.	%	No.	%	No.	%	No.	%	No.	%
HAMMERSMITH										
Private landlords & developers										
Conversion	295		852		798		210		2155	
Improvement	179		193		144		118		634	
Total	474	54.3	1045	70.5	942	64.7	328	47.4	2789	61.9
Owner occupiers										
Conversion	62		109		147		97		415	
Improvement	231		322		328		252		1133	
Total	293	33.6	431	29.1	475	32.6	349	50.4	1548	34.4
Housing Assocs.										
Conversion	4		1		0		14		19	
Improvement	7		1		0		0		8	
Total	11	1.3	2	0.1	0		14	2.0	27	0.6
Local Authority										
Conversion	89		5		27		0		121	
Improvement	6		0		13		1		20	
Total	95	10.9	5	0.3	40	2.7	1	0.1	141	3.1
All owners										
Conversion	450		967		972		321		2710	
Improvement	423		516		485		371		1795	
Total	873		1483		1457		692		4505	
% Group A boroughs	12.6		13.5		11.4		6.7		11.0	
% Greater London	7.6		7.3		6.2		2.8		5.6	
KENSINGTON & CHELSEA										
Private landlords & developers										
Conversion	409		841		830		792		2872	
Improvement	25		49		40		33		147	
Total	434	58.3	890	69.7	870	70.5	825	82.7	3019	71.0
Owner occupiers										
Conversion	53		87		85		79		304	
Improvement	33		39		78		58		208	
Total	86	11.6	126	9.9	163	13.2	137	13.7	512	12.0
Housing Assocs.										
Conversion	204		202		195		36		634	
Improvement	20		0		9		0		29	
Total	224	30.1	202	15.8	201	16.3	36	3.6	663	15.6
Local Authority										
Conversion	0		59		0		0		0	
Improvement	0		0		0		0		0	
Total	0	0	59	4.6	0	0	0	0	59	1.4
All owners										
Conversion	666		1189		1107		907		3869	
Improvement	78		88		127		91		384	
Total	744		1277		1234		998		4253	
% Group A boroughs	9.4		11.7		9.3		11.7		10.6	
% Greater London	5.7		6.3		5.1		4.8		5.4	

	1970 No.	1970 %	1971 No.	1971 %	1972 No.	1972 %	1973 No.	1973 %	Total No.	Total %
WESTMINSTER										
Private landlords & developers										
Conversion	282		546		748		728		2304	
Improvement	145		225		145		107		622	
Total	427	65.4	771	60.1	893	74.6	835	69.1	2926	67.4
Owner occupiers										
Conversion	6		18		36		78		138	
Improvement	36		36		12		26		112	
Total	42	6.4	54	4.2	48	4.0	104	8.6	250	5.8
Housing Assocs.										
Conversion	20		250		70		119		459	
Improvement	52		0		0		9		61	
Total	72	11.0	250	19.5	70	5.8	128	10.6	520	12.0
Local Authority										
Conversion	52		178		48		77		355	
Improvement	60		30		138		64		292	
Total	112	17.2	208	16.2	186	15.5	141	11.7	647	14.9
All owners										
Conversion	360		992		902		1002		3256	
Improvement	293		291		295		206		1085	
Total	653		1283		1197		1208		4341	
% Group A boroughs	9.4		11.7		9.3		11.7		10.57	
% Greater London	5.7		6.3		5.1		4.8		5.4	
GROUP A BOROUGHS										
Private landlords & developers										
Conversion	2156		4560		5315		3652		15683	
Improvement	919		1562		1485		1191		5157	
Total	3075	44.3	6111	55.7	6810	53.1	4843	47.1	20840	50.8
Owner occupiers										
Conversion	324		728		952		917		2921	
Improvement	1076		1603		2187		2467		7333	
Total	1400	20.2	2331	21.2	3139	24.5	3384	32.9	10254	
Housing Assocs.										
Conversion	737		1132		1162		700		3731	
Improvement	99		19		116		72		306	
Total	836	12.0	1151	10.5	1278	10.0	772	7.5	4037	9.8
Local Authority										
Conversion	1041		1088		1018		590		3737	
Improvement	587		295		597		704		2183	
Total	1628	23.5	1385	12.6	1615	12.6	1294	12.6	5920	14.4
All owners										
Conversion	4258		7508		8447		5859		26072	
Improvement	2681		3479		4385		4434		14979	
Total	6939		10987		12832		10293		41051	
% Greater London	60.1		53.9		54.7		41.1		51.0	
GREATER LONDON										
All owners										
Conversion	6514		11016		12890		11031		41451	
Improvement	5038		9359		10561		14044		39002	
Total	11552		20375		23451		25075		80453	

KEY

HAMMERSMITH

1 Addison
2 Avonmore
3 Broadway
4 Brook Green
5 Colehill
6 College Park and Old Oak
7 Coningham
8 Crabtree
9 Gibbs Green
10 Grove
11 Halford
12 Margravine
13 Parsons Green
14 St.Stephens
15 Sandford
16 Sherbrooke
17 Starch Green
18 Sulivan
19 Town
20 White City
21 Wormholt

KENSINGTON AND CHELSEA

22 Brompton
23 Cheyne
24 Church
25 Earls Court
26 Golborne
27 Hans Town
28 Holland
29 Norland
30 North Stanley
31 Pembridge
32 Queens Gate
33 Redcliffe
34 Royal Hospital
35 St.Charles
36 South Stanley

WESTMINSTER

37 Baker Street
38 Cavendish
39 Charing Cross
40 Church Street
41 Churchill
42 Harrow Road
43 Hyde Park
44 Knightsbridge
45 Lancaster Gate
46 Lords
47 Maida Vale
48 Millbank
49 Queens Park
50 Regents Park
51 Regent Street
52 Victoria Street
53 Warwick
54 Westbourne Park

BRENT

55 Alperton
56 Barham
57 Brentwater
58 Brondesbury Park
59 Carlton
60 Chamberlayne
61 Church End
62 Cricklewood
63 Fryent
64 Gladstone
65 Harlesden
66 Kensal Rise
67 Kenton
68 Kilburn
69 Kingsbury
70 Manor
71 Mapesbury
72 Preston
73 Queens Park
74 Queensbury
75 Roe Green
76 Roundwood
77 St.Raphael
78 Stonebridge
79 Sudbury
80 Sudbury Court
81 Tokyngton
82 Town Hall
83 Wembley Central
84 Wembley Park
85 Willesden Green

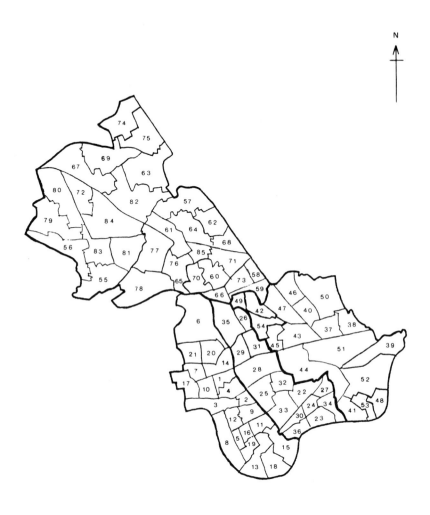

N

Boundaries

London boroughs

Wards

0   1

Mile

APPENDIX F   RELATIONSHIP BETWEEN REHABILITATION-NEED INDEX AND
              APPROVAL OF IMPROVEMENT GRANTS, INNER WEST LONDON
              BOROUGHS AND BRENT

Ward	Rehabilitation need-index	% households receiving improvement grants 1970-73
* Kilburn	51 678.5	0.8
* Mapesbury	49 361.6	0.9
* Queens Park	48 205.1	0.6
Harrow Road	47 919.6	11.1
* Harlesden	47 691.7	0.6
* Kensal Rise	47 569.9	0.5
Coningham	46 421.4	9.6
Addison	46 421.4	8.3
Golborne	46 284.0	0.4
Brook Green	45 433.9	11.3
St.Stephens	44 713.8	3.0
College Park & Old Oak	44 713.8	2.3
Westbourne	44 041.5	6.4
* Willesden Green	44 142.1	1.2
Grove	43 102.7	9.9
Warwick	41 325.0	7.0
Colehill	40 923.1	6.8
* Stonebridge	40 508.9	1.3
* Manor	40 393.7	0.5
Earls Court	40 186.4	4.1
Sherbrooke	40 075.2	8.6
Gibbs Green	40 044.6	6.2
Pembridge	39 782.4	5.9
Halford	39 642.6	6.8
Lancaster Gate	39 311.5	4.6
* Cricklewood	39 297.5	0.1
* Roundwood	39 247.8	0.1
* Brondesbury Park	39 239.6	1.5
Brompton	39 120.0	4.3
Redcliffe	38 875.6	7.7
White City	38 464.1	2.9
Town	38 462.1	11.0
St.Charles	36 220.5	6.1
Avonmore	35 604.6	3.5
Sandford	35 490.5	11.7
Margravine	35 486.3	6.9
Sulivan	35 166.7	9.5
Starch Green	34 580.3	4.8
* Carlton	34 485.6	0.9
* Chamberlayne	34 236.1	0
* Wembley Central	33 518.3	0.7
* Church End	33 470.7	1.9
Queens Park	32 971.8	0.6
Norland	32 607.3	11.4
Wormholt	32 468.8	3.6
Maida Vale	31 996.7	9.4
Parsons Green	31 301.8	7.6
* St.Raphael	30 408.3	0.4
Crabtree	30 200.0	5.8

Ward	Rehabilitation need-index	% households receiving improvement grants 1970-73
Broadway	30 661.4	5.8
Hyde Park	29 970.0	3.8
Queens Gate	29 950.4	3.6
Millbank	28 554.2	0
* Brentwater	28 554.2	0
Churchill	27 904.8	6.1
Holland	27 441.7	4.6
Baker Street	27 307.5	2.7
South Stanley	27 125.9	1.8
* Gladstone	27 123.4	0.3
Church Street	26 896.9	2.0
* Alperton	26 284.1	0.1
* Tokyngton	25 793.2	0.1
* Barham	23 692.6	0.1
Cheyne	23 164.8	4.6
Royal Hospital	22 481.4	3.9
Regent Street	22 275.4	4.7
Victoria Street	22 192.2	1.3
North Stanley	21 670.4	8.3
* Roe Green	20 714.9	0.1
* Queensbury	20 252.5	0.1
Hans Town	20 092.1	1.3
* Wembley Park	19 648.0	0.3
Charing Cross	19 273.9	0
Knightsbridge	19 036.2	1.8
* Fryent	18 785.7	0.1
Regents Park	18 547.0	3.6
Lords	17 744.1	5.3
Church	17 046.8	1.7
Cavendish	16 563.9	3.9
* Town Hall	16 430.7	0
* Sudbury Court	16 026.6	0
* Kingsbury	15 874.0	0
* Sudbury	15 288.6	0.1
* Preston	14 126.7	0
* Kenton	10 609.3	0.1

* Ward of the L.B. Brent

IMPROVEMENT GRANT APPROVALS TO DIFFERENT HOUSEHOLD
TENURE GROUPS IN THE HAMMERSMITH GIAs, 1970-73

	1970		1971		1972		1973		Total	
	No.	%	No.	%	No.	%	No.	%	No.	%
HAMMERSMITH GIAS										
Private landlords &										
developers										
Conversion	18	19.8	49	38.9	22	34.4	15	30.6	94	29.4
Improvement	11	12.1	16	12.7	14	21.9	2	4.1	43	13.4
Total	29	31.9	65	51.6	36	56.3	17	34.7	137	42.8
Owner occupiers										
Conversion	8	8.8	20	15.9	9	14.0	10	20.4	27	14.7
Improvement	54	59.3	41	32.5	19	29.7	22	44.9	136	42.5
Total	62	68.1	61	48.4	28	43.7	32	65.3	183	57.2
All owners										
Conversion	26	28.6	69	54.8	31	48.4	25	51.0	141	44.1
Improvement	65	71.4	57	45.2	33	51.6	24	49.0	179	55.9
Total	91	100.0	126	100.0	64	100.0	49	100.0	320	100.0
MASBRO ROAD GIA*										
Private landlords &										
developers										
Conversion	6	17.1	21	34.4	8	26.7	6	22.2	31	21.7
Improvement	8	22.9	8	13.1	5	16.0	0	0	21	14.7
Total	14	40.0	29	47.5	13	43.3	6	22.2	52	36.4
Owner occupiers										
Conversion	0	0	11	18.0	6	20.0	5	18.5	22	15.4
Improvement	21	60.0	21	34.4	11	36.7	16	59.3	69	48.3
Total	21	60.0	32	52.5	17	56.7	21	77.8	91	63.6
All owners										
Conversion	6	17.1	32	52.5	14	46.7	11	40.7	53	37.1
Improvement	29	82.9	29	47.5	16	53.3	16	59.3	90	62.9
Total	35	100.0	61	100.0	30	100.0	27	100.0	143	100.0
MOORE PARK GIA										
Private landlords &										
developers										
Conversion	12	21.4	28	43.1	14	41.2	9	40.9	63	35.6
Improvement	3	5.3	8	12.3	9	26.4	2	9.1	22	12.4
Total	15	26.8	36	55.4	23	67.6	11	50.0	85	48.0
Owner occupiers										
Conversion	8	14.3	9	13.8	3	8.8	5	22.7	25	14.1
Improvement	33	58.9	20	30.8	8	23.6	6	27.3	67	37.9
Total	41	73.2	29	44.6	11	32.4	11	50.0	92	52.0
All owners										
Conversion	20	35.7	37	56.9	17	50.0	14	63.6	88	49.7
Improvement	36	64.3	28	43.1	17	50.0	8	36.4	89	50.3
Total	56	100.0	65	100.0	34	100.0	22	100.0	177	100.0

* The Masbro Road GIA was not declared until 1971. Data for 1970
related to the area which subsequently became the GIA.

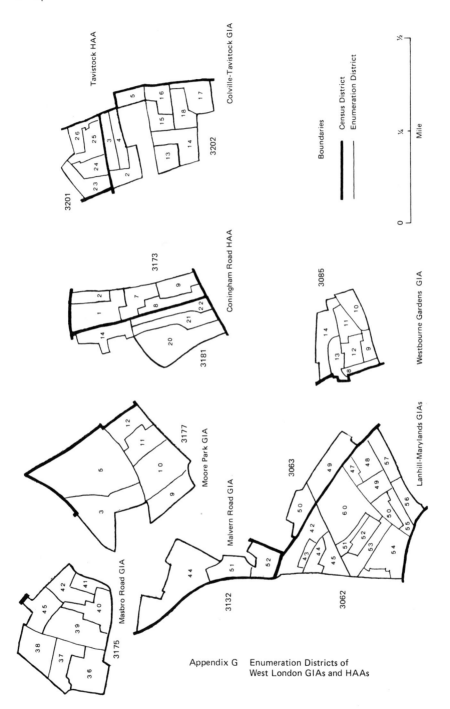

N ←

Tavistock HAA

Colville-Tavistock GIA

26 25 3
24   4   5   16 17
23 2   13 14 15 18
3201   3202

Coningham Road HAA

3173
14 1   2   7   8   9
20 21 22
3181

Westbourne Gardens GIA

3085
14 13 11 10
8   12 12 9

Moore Park GIA

3177
5   3   11 12
9   10

Malvern Road GIA

Lanhill-Marylands GIAs

3063
50 49 47 48 57
60 49 50
42 51 52 53 50 56
43 44 45 54 55
51
52
3132   3062

Masbro Road GIA

3175
38 45 42 41
37 39 40
36
44 51

Boundaries
━━━ Census District
━━ Enumeration District

0   ¼   ½
Mile

Appendix G   Enumeration Districts of
West London GIAs and HAAs

241

APPENDIX I   RELATIONSHIP BETWEEN REHABILITATION-NEED INDEX AND
                  APPROVAL OF IMPROVEMENT GRANTS, WEST LONDON GIAS & HAAS

Census District	ED	GIA/HAA	RNI	% Households Receiving Improvement Grants 1970-73
3175	36	MR	52 364	4.5
3085	10	WG	51 191	0.8
3062	45	LM	49 479	4.3
3062	50	LM	48 065	7.9
3062	47	LM	47 669	10.2
3085	8	WG	46 600	20.4
3062	52	LM	43 681	5.5
3085	13	WG	43 481	6.1
3062	51	LM	42 936	4.7
3062	48	LM	42 895	5.0
3062	57	LM	42 571	9.4
3202	18	CT	42 411	7.1
3181	22	CR	42 032	4.4
3175	42	MR	41 300	33.7
3202	3	T	41 252	2.7
3202	14	CT	41 015	22.1
3132	51	MVR	40 423	6.0
3062	44	LM	40 287	7.4
3062	56	LM	39 971	5.5
3202	4	T	39 953	5.1
3202	16	CT	39 603	3.7
3181	20	CR	39 513	7.7
3062	55	LM	38 905	4.7
3202	2	T	38 863	1.9
3063	50	LM	38 582	0.6
3201	24	T	38 432	0.6
3181	14	CR	38 098	4.1
3132	44	MVR	38 013	0
3201	26	T	37 601	4.8
3085	11	WG	37 432	6.6
3202	5	T	37 387	1.1
3175	41	MR	37 305	15.5
3062	43	LM	37 198	6.4

Census District	ED	GIA/HAA	RPI	% Households Receiving Improvement Grants 1970-73
3062	56	LM	53 085	5.5
3202	3	T	52 554	2.7
3202	4	T	52 553	5.1
3173	8	CR	52 525	0.5
3173	7	CR	52 409	1.2
3085	10	WG	52 343	0.8
3202	14	CT	51 951	22.1
3062	47	LM	51 801	10.2
3173	1	CR	51 690	2.8
3175	42	MR	51 441	15.5
3201	25	T	51 360	2.8
3202	18	CT	51 180	7.1
3202	16	CT	51 179	3.7
3062	55	LM	50 877	4.7
3062	57	LM	50 782	9.4
3085	8	WG	50 450	20.4
3062	48	LM	50 223	5.0
3202	15	CT	49 447	6.2
3202	5	T	48 390	1.1
3062	52	LM	48 268	5.5
3062	45	LM	48 025	4.3
3132	44	MVR	47 674	0
3181	22	CR	47 663	4.4
3202	2	T	47 593	1.9
3132	51	MVR	47 296	6.0
3062	43	LM	47 042	6.4
3085	13	WG	46 956	6.1
3201	26	T	46 433	4.8
3201	24	T	44 355	0.6
3062	44	LM	44 121	7.4
3085	11	WG	44 085	6.6
3181	21	CR	41 741	7.9

CR   Coningham Road
CT   Colville-Tavistock
LM   Lanhill-Marylands
MP   Moore Park
MR   Masbro Road
MVR Malvern Road
T   Tavistock
WG   Westbourne Gardens

APPENDIX J   RELATIONSHIP BETWEEN REHABILITATION POTENTIAL INDEX
AND APPROVAL OF IMPROVEMENT GRANTS, WEST LONDON
GIAS & HAAS

Census District	ED	GIA/HAA	RPI	% Households Receiving Improvement Grants 1970-73
3177	11	MP	107 917	74.7
3177	10	MP	99 306	46.4
3175	39	MR	88 121	33.3
3177	12	MP	87 615	59.2
3202	17	CT	82 427	12.1
3085	14	WG	80 439	3.5
3177	5	MP	80 273	10.0
3173	2	CR	70 009	1.3
3175	38	MR	78 809	21.4
3132	52	MVR	76 321	4.1
3175	37	MR	75 035	21.7
3202	13	CT	71 639	10.0
3175	45	MR	67 011	11.9
3062	54	LM	65 599	1.9
3181	21	CR	62 829	5.6
3177	9	MP	62 548	46.6
3175	36	MR	61 096	4.5
3062	53	LM	61 044	12.4
3085	12	WG	58 736	2.8
3175	40	MR	58 635	25.5
3062	42	LM	58 472	13.3
3062	49	LM	57 491	2.9
3177	3	MP	56 698	6.9
3063	49	LM	56 662	3.2
3173	09	CR	56 119	1.2
3062	51	LM	55 946	4.7
3201	23	T	55 623	2.0
3062	60	LM	55 492	3.6
3181	20	CR	55 337	7.7
3063	50	LM	54 490	0.6
3175	42	MR	53 652	33.7
3181	14	CR	53 581	4.1
3085	9	WG	53 362	0

Census District	ED	GIA/HAA	RNI	% Households Receiving Improvement Grants 1970-73
3175	45	MR	37 015	11.9
3201	25	T	37 011	2.8
3085	12	WG	35 734	2.8
3132	52	MVR	35 664	4.1
3175	38	MR	35 017	21.4
3063	49	LM	34 309	3.2
3062	49	LM	34 143	2.9
3202	15	CT	33 598	6.2
3062	53	LM	33 587	12.4
3062	42	LM	33 065	13.3
3202	17	CT	32 196	12.1
3177	9	MP	32 179	46.6
3173	02	CR	31 946	1.3
3062	54	LM	31 030	1.9
3062	60	LM	30 130	3.6
3201	23	T	29 924	2.0
3175	39	MR	28 031	33.3
3173	01	CR	27 683	2.8
3177	5	MP	26 326	10.0
3175	37	MR	25 393	21.7
3202	13	CT	24 997	10.0
3085	9	WG	24 416	0
3181	21	CR	23 107	5.6
3177	12	MP	18 949	59.2
3177	10	MP	17 469	46.4
3177	11	MP	16 318	74.7
3173	08	CR	15 919	0.5
3085	14	WG	13 884	3.5
3175	40	MR	13 812	26.0
3177	3	MP	12 816	6.9
3173	09	CR	12 457	1.2
3173	07	CR	9 755	1.2

CR   Coningham Road
CT   Colville-Tavistock
LM   Lanhill-Marylands
MP   Moore Park
MR   Masbro Road
MVR   Malvern Road
T   Tavistock
WG   Westbourne Gardens

QUESTIONNAIRE

Name of interviewer(s)..

Date of interview..

GIA/HAA..

Initials of interviewee ....

Address of interviewee...

Question:

1   How long have you (and your household)
    resided at this address?
                                  ....

2   Are you (a) an owner occupier? ....

            (b) a tenant of unfurnished
                accommodation?   ....

            (c) a tenant of furnished
                accommodation?   ....

3   Are you a tenant of a housing association? ....

4   If yes, of which housing association are
    you a tenant?   ....

5   Is your dwelling shared with another household? ....

6   If yes, are the following amenities shared?

            (a) Hot water   ....

            (b) Bath or shower ....

            (c) Inside W.C.   ....

            (d) All three   ....

7   Is your dwelling without exclusive use of:-

            (a) Hot water   ....

            (b) Bath or shower ....

            (c) Inside W.C.   ....

            (d) All three   ....

8   What are the occupations of males in the household (15-65 years)?
    ....
    ....
    ....

9   What is the occupation of the head of the household
     if different from '8'?

     ....

10   How many car owners or car users are there in the
     household?   ....

11   What are the ages of persons in the household?

                         Please signify male (m) or female (f)

     0-4   _____

     5-14   _____

     15-19   _____

     20-39   _____

     40-64   _____

     Over 64   _____

12   What is the approximate wage or salary of the working male or
     head of the household? (Please tick)

     Up to £1,000   p.a.   Up to £19 per week
     £1,000-£1,500 p.a.   £20-£29   "   "
     £1,500-£2,300 p.a.   £29-£43   "   "
     £2,300-£3,000 p.a.   £43-£57   "   "
     £3,000-£5,000 p.a.   £58-£96   "   "
     Over £5,000   Over £96   "   "

References

Abu-Lughod, J., (1960) 'A Survey of Centre-city Residents', in Foote, N.,
N. et al., Housing Choices and Housing Constraints, McGraw, New York.
Alonso, W., (1960) 'A theory of the urban land market's Regional Science
Association, Papers and Proceedings, 6 (1964) Location and Land Use,
Towards a General Theory of land rent, Harvard University Press,
Cambridge, Mass.
Amery, J., (1972a) Speech to National House-Builders' Registration
Council, 1 November 1972 (1972b) Parliamentary Debates (Hansard)
House of Commons Official Report, vol.845.
Anderson, J. and Williams, T., (1971) Living in Central London - A
Survey of Population, Housing and Employment in Westminster, Report to
the City of Westminster, Department of Architecture and Planning.
Anderson, T.R., (1962) 'Social and Economic Factors Affecting the
Location of Residential Neighbourhoods'; Papers and Proceedings of the
Regional Science Association, vol.9.
'Argus', (1970) 'Poor results produced by out of context schemes';
Municipal Engineering, vol.147.
Association of Public Health Inspectors, (1972) Memorandum to the
Department of the Environment.
Babbage, A.G. (1973) 'House Improvement in Stress Areas'; Environmental
Health, vol.81.
Bermant, C., (1973) 'East End goes West'; Observer Magazine, 30
September 1973.
Burgess, E.W., (1925), 'The Growth of the City'; in Park, R.E., et al.,
The City, University of Chicago Press, Chicago.
Buttimer, A., (1969) 'Social Space in Interdisciplinary Perspective';
Geographical Review, vol.59.
Central Housing Advisory Committee (Ministry of Housing and Local
Government), Housing Management Sub Committee, (1969) Council Housing:
Progress, Procedures and Priorities, Ninth Report.
Cherry, G., (1970) Town Planning in its Social Context, Leonard Hill,
London.
Cobbold, D., (1972) quoted by Marks, L., 'Speculators cash in on housing
grants'; Observer, 17 April 1972.
Counter Information Services, (1973) The Recurrent Crisis - CIS Anti-
Report on the Property Developers, London.
Coward, J., (1972) quoted in Marks, L., 'Speculators cash in on housing
grants'; Observer, 17 April 1972.
Crosland, A., (1972) 'Housing and Equality', Guardian, 15 June 1972.
(1974) Parliamentary Debates (Hansard), House of Commons Official
Report, vol.873.
Crossman, R.H.S., (1969) Speech to Association of Public Health
Inspectors Conference, Eastbourne.
Davis, O.A. and Whinston, A.B., (1961) 'The Economics of Urban Renewal',
in Wilson, J.Q. (ed.) (1966) Urban Renewal - The Record and the
Controversy, Harvard University Press, Cambridge, Mass.
Dennington Report, (1966) (Our Older Homes: A Call for Action).
Department of Economic Affairs, (1965) The National Plan, Cmnd.2764.
Department of the Environment, (1971) Fair Deal for Housing (Report of

the Francis Committee), Cmnd.4728.   (1971) <u>Housing Condition Survey</u>.
(1973) <u>Better Homes - the next priorities</u>, Cmnd.5339.   (1973)
<u>Circular 99/73</u>, House and Area Improvement, <u>Circular 13/75</u> Housing Act
of 1974: Renewal Strategies (1975) <u>Some Social Implications of</u>
<u>Improvement Policy in London</u>.
Dimson, G., (1974a) quoted by Willcox, D., 'Twilight homes Bill only a
    tickle', Evening Standard, 25 January 1974. (1974b) quoted in GLC
    Press Office, <u>GLC Announce Strategic Housing Plan for London</u>,
    17 October 1974.   (1974c) <u>A Strategic Housing Plan for London</u>; Town
    and Country Planning Association Conference, London.
Donnison, D.V., (1967) <u>The Government of Housing</u>, Penguin, Harmondsworth.
Dugmore, K. and Williams, P., (1974) 'Improvement Grants'; <u>Area</u>,
    Institute of British Geographers, vol.6.
<u>Economist</u>, (1977) 'London's burning! London's burning!   A Survey';
    vol.261, 1 January 1977.
Ellis, R.H., (1967) 'Modelling of household location: a statistical
    approach'; Highway Research Record, vol.207.
Estates Gazette (1972) 'Improvement Grants', vol.224.
Evans, A.W., (1973) <u>The Economics of Residential Location</u>, Macmillan,
    London.
Eversley, D., (1973) 'Problems of Social Planning in Inner London'; in
    Donnison, D. and Eversley, D. (1973) <u>London: Urban Patterns, Problems</u>
    <u>and Policies</u>, Heinemann Education, London.
Francis Report, (1971) (<u>Fair Deal for Housing</u>) Cmnd.4728.
Garner, B.J., (1968) 'Models of Urban Geography and Settlement Location';
    in Chorley, R.J. and Haggett, P. (eds.),   (1968) <u>Socio-Economic</u>
    <u>Models in Geography</u>, Methuen, London.
Glass, R. and others, (1963) <u>London: Aspects of change</u>, MacGibbon and
    Kee, London.
GLC, (1966) Land Use Survey.   (1967) <u>Family Expenditure Survey</u>.
    (1969) <u>Ibid</u>. <u>Greater London Development Plan: Report of Studies</u>.
    (1970a) <u>The Condition of London's Housing - A Survey</u>; Department of
    Planning and Transportation.   Intelligence Unit Research Report No.4.
    (1970b) <u>The Characteristics of London's Households</u>; Department of
    Planning and Transportation Intelligence Unit, Research Report No.5.
    (1970c) <u>Tomorrow's London</u>.   (1973) <u>Annual Abstract of Statistics</u>.
    (1974) <u>Ibid</u>; <u>Strategic Housing Plan for London</u>.   (1976) <u>Annual</u>
    <u>Abstract of Statistics</u>.
Greenwood, A., (1969a) Parliamentary Debates (Hansard), <u>House of Commons</u>
    <u>Official Report</u>, vol.777 (1969b) Parliamentary Debates (Hansard) <u>House</u>
    <u>of Commons Standing Committee F, Housing Bill</u>, 1st through 20th
    Sitting.   20 February - 6 May.
Hall, P., (1963) <u>London 2000</u>, Faber, London.
Hamnett, C., (1973) 'Improvement grants as an indicator of gentrification
    in inner London'; <u>Area</u>, Institute of British Geographers, vol.4.
Harris, M., (1973) 'Some aspects of social polarisation'; in Donnison,
    D. and Eversley, D. (1973) <u>London: Urban Patterns, Problems and</u>
    <u>Policies</u>, Heinemann Education, London.
Hillman, J., (1969) 'New homes for old - when?; <u>Observer</u> 2 February
    1969.
Holmes, C., (1972) C. Holmes: <u>Evidence to Greater London Development</u>
    <u>Plan</u>.   (1974) A Strategy for London's Housing; Town and Country
    Planning Association Conference, London.
Hoover, E.M. and Vernon, R., (1959) <u>Anatomy of a Metropolis</u>, Harvard
    University Press, Cambridge, Mass.
House of Commons, (1973) <u>Tenth Report of the Expenditure Committee</u>,
    <u>Environmental and Home Office Sub-Committee; session 1972/1973</u>.

1, 2, and 3, H.C. vol.349.   Memorandum by the London Borough of
Hammersmith (M.16).   Memorandum by the Association of Municipal
Corporations (M.21).   Memorandum by the London Boroughs' Association
(M.22).   Memorandum by the Royal Town Planning Institute (M.25).
Supplementary Memorandum by the Department of the Environment (M.41).
Hoyt, H., (1939) The structure and growth of residential neighbourhoods
in American cities, Federal Housing Administration, Washington.
Jacobs, J., (1961) The Death and Life of Great American Cities, Random
House, New York.
Jenkins, S., (1975) Landlords to London, Constable, London.
Kelly, F., (1971) Classification of the London Boroughs; GLC Intelli-
gence Unit, Research Report, No.9.
Kensington and Chelsea (The Royal Borough of), (1972) The Colville
Tavistock Study.
Kilroy, B., (1972a) 'Improvement Grants Threaten North Kensington';
Housing Review, vol.21.   (1972b) quoted in Marks, L., 'Speculators
cash in on housing grants'; Observer, 17 April 1972.
Layfield Committee (1973) Greater London Development Plan.   Report of
the Panel of Inquiry Department of the Environment.
Lomas, G.M., (1974) London after Layfield; Town and Country Planning
Association Conference, London.
Malcolmson, P.E., (1975) 'Getting a Living in the Slums of Victorian
Kensington'; The London Journal, vol.1.
Medhurst, D.F. and Lewis, J. Parry, (1969) Urban Decay, Macmillan,
London.
Merrett, S., (1976) 'Gentrification'; in Edwards, M., Gray, F.,
Merrett, S. and Swann, J. (eds.), Housing and Class in Britain.   A
second volume of papers presented at the Political Economy of Housing
Workshop of the Conference of Socialist Economists, London.
Milner Holland Report, (1965) (Report of the Committee on Housing in
Greater London).
Ministry of Health, (1948) Circular 40/48; Building Licensing: Defence
Regulations 56A.   (1949) Circular 90/94; Housing Act of 1949.
Ministry of Housing and Local Government, (1953) Housing - The Next
Step, Cmnd.8996.   (1955) Slum Clearance (England and Wales), Cmnd.9593
(1965) The Housing Programme, 1965 to 1970, Cmnd.2838.   (1967) Housing
Condition Survey.   (1968) Old houses into new homes, Cmnd.3602.
(1969) Circular 64/69, Housing Improvement.   Circular 65/69, Area
Improvement.
Ministry of Housing and Local Government, Central Housing Advisory
Committee, (1966) Our Older Homes: A Call for Action (Report of the
Sub-Committee on Standards of Housing Fitness, Chairman, Mrs E.
Dennington).
Morton, J., (1971) 'Housing'; in Hillman, J. (ed.), Planning for London,
Harmondsworth.
Muchnick, D.M., (1970) Urban Renewal in Liverpool - Occasional Papers
on Social Administration 33.
Muth, R.F., (1969) Cities and Housing, University of Chicago Press,
Chicago.
Needleman, L., (1965) The Economics of Housing, Staples Press, London.
Nevitt, A.A., (1965) Housing Taxation and Subsidy, Nelson, London.
North Islington Housing Rights Project (1974), Housing Action Areas and
the Compulsory Purchase Question.
Notting Hill Peoples' Association Housing Group, (1972) Losing Out - A
Study of Colville and Tavistock.
Olsen, D.J., (1976) The Growth of Victorian London, Batsford, London.
Pahl, R., (1970) Patterns of Urban Life, Longman, London.

Pickup, D., (1974) 'Housing Action Areas: The Provisions of the Housing Act, 1974'; Housing Review, vol.24.

Pimlico Neighbourhood Aid Centre Housing Group and Pimlico Tenants and Residents Association, (1973), Pimlico – Houses for People not Profit, London.

Rayner, R. and Raynsford, D., (1972) 'Speculators' Paradise'; Municipal and Public Services Journal, vol.80.

Redpath, R., (1974) 'The hard case for community'; New Society, vol.30.

Reeder, D.A., (1968) 'A Theatre of Suburbs: Some Patterns of Development in West London, 1801-1911'; in Dyos, H.J., (ed.) The Study of Urban History, Edward Arnold, London.

Report of the Committee on Housing in Greater London (Chairman: Sir Milner-Holland Q.C.), (1965).

Report of the Ministry of Housing and Local Government 1950/51 to 1954, (1955) Cmnd.9559.

Rippon, G., (1973) quoted in McKie, D., 'Rippon signals a retreat from big urban planning'; Guardian, 11 September 1973.

Rose, H., (1968) The Housing Problem, Heinemann Education, London.

Rothenberg, J., (1967) Economic Evaluation or Urban Renewal, The Brookings Institution, Washington, DC.

Schnore, L.F., (1954) 'The Separation of Home and Work: A Problem for Human Ecology'; Social Forces, vol.32.

Shelter – National Campaign for the Homeless, (1972). Home Improvement – People or Profit. (1973) A new deal for furnished tenants. (1974) quoted in Hoggart, S. 'Housing Bill gives power to councils'; Guardian, 19 April 1974.

Shore, P., (1976) Speech in Manchester, 17 September 1976.

Stone, P.A., (1964) 'The Price of sites for Residential Building'; Estates Gazette, vol.189. (1970a) 'Housing Quality: The Seventies Problem'; Building Societies Gazette, June. (1970b) Urban Development in Britain, Costs and Resources, 1964-2004. 1: Population, Trends and Housing, University of Cambridge Press, Cambridge.

Summerson, J., (1969) Georgian London, Penguin, Harmondsworth.

Sunday Times, 'Losers in the housing game'; 29 October 1972.

Treasury, (1947) Capital Investment in 1948; Cmnd.7268. (1975) Public Expenditure to 1978-79; Cmnd.5879.

Walker, P., (1969) quoted in The Housing Research Foundation, (1970) Home Ownership in England and Wales. (1970) Press Notices No.98, Ministry of Housing and Local Government. (1972) Parliamentary Debates (Hansard), House of Commons Official Report, vol.845.

Waroff, D., (1973) 'Coming up in the world', Financial Times; 13 January 1973.

Westminster (City of) (1970) North Westminster Study. (1972) The Central London Housing Study; Development Plan Research Report R.1. Housing in Westminster; Development Plan Research Report, R.2. (1974) Review of Improvement Policy in Lanhill and Marylands General Improvement Areas; Joint Report of Architecture and Planning and Director of Housing.

Westminster Council of Social Service (1974) The Report on the Decline of Low Rented Accommodation in Westminster.

Williams, P., (1975) The Role of Institutions in the Inner London Housing Market: The Case of Islington. Institute of British Geographers Conference, Oxford.

Willmot, P. and Young, M., (1973) 'Social Class and Geography'; in Donnison, D. and Eversley, D. (eds.) London: Urban Patterns, Problems and Policies, Heinemann Education, London.

Wingo, L., (1961a) Transportation and Urban Land, Resources for the

Future, Washington, DC.   (1961b) 'An Economic Model of the Utilisation of Urban Land for Residential Purposes'; <u>Papers and Proceedings of the Regional Science Association</u>, vol.7.

Young, D., (1972) Speech in Leeds, quoted in the <u>Observer</u>, 10 December 1972.

Young, M. and Willmott, P., (1957) <u>Family and Kinship in East London</u>, Routledge and Kegan Paul, London.

Index

Abu-Lughod (1960) 56
Addison 112, 115
Alonso (1960) 5
Amery, Mr Julian (1972a) 23,
  (1972b) 24, 67
Anderson (1962) 38
Anderson and Williams (1971) 128
Annual Abstract of Statistics
  (GLC) 131, (1970-73) 83,
  (1974) 42, (1975) 76, (1976) 58
Argus (1970) 64
Artisans Dwellings Act of 1868 11
Assisted Areas 19
Association of Municipal
  Corporations 25
Association of Public Health
  Inspectors 25

Babbage (1973) 19-20, 22, 221
Baker Street 121
Banks 65
Barnsbury 62-3, 74
Barnsbury Action Group 67
Barnsbury Association 63, 67
Battersea 62
Bayswater 73, 78
Belgravia 78
Bermant (1973) 24
Bethnal Green 38
Bid-rent 5
Blight 31, 39
Blighted conditions 3
Brent 44, 49, 53, 72, 79, 83, 85,
  91, 111-12, 115, 127, 170-72, 207
Brentwater 126
Brompton 112, 121
Brondesbury Park 101, 112
Brook Green 97, 101, 112, 115,
  127, 177
Brown Ban 65
Building industry 14, 32-33
Building society/societies 60,
  65, 74
Burgess (1923) 1, 3, 41, 115, 119,
  228
Buttimer (1969) 38

Camden 68-9, 73-4
Camden Town 68, 74

Canonbury 63, 74
Carlton 177
Census 1961 6, 112
        1966 41, 53, 172
        1971 53, 60, 79, 105, 111,
               115, 163, 172, 192,
               196
Central area 4, 8
Central Business District (CBD) 3,
  56-7, 115
Central Housing Advisory Committee
  (1969) 58
Central London Housing Study (1972)
  223
Central Residential Area 115, 119,
  121
Central Residential District 41-2
Certificate of provisional approval
  26
Chalk Farm 74
Channon, Mr Paul 26
Characteristics of London Households
  (GLC, 1970) 49
Charing Cross 19
Chelsea 62, 220
Cherry (1970) 36
Chicago 1, 3, 56, 115
Church 121
Church Commissioners 62
Church End 101
Circular 40/48 (Ministry of Health)
          11
          90/49 (Ministry of Health)
          12
          64/69 (Ministry of Housing
          and Local Government)
          17, 36
          99/73 (Department of the
          Environment) 26
          13/75 (Department of the
          Environment) 10, 28
City (of London) 65, 78, 119
Clearance 8, 10, 27
Clearance schemes 23, 65
Clydeside 6
Cobbold, Mr David 69
Colehill 112, 115
College Park and Old Oak 112

255

Colville-Tavistock (GIA) 131, 136,
  114-5, 150, 170, 172-3, 188, 192,
  196, 207, 211, 219, 221-3
Colville Tavistock Study (1972)
  221-2
Community/communities 23, 24, 26-7,
  38-9, 67
Commuter costs 4
       travel 4
       zone 3
Commuting 5, 42, 66, 227
  costs 5
Compulsory acquisition 70, 223
  purchase 8, 11, 17, 24, 27, 40,
    70
  purchase orders 26, 28-9, 63, 69
Concentric zone model 1, 41
Condition of London's Housing
  (GLC, 1970) 44, 129
Conningham Road 101, 112, 115, 177
Coningham Road (HAA) 131, 145, 154,
  163, 172, 177, 188, 192, 196, 207,
  211, 221
Conservation 8, 67
Conservative Government/party 12,
  17, 24, 33, 39, 62, 70
Construction industry 29
Controlled tenancies 16, 20
Conversion(s) 11, 13, 15-17, 36,
  41, 44, 64, 67, 74-5, 91, 97, 101,
  119, 121, 127, 129, 136, 144, 222,
  226
  works 221
Counter Information Services (1973)
  63, 66
Coward (1972) 67
Crabtree 121, 126
Cricklewood 112, 126
Crosland, Mr Anthony (1972) 19, 23
  (1974) 27
Crosman, Mr Richard (1969) 37

Davis and Whinston (1961) 30-1, 57,
  145
Decentralisation 29, 73
Deeplish (Rochdale) 83
Demolition(s) 8, 10, 71
Dennington Committee 19
Department of the Environment 17,
  20, 25, 31-2, 69, 75, 83, 101
Developers 19-20, 23, 34, 36, 63,
  66-7, 69-70, 74, 85, 97, 101, 105,
  111, 129, 131, 136, 144
Development Areas 15-16
Dimson, Mrs Gladys (1974a) 27,
  (1974b) 71

Discretionary grant(s) 15-16, 22,
  75
Displaced households 10
Displacement 72, 128, 223-4
Donnison (1967) 57
Dugmore and Williams (1974) 74

Ealing 53
Earls Court 112
Economist, The (1977) 41, 56
Elasticity of demand 6, 56
Electoral Registers 207
Estate agents 34, 36, 66
Estates Gazette, The (1972) 23
Evans (1973) 4, 6-7, 56-7
Eversley (1973) 42

Fair rent(s) 16, 20, 207, 211,
  219, 223
Family Expenditure Survey (GLC 1967)
  65, 220 (1975) 56
Filtering hypothesis 33
Filtration 24
Francis Committee 58, 60
Fulham 79

Garden City Movement 11
Garner (1968) 1
General Improvement Areas (GIAs)
  16-17, 19, 23, 25-6, 28, 40, 70,
  131, 136, 144-5, 150, 154, 159,
  161, 163, 170-3, 177, 188, 192,
  196, 202, 207, 211, 219-24, 226-8
Gentrification 25, 34, 36, 57,
  62-3, 66-7, 73-5, 111, 121, 126-7,
  129, 161, 163, 170-1, 188, 192,
  219, 223-4
Ghettoes 24, 72
Gibbs Green 112
Glass (1963) 62
Golborne 112, 121, 170
Great Britain 8, 60
Great Estates 78, 115, 119
Greater London 6, 58, 65, 67, 73,
  79, 83, 119, 131, 136, 211, 220
Greater London Council (GLC) 41,
  44, 49, 53-4, 62, 64-5, 67, 71-3,
  85, 97, 111-12, 222-3, 227
Greater London Development Plan
  Inquiry 66
  Report of Studies (1969) 53
Green Belt 54, 60
Greenwich 73
Greenwood, Mr Anthony (1969a) 15, 33
  (1969b) 17
Gross value(s) 172, 207, 211, 219

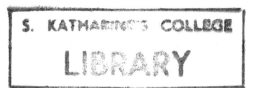